Spectral Dickens

Manchester University Press

Series editors: Anna Barton, Andrew Smith

Editorial board: David Amigoni, Isobel Armstrong, Philip Holden, Jerome McGann, Joanne Wilkes, Julia M. Wright

Interventions: Rethinking the Nineteenth Century seeks to make a significant intervention into the critical narratives that dominate conventional and established understandings of nineteenth-century literature. Informed by the latest developments in criticism and theory the series provides a focus for how texts from the long nineteenth century, and more recent adaptations of them, revitalize our knowledge of and engagement with the period. It explores the radical possibilities offered by new methods, unexplored contexts, and neglected authors and texts to re-map the literary-cultural landscape of the period and rigorously re-imagine its geographical and historical parameters. The series includes monographs, edited collections, and scholarly sourcebooks.

Already published

Engine of modernity: The omnibus and urban culture in nineteenth-century Paris   Masha Belenky

Pasts at play: Childhood encounters with history in British culture, 1750–1914
Rachel Bryant Davies and Barbara Gribling (eds.)

The Case of the Initial Letter: Charles Dickens and the politics of the dual alphabet   Gavin Edwards

Spain in the nineteenth century: New essays on experiences of culture and society
Andrew Ginger and Geraldine Lawless

Instead of modernity: The Western canon and the incorporation of the Hispanic (c. 1850–75)
Andrew Ginger

Creating character: Theories of nature and nurture in Victorian sensation fiction   Helena Ifill

Margaret Harkness: Writing social engagement 1880–1921   Flore Janssen and
Lisa C. Robertson (eds.)

Richard Marsh, popular fiction and literary culture, 1890–1915: Re-reading the fin de siècle
Victoria Margree, Daniel Orrells, and Minna Vuohelainen (eds.)

Charlotte Brontë: Legacies and afterlives   Amber K. Regis and Deborah Wynne (eds.)

The Great Exhibition, 1851: A sourcebook   Jonathon Shears (ed.)

Interventions: Rethinking the nineteenth century   Andrew Smith and Anna Barton (eds.)

Counterfactual Romanticism   Damian Walford Davies (ed.)

Marie Duval: Maverick Victorian cartoonist   Simon Grennan, Roger Sabin, and Julian Waite

Spectral Dickens
The uncanny forms of novelistic characterization

Alexander Bove

Manchester University Press

Copyright © Alexander Bove 2021

The right of Alexander Bove to be identified as the author of this work has been asserted by him in accordance with the Copyright, Designs and Patents Act 1988.

Published by Manchester University Press
Oxford Road, Manchester M13 9PL
www.manchesteruniversitypress.co.uk

British Library Cataloguing-in-Publication Data
A catalogue record for this book is available from the British Library

ISBN 978 1 5261 4793 6 hardback
ISBN 978 1 5261 7454 3 paperback

First published 2021
Paperback published 2023

The publisher has no responsibility for the persistence or accuracy of URLs for any external or third-party internet websites referred to in this book, and does not guarantee that any content on such websites is, or will remain, accurate or appropriate.

Typeset by Newgen Publishing UK

Contents

List of figures vi
Acknowledgments ix

Introduction: an uncanny ontology of characterization 1

Part I: Spectral mimesis: portraits, caricature, and character 29

1 Mimesis's ghosts: caricature and anamorphosis 31
2 Spectral character: dreams, distortion, and
  the (cut of the) Real 54

Part II: "Moor eeffocish things": effigy and the bourgeoisie 81

3 Where "the specular becomes the spectral" in *The Old
  Curiosity Shop* and *Dombey and Son* 83
4 Imagos, dolls, and other gazing effigies in *Bleak House* 128

Part III: Beyond the realism principle: spectral materiality 157

5 Dream as spectral form in *Bleak House* and the comic
  surplus of Micawber in *David Copperfield* 159
6 The "as if" hauntology of *Little Dorrit* and the uncanny
  dream of the three fathers 199

Bibliography 223
Index 229

Figures

1. Honoré Daumier, "Les Poires" (The Pears), lithograph published in *La Caricature*, 1831 (courtesy of the Met Collection) — 35

2. Charles Philipon, "Croquades faites à l'audience du 14 nov." (Jibes Made at the Hearing of 14 Nov.), sketch, 1831 (courtesy of the British Museum Collection) — 37

3. J. J. Grandville, "Man and Animal Portraits Compared," lithograph in *Le Magasin pittoresque*, 1844 (author's personal collection) — 40

4. J. J. Grandville, "Premier Rêve, Crime et expiation" (First Dream: Crime and Atonement), wood engraving illustration (from lithograph on wove paper) in *Le Magasin pittoresque*, July 1847 (courtesy of the Met Collection) — 41

5. J. J. Grandville, "Second Rêve, Une promenade dans le ciel" (Second Dream: A Promenade Through the Sky), engraving (from lithograph on wove paper) in *Le Magasin pittoresque*, 1847 (courtesy of the Met Collection) — 42

6. J. J. Grandville, "Un peintre, à cheval sur son dada raphaélique" (A Painter Astride His Raphael Hobby Horse), lithograph illustration in *Un Autre Monde*, 1843 (author's personal collection) — 47

7. J. J. Grandville, "Il a beau faire, il n'aura pas la croix" (No Matter How Hard He Tries, He Will Not Find the Cross), lithograph illustration in *La Caricature*, 1832 (author's personal collection) — 55

Figures

8   Phiz (Hablot K. Browne), "The Valentine," etching for *The Pickwick Papers*, 1837 (courtesy of the Rare and Special Books Collection of the University Libraries, University at Buffalo, State University of New York)   64

9   Phiz (Hablot K. Browne), "The Trial," etching for *The Pickwick Papers*, 1837 (courtesy of the Rare and Special Books Collection of the University Libraries, University at Buffalo, State University of New York)   69

10 Honoré Daumier, "Le Ventre Législatif" (The Legislative Belly), lithograph on wove paper, 1843 (courtesy of the Met Collection)   73

11 Phiz (Hablot K. Browne), "Pickwick Sits for His Portrait," etching for *The Pickwick Papers*, 1837 (courtesy of the V & A Collection)   78

12 Honoré Daumier, "Masques de 1831" (Masks of 1831), lithograph published in *La Caricature* March 8, 1832 (courtesy of the Met Collection)   90

13 Phiz (Hablot K. Browne), "Revenge Is Sweet," engraving for *The Old Curiosity Shop*, 1840   99

14 Phiz (Hablot K. Browne), "Captain Cuttle Consoles His Friend," etching for *Dombey and Son*, 1846 (courtesy of the Rare and Special Books Collection of the University Libraries, University at Buffalo, State University of New York)   107

15 Phiz (Hablot K. Browne), "The Wooden Midshipman on the Lookout," etching for *Dombey and Son*, 1847 (courtesy of the Rare and Special Books Collection of the University Libraries, University at Buffalo, State University of New York)   108

16 Phiz (Hablot K. Browne), "The Lord Chancellor Copies from Memory," etching for *Bleak House*, 1853 (courtesy of the Rare and Special Books Collection of the University Libraries, University at Buffalo, State University of New York)   142

Figures

17 Phiz (Hablot K. Browne), "The Appointed Time," etching for *Bleak House*, 1853 (courtesy of the Rare and Special Books Collection of the University Libraries, University at Buffalo, State University of New York) — 144

18 Phiz (Hablot K. Browne), "A New Meaning in the Roman," dark plate etching for *Bleak House*, 1853 (courtesy of the Rare and Special Books Collection of the University Libraries, University at Buffalo, State University of New York) — 145

19 Phiz (Hablot K. Browne), "Tom-All-Alone's," dark plate etching for *Bleak House*, 1853 (courtesy of the Rare and Special Books Collection of the University Libraries, University at Buffalo, State University of New York) — 149

20 Honoré Daumier, "Ah His! ... Ah His! Ah His!" (Heave-Ho! ... Heave-Ho! Heave-Ho!), lithograph published in *La Caricature*, July 19, 1832 (author's personal collection) — 152

Acknowledgments

My deepest gratitude—more than I can possibly put into words here—goes to the two people who most inspired this book through their teaching, writings, conversations, and lifelong friendship: Professor Julia Prewitt Brown and Professor David Wagenknecht, both of Boston University. Their influence and inspiration go far beyond these pages, but suffice it to say that my fascination with Dickens and Lacan, along with many other things, can be traced back to these wonderful human beings. I also owe a very special thanks to Howard Eiland, whose boundless hospitality and intellectual generosity provided the occasion for many inspirational discussions of Walter Benjamin, the Frankfurt School, J. J. Grandville, illustration, film, and many other things that fostered the seeds of this book.

I would never have been able to bring this work—a labor of love long in the making—to fruition, were it not for the constant encouragement and unfaltering support of my mother and father, who never failed to show enthusiasm for my work and ideas, and the always solid advice of my sister, Andrea, over the years and at pivotal moments in my life. I am also deeply grateful to two of my dearest friends, fellow writers, and colleagues, Michael Arner and Keith Leslie Johnson, for the many hours we spent together in Boston discussing theory and for all the ways in which they have challenged and influenced my thinking.

Finally, this book is for my wife Amanda, whose presence is there in every word on every page.

Introduction: an uncanny ontology of characterization

> To haunt does not mean to be present, and it is necessary to introduce haunting into the very construct of a concept. Of every concept, beginning with the concepts of being and time. That is what we would be calling here a Hauntology. Ontology opposes it only in movement of exorcism. Ontology is a conjuration. (Derrida, *Specters* 202)

> The uncanny is always at stake in ideology—ideology perhaps basically consists of a social attempt to integrate the uncanny, to make it bearable, to assign it a place, and the criticism of ideology is caught in the same framework if it tries to reduce it to another kind of content or to make the content conscious and explicit. (Dolar 19)

A new art form, without an origin (or originator)

> Dickens, almost accidentally, as it were, created a new art form in his simultaneous composition of the texts for the novel's parts and supervision of its illustrations. But new as the art form was, both he and his most frequent illustrator, Hablot Browne, drew on a rich set of iconographic traditions. (Steig 7)

Despite being the Victorian novelist perhaps best known for his invention of characters, Dickens has, strangely enough, always presented a challenge to critical studies of characterization. At times this difficulty in explaining Dickens's elusive characterization is attributed to a flaw on the part of the author himself, rather than to a deficiency in the theory, so that Dickens has not infrequently been considered, for instance, a "failed realist" rather than a radically idiosyncratic novelist writing in the age of realism. On the other hand, some of the most insightful and groundbreaking work in this area is by authors—G. K. Chesterton, Steven Marcus, Garrett Stewart, and John Bowen to name but a few—who seem uninterested in formulating a unified or systematic theory of characterization. Either way, Dickens's characters continue to haunt critics in their ability to inspire imaginative and nuanced critical responses and yet elude systematization. My assumption here is that it is precisely these *resistances* that Dickens's characters offer to theorization that present an opportunity to rethink the very idea of characterization as such. But what kind of characterization would we be rethinking here? Novelistic characterization, whose medium is words? One belonging to the illustrated novel, made up of words and images whose relation tends to go under the aegis of iconography or iconology? Or one belonging to some "new art form" that, as Steig suggests, Dickens (and Phiz) invented, and perhaps still itself remains elusive and under-theorized—even unrecognized?

The history of modern studies of fictional characterization has, in the broadest sense, traditionally been divided between two camps: on one side there are structuralist and poststructuralist-inspired theories that see character as inextricable from forms of representation like plot, narrative, and language; on the other side, there are mimesis-bound theories that see characters as "autonomous" from structure and plot, as "life-like" reflections of "real-world" persons or selves. Scholarship that addresses characterization in the Victorian novel, like that of most other literary periods and genres, may be self-conscious about this framework or it may be indifferent to it, but it rarely if ever breaks away from it or forges new ground in this regard. And yet little has been said about the limits this semiotic dichotomy places on critical thought and theorization regarding the range of representational modalities it recognizes within the novel form, let alone how a novelist like Dickens eludes these coordinates in very literal and obvious ways. And it is not difficult to see how either side may seem reductive and, well, one-sided: in his classic post-structuralist study of novelistic characterization, *The Form of the Victorian Novel*, for instance, J. Hillis Miller claims that "far from affirming the independent existence of what he describes, Dickens's narrator betrays in a number of ways the fact that fictional characters and their world are made only of words" (36). This formulation, which well encapsulates the traditional debate, assumes a framework that has only oppositional reference points, an external "independent existence" and a self-referential "world ... of words," and indeed obscures the obvious presence of the nontextual elements of characterization in Dickens's novel, the *illustrations*, which in turn leaves little place for the idea that *visual* forms of representation could (equally) have an *intrinsic* role in this supposedly exclusive linguistic world.

Introduction

Somewhat ironically, Miller went on to write a good deal (and very insightfully) about Dickens's illustrators Cruikshank and Phiz, but even then his criticism never took into account the idea that Dickens's words could, as such, actually draw on techniques of visual representation for means of evoking subjectivity. One reason may be that Miller's analysis of the illustrations was framed in terms of an *iconology*, which led him to compare word and image ultimately on the grounds of structure, each, that is, as an abstract and reified "sign": "The interference of picture and text with one another, *their* dialogic relation, in any situation in which they are set side by side, arises not from the fact that they are different media that produce meaning differently, but from the fact that they work in the same way to produce meaning as designs that are signs" (*Illustration* 95). *Do* all types of signs, whether linguistic or imagistic, "work in the same way to produce meaning"? Is this question/representational aporia formulated in the right way? Miller's formulations here are very telling and, indeed, a great starting point for rethinking our ontology of characterization. To cut ahead for a moment, I would like to suggest here that we should stop thinking of different forms of representation, such as words and pictures no less than novels and films, as being "set side by side" but in fact as *haunting and haunted by one another*—even in some cases where there are no illustrations present, perhaps above all in such cases. Can we speak of *absent* illustrations in a text? Later in this book I will suggest that many of Dickens's scenes and characters are haunted by lithographs of French artists like Daumier and Grandville. "Side by side" opposes these media, in Miller's formulation, only to then efface their difference through a sort of semiotic vanishing point, whereas I find it much more useful to see each sign-system as multiple and various within themselves, and yet fundamentally (and this is the key point here) other to each other and *therefore to themselves*—each as marked by its own non-self-identity or "*out-of-jointness*," to use Derrida's hauntological term, which puts them into antagonism with each other. These *differences* or *antagonisms* within and between forms of representation, their otherness to each other and to themselves, is, I argue, the very thing that grounds characterization in an ethics/hauntology and that allows me to distinguish between multiple forms of representation, most importantly between institutionalized forms (such as mimesis and realism) and counter-representational or *spectral forms* (such as caricature and anamorphosis), beyond the internal/external opposition that has limited studies of characterization.

Assumed in any theory of characterization, and in fact in any discussion of character, is a whole panoply of underlying concepts having to do with subjectivity, the subject, the difference between subjects and objects, personhood and the politics of the person, the psyche, etc. If we lump these concepts and fields under the blanket idea of the subject, we can see that the dichotomy in approaches to characterization reflects an interesting dichotomy in relation to the approaches to the subject they draw on implicitly or explicitly. Whereas the structuralists tended to evade the need to appeal to theories of the subject by shifting the focus onto language and semiotic theory, mimetic approaches tend almost by definition to imply an emphasis on the ego (in some named or unnamed form) as the center and ground of the subject. Attempts to think through this opposition, especially in earlier criticism on characterization informed by post-structuralism, often tended only to reinforce it. Robert Higbie's comprehensive early study *Character and Structure in the English Novel* (1984), which focuses intensely on Austen and Dickens as illustrating opposite types of characterization in the novel, proves a demonstrative example. Higbie, whose approach is ostensibly linguistic at heart but draws heavily on an American version of Freud, very tellingly makes the relationship of the subject to desire (and the extent to which it is sublimated) central to his concept of characterization, distinguishing categorically between Dickens's "unresolved characters" and Austen's "conscious characters":

> Unresolved characters like those in Dickens differ from conscious characters, then, in that they *cannot function as subjects as adequately* as conscious characters can. That is, the desire they serve cannot be sublimated or controlled enough to be accepted and used fulfillingly by the self. Thus their desire remains fairly negative, not reconciled to control, often irrational, even violent. (123, emphasis added)

It is easy to see from our vantage point that Higbie's use of Freud and structuralism is dated and in fact in some ways more reflective of a historicist ideology, but in fact the very schematic way in which Higbie establishes an opposition in the novel tradition between the psychological innerness of Richardson's characters as "subject" characters (culminating in Austen) and the comic externality of Fielding's characters, as "object" characters (culminating in Dickens), strips bear, as it were, the skeletal structure at the core of many of the unacknowledged assumptions about character informing much of the criticism on characterization to this day and its ontological/ideological implications. Higbie's approach, that is, privileges a potentially fully self-present ego as a model of the subject, despite its ostensible appeal to Freudian terminology on the one

Introduction

hand and structuralism on the other, a concept of the "self" ideologically deeply rooted in an ideal of control and mastery (especially mastery of pleasure), as well as productive rationality, leading to a scale according to which certain subjects (i.e., Dickens's characters by nature) are in fact *less* (ontologically) *subjects* and more like *objects*, or like partial (quasi-) subjects conceived as ontologically diminished persons (subjects minus their "full" consciousness and thus presence). Higbie's classic study inadvertently shows us how much our approach to characterization is inextricably bound up with ethics, ideology, and ontology. Moreover, many of the more recent and more theoretically sophisticated psychoanalytic approaches to characterization in the Victorian period are still haunted by this kind of out-of-date American ego psychology inasmuch as there is a sense that characters that are not subjectivized in a preconceived way are not "adequately" or "fully" subjects (for instance in Audrey Jaffe's influential *Vanishing Points: Dickens, Narrative, and the Subject of Omniscience*). Yet one can immediately see how more recent psychoanalytically informed critical approaches could potentially provide the direction for a way out of the structure/ego dichotomy. In fact, much of the psychoanalytically informed Victorian criticism of the last two decades or so has moved in this direction, though, as I have just suggested, it does not go nearly far enough, often remaining partly influenced by American ego-psychology or especially by unconsidered New Historicist influences. My project is thus to resituate the framework within which we conceive of character in Dickens's novels in terms of an openness to other (for instance visual or nonmimetic) forms of representation and to truly *other* conceptions of subjectivity (not grounded in the ego, even if in contradistinction to it, or as "external")—for which I need to turn to the idea of hauntology.

Hauntology and character

The framework, then, within which we theorize character—and indeed think about and write about character in general—comes down to us already structured by this opposition between a *mimetic* concept of character, for which character is a direct simulacrum of a person defined as a conscious self-present ego, on the one hand, and a *structural* concept on the other, for which character is a pure representation, a play or effect of a signifying system that disposes of any appeal to the "real" or to real *subjectivity* at all. What should stand out here, though, after the preceding discussion, is the strange asymmetry of this opposition, mimesis versus structure. Is structure really the "opposite" of mimesis? Mimetic character is supposedly attached to a "real" referent, the approximation of a person, whereas structural approaches circumvent the problem of the real with a linguistically grounded ontology, immanent or "internal" to the representation itself (both they and their world are self-referential and "made only of words"); so in the ontological sense, the opposition seems at first glance to function adequately and to make sense critically. And yet, mimesis can be identified primarily by two key factors: the form of representation (frequently associated with some form of *realism*), and in the case of characterization, a concept of the subject or self (a "person") associated with self-presence and ego (not to mention ideologies of personhood). Here is where the opposition seems asymmetrical because structuralism is neither in itself, nor intrinsically linked to, a *form* of representation; nor is it *necessarily associated* with a particular concept of subjectivity. If anything, it carries the connotation of being an "objective" or "external" view of a person that lacks "access" or suggests a lack of "innerness" or fullness of subjectivity (as Higbie supposes), defined as it is by the system or "structure" of signs themselves and not in terms of the referents, let alone the "persons" it represents. Some critical questions arise from looking at the asymmetry in this way. One would be: what other forms of representation *do* "oppose" or act as "other" to mimetic forms of representation? One might, for instance, describe nonmimetic characters from a novel or film as "very dreamlike" or "fantastic," but these adjectives are not attached to any given form of representation (for which we have a specific name) in the way that "very realistic" would seem to necessarily imply mimesis, while available descriptive nonmimetic categories like fantasy, gothic, or melodrama all refer to *genres* and not *forms* of representation. Another question would be: What *other* means of thinking subjectivity, as opposed to egocentric and presence-based models, can help inform theories of characterization that take medium and representation into account?

A recent revival in theories of characterization in the novel has brought this dichotomy to the foreground, but has not really been able to formulate the problem in such a way as to bring about some working through or beyond it. John Frow is the best illustration of this: his epic study of characterization, *Character and Person*, gets to the core of the whole tradition of characterization studies and best articulates the aporia we are essentially dealing with here, though without really reframing it himself. The aporia underlying the different approaches, as Frow does well to see from the outset, is an ontological one, and according to Frow presents us

Introduction

with a double bind. Frow's deliberations on the ontological nature of the problem are worth quoting at length here:

> This is the first part of the problem we encounter when we try to understand the nature of fictional character: these figures are made of words, of images, of imaginings; they are not real in the way that people are real. The second part of the problem is this: why and how do we endow these sketched-in figures with a semblance of reality? Why are we moved by these ontologically hybrid beings that people the pages of novels or the spaces of theater of the storyline of films? What makes us imagine that these clusters of words or images are in some way like persons? (1)

There is a kind of hermeneutic, searching element to Frow's approach that makes it both compelling and fruitful, but it is interesting that rather than questioning the ontological aporia on ontological grounds, Frow temporally displaces it: "first" of all characters are put safely into the realm of representation, they are "not real" in any literal sense, and only *then* (the "second part of the problem") do they compel us to see and think of them as "real" persons. In order to pursue the complex ontological question at stake here we will have to rethink this opposition between a "real person" and a "fictional character" as a purely imaginary copy or simulacrum of a real person—an opposition depending on a rather surprisingly simplified idea of *presence* given the last few decades of literary theory and continental philosophy. In order to reframe our conceptualization of character, we would have to subject some of these concepts to more rigorous analysis, including and perhaps above all the question of the *real*. Instead, Frow sees characters as "ontologically hybrid" beings that span across the two categories, sharing some qualities of each, and yet remaining always "made of words," "not real."

Frow's innovation, then, is interestingly to reformulate the opposition sketched out here between structure and mimesis in terms of "structuralist reduction" and "humanist plenitude" (17) and he attempts to navigate some ways beyond the dichotomy by displacing them onto different objects: "One way of moving beyond the tied dichotomy of structuralist reduction and humanist plenitude (of the *actant* and the fully human character) is to recognize that these models of fictional agency apply to different objects, and thus recast them as difference levels of analysis" (17). But again here we are diverted from the fundamental question of ontology, since the "object" of representation is already presumed to be a "model of" something real, a "fictional agency" as opposed to a "real" one. Frow himself is certainly attuned to this, and he himself criticizes Alex

Woloch for attaching character, as person, to a hierarchical grounding in presence: "Underlying Woloch's systematic attempt to overcome the poles of structuralist reduction and humanist plenitude, however, is a deeply problematic insistence on the fullness of being that underlies character, a sense that the asymmetry of attention to major and minor characters somehow represents a repression of the 'potentially full human beings' of narrative," which Frow insists is in fact "no more than a function of the fictional universe" (23). We can thus see how Frow can only critique Woloch's implicitly ontological (although, granted, less self-consciously so) position by recourse to another ontologically grounded critique that is still no less bound to the dichotomy of real versus simulacrum. In other words, Frow can rationalize ("demystify") presence as a "function of the fictional universe," but he can't escape it because he doesn't allow for its own inherent antagonism, its own haunted ontology.

More broadly, Frow's overall approach to characterization takes its strength from its multiplicity and flexibility, rather than from systematicity and uniformity, grounded as it is in his discussion of various tropes and concepts that work to form characters that generate an attachment and investment comparable to "real" persons, such as: "figure," "interest," "person," "type," etc. (which name and structure his chapters). In this way he is successful insofar as we get a kind of Deleuzian material critique of character, but we can never really escape "ontological hybridity" as a means of "holding together" different "ways of thinking" about character: the reduction to structure versus the "plenitude" of presence (25). But these two ways are, again, at bottom just another means of repeating the ontological aporia that the problem of character inevitably entails. Characters, on the one hand, are generated by structure and narrative sequencing: "As figure, [character] is a dimension of the compositional structure of a text; a moment of an action sequence which both derives and acquires attributes from the sequence" (24). On the one hand, and in tension with this structuralist aspect, "character is, in certain respects, also the analogue of 'real' persons, conforming more or less closely and more or less fully to the schemata that govern ... what it means to be a person and to have a physical body, a moral character, a sense of self," etc. (24). As such, there is always something ontologically lacking, an ontological *secondariness*, when it comes to character; in short, says Frow, "[character] is of the order of representation rather than the order of the real" (25). In other words, "ontological hybridity" is merely a means for Frow to have his cake and eat it, to straddle an aporia without thinking its antagonism—without coming to terms with the fact that the "order of the real"

8

is the *internal* limit concept for characterization, rather than filling in the aporia with a concept still determined by its logic.

But is there a way for us to approach this aporia without rationalizing it, or conjuring it away? Is there a way to incorporate this seemingly ineluctable problem of the "order of the real" into the very concept of character itself, or into a theory of character that does not rely on presence as an external limit point or ground? How much do we know about the relation *between* these two orders, real and representation? Are not characters of the order of the real at least *as* characters? Is not the concept of *person* of the order of representation in often literal ways, for instance legally, politically, (auto)biographically? In short, the first step, I am suggesting, is to see the *order of the real*, and the idea of the "real person," not as an external limit point, but as a *spectral other* that will always haunt character's ontological status within the order of representation—and will always *be haunted itself by the order of representation*.

However we might want to be dismissive of or brush aside these questions, perhaps as belonging to some field other than our own, they are questions we need to at least properly formulate if we are going to try to tackle the "problem" of character (as Frow puts it) in a way that can move beyond the traditional limit concepts of literary theory. Anyone specializing in the field of literature should readily admit, or at least be prepared to carefully consider, that we cannot simply "remove" representation from reality in order to separate them and speak of them as different "orders" sustaining the purity of some ideal reality or "real" referent beyond and independent of representation. Instead of brushing aside this complex relationship, we need to think of this grounding concept of *the Real*, as that which representation seems to distinguish itself (or externalize itself) from ontologically, in its various dimensions. If character is a simulacra of a "real" subject (a person, for instance), then what is the relation of the *subject* (or *person*) to this "real"—do they wholly overlap and encompass each other without remainder? If so, how and why would the subject "have" (or *need*) language (representation) to access this real? Inversely, if character/simulacra is merely a "cluster of words," made only of language *and so not of the order of the real*, what is the relation of the "*real*" subject, as such, to words? And underlying all this: *What is the relation of language to the Real?* Is it merely a given that the former reflects the latter as a distinct "order"? These are of course by no means new or unasked questions, and this is precisely why *Lacanian psychoanalysis*, which grows out of these question about the signifier and it's relation to the subject, is so useful here—and Lacan's concept of the Real is precisely what captures the fundamental elusiveness of this limit point, this *manqué-être*, this something/nothing/being "beyond representation" and its paradoxically ontological, epistemological, psychological, and political status. Literary criticism understandably tends to want to repress or "exorcise" (as Derrida would have it) this problematic specter of referentiality, but when we do so it only returns in the form of other specters. As Dolar points out, we want to "assign" this uncanny ontology a more rational and conscious place to make it "bearable," which as I have tried to show is ineluctably an act caught up in a framework of ideology.

Fortunately this territory has been extensively and productively explored and mapped out by Lacanian psychoanalytic theory. Žižek's concept of Disparity, for example, provides a useful metaphor for thinking about the relational dimensions between the subject, language, and the Real. One of the basic insights of Lacan on which he bases his whole systematic decentering of the subject is that language is not merely an objective thing to be included among other objects within reality, since in fact this very reality is always already constituted for the subject by language, and the Real is ultimately precisely the disparity, the nonidentity, or element of nonrelation between reality and itself: "One cannot include language into reality since what appears to us as reality is already transcendentally constituted through a horizon of meaning sustained by language" (*Disparities* 70). Žižek's discussion of Disparity also nicely crystalizes why the recent trend in psychoanalytic criticism is called "psychoanalytic materialism," because in opposition to the so called New Materialisms (e.g., object-oriented ontology), which sees its "materialism" as a form of object-oriented *realism*, or "speculative realism," psychoanalysis distinguishes the subject from the object as that which introduces Disparity, or antagonism, into the order of reality as such. As Žižek puts it, "We have to introduce here the distinction between the transcendentally constituted phenomenon reality and the Real: the way to be a consequent materialist is not to directly include the subject into reality, as an object among objects, but to bring out the Real of the subject, the way the emergence of subjectivity functions as a cut in the Real" (*Disparities* 70). In this sense, the Real is not so much an ontological concept as an ontoethical one, or more precisely the vanishing point between ontology and ethics (since without it we are at a loss to accommodate the idea of ontological difference); the Real "is a convulsion, a stumbling block of the space of being," as Zupančič so wonderfully put it (43). The Real is precisely where the nonrelation, the uncanny out-of-jointness, between the symbolic and being is articulated: "There is only being in the

Introduction

symbolic—*except that there is the Real*" (Zupančič 42), which is also perhaps what so worried Frow about Woloch's sense of potential ontological "plenitude" within representation.

Frow, as I have tried to demonstrate, has brought to the surface, as it were, more saliently than any other critic on characterization, how ontological opposition (manifested as of real/copy, absent/present, being/imaginary, etc.) remains an elusive limit-point that determines and haunts our concept of fictional character; yet his theoretical framework, being determined by this limit-point, cannot situate us to think this opposition as such, or more specifically, as the *antagonism of all realism*, ontological difference. The antagonism is not a "thing" that can be stitched together with, for instance, hybridity (or obfuscated by hierarchies like original/copy), but is a *specter* haunting it from within, an intrinsic lack that functions as a (non)object preventing the "real thing" or "real person" from ever being a complete-present-Being. For Lacan, as Žižek's concept of Disparity illustrates, the Real *is* this very antagonism, this "disparity between part of a thing and nothing … It is at this level that we should locate ontological difference: reality is partial, incomplete, inconsistent, and the Supreme Being is the illusion imagined in order to fill in (obfuscate) this lack, this void that makes reality not-all" (Žižek, *Disparities* 21). This last point is crucial because it speaks to the way our drive to subjectivize the world—and thus fiction, fictional character, etc.—is structurally determined by the fundamentally desubjectivizing relation between being ("reality") and language. The subject *occupies* this position of the cut in being relative to language, not some position *in the real* as self-present reality, and this very cut or lack *as an uncanny disparity* or not-all, compels us to fill it in with "plenitude," with presence, as a means of avoiding its intrinsic *ontological uncanniness*. In other words, in this way, seeing character as an ontologically secondary simulacrum, or an ontological hybrid, itself creates a sense of "plenitude" for the "real"/original status of the person.

And yet, we nevertheless can and do also sometimes perceive characters as *uncanny forms*—not as safely confined to the "order of representation," but as *haunting us* with our own lack of presence *from within* that safely defined "order of the real." And of course while many forms of characterization appeal in their very construction to mimetic impulses towards plentitude (or as Audrey Jaffe puts it, to the dream, the fantasy of the real), other forms of characterization, which are less theorized, push towards this uncanny gap in being that I am referring to as the Real. These are, I am suggesting, nowhere better articulated than in Dickens's works and in the modes of characterization that were influenced directly and indirectly by his work. Dickens, that is, marks an uncanny departure from the subjective/objective, internal/external trajectory of characterization in the history of the novel as sketched out, for instance, by Higbie—not as a force for one side or the other, or as some synthesis of the two, but in his development of forms of character that haunt us with the specters of subjectivity. Dickens's characters are grounded in an uncanny ontology and develop the forms of this uncanny ontology in a variety of new, nonmimetic forms of representation that he perhaps partly stumbled upon in his "new art form," with its strange and unexpected, unplanned for internalization of the visual medium into the novel, not to mention his journalistic sketches, his temporal rhythms for composition punctuated with coordinating illustrations and text, and his contemporaneity with the invention of the lithograph, with its own internal verbal/visual dimension articulated especially in political caricature. Others have located this uncanny historical departure in various historical/biographical ways: Steven Marcus, for instance, attributes Dickens's strangely "material" relation to language to his youthful encounter with shorthand stenography ("Language into Structure"); Chesterton attributes the fluidity in Dickens's prose between subjects and objects (people and things) to his "walking dreamily" though the streets alone as a child on his way to the blacking factory (*Collected Works*); Daniel Novak sees in Dickens's strange and paradoxical realism his obsession with art models and its relation to the budding technology of photography. I will touch on many of these ideas in the chapters that follow, but for me, trying to posit a literal historical explanation for the uncanny breakthrough of Dickens's characters, or to "make the [uncanny] content [rather than its form] explicit and conscious" as Mladen Dolar points out, is only to place this break back into another ideological framework. Instead I will explore the ontological role of the uncanny as such.

Uncanny ontology: subjectivity, the cut of the Real

Freud's concept of the uncanny comes at a crucial juncture in his *oeuvre*, marking a point at which his model of the human psyche is disrupted from within by an external foreign entity, hinted at in his essay "The Uncanny" (1919) through the concept of *repetition compulsion* and developed as the *death drive* that opposes both the reality principle and the pleasure principle in his subsequent work *Beyond the Pleasure Principle* (1920). In his seminal essay "The Uncanny," Freud defines the uncanny as a play between the familiar and the strange or secret—or as he puts it, as "the secretly

Introduction

familiar"—between the homely (*heimlich*) and the *un*homely (*unheimlich*), which arises when, through an elusive repetition known as the return of the repressed, a forbidden/repressed/secretly known thing "comes to light" as such. But the concept of the death drive, which is attached to the uncanny through the harmony between the two works, makes the concept even more suggestive and ontological, which is why it has had such a rich and diverse history in philosophy and critical thought since the essay was published. Thus as a liminal dimension wavering or flickering between oppositions—strange/familiar, self/other, subject/object, and even life/death—yet reducible to neither side, the uncanny provides a unique horizon within which to reconsider the ontological dimensions of characterization. That is, with its strange *undecidability* between external and internal, the uncanny provides a new opportunity to resituate our understanding of character as a "hybrid" or as somehow divided between this ontological division of objective structure (a cluster of words, images, etc.) and subjective "plentitude" (ego and imitated presence).

The paradoxically deferred temporality of the uncanny, what Freud termed "repetition compulsion" or "return of the repressed," is one of its most important dimensions as a concept that disrupts the traditional dichotomy of mimesis's original/copy dynamics. What is it about the uncanny that makes it, by definition, *return* or repeat? Derrida puts it another way: what is uncanny is *always already a repetition*, even upon its first "visit." Like the ghost in *Hamlet*, it always seems to be "coming back" from somewhere, some beyond. In fact, as Freud formulates it in his famous essay, the return of the repressed in the case of uncanny is always essentially traceable to a moment in the history of the subject that logically precedes the relation between *inside* and *outside*, or self and Other; in other words, the repetition can have no "origin" in relation to a self that did not as such exist. Both the "castration complex" and "primary narcissism," the two forms of repressed material most associated with the uncanny by Freud, refer implicitly to a *cut* that establishes a relation between inside and outside of the subject's body and psyche, but that, precisely because it plays the role of positing this structure in the "first place," as it were, always threatens to "return" to the status of the (now repressed or forgotten) nonrelation. The different forms of the return of the repressed Freud provides as examples are all, as he puts it, "harkening back to particular phases in the evolution of the self-regarding feeling, a regression to a time when the ego had not yet marked itself off sharply from the external world and from other people" ("The Uncanny" 212). What is touched by the uncanny, we could say, always bears the mark of this cut, this (impossible) known within the unknown, the foreign and strange within the familiar, which threatens to undo the very distinction between the separate categories precisely by introducing a cut, an out-of-jointness (to borrow Derrida's phrase) into the telos of the subject, its narrative formation of self-identity, which is why Freud's tracing of the uncanny to castration and narcissism is always already a mark of *symbolic castration* (what I will call later a *desubjectification* that always haunts subjectification). The uncanny as such introduces this real/representation antagonism into the very heart of the ("real") subject.

It is thus this concept of *desubjectification* that takes the concept of character *beyond the representation/real dichotomy*, as this desubjectification, this cut of the Real beyond the being/symbolic relation, is at stake, and indeed ontologically determinative, in both character and subject; it is in a sense their vanishing point in the Real where one converges into the other in a missing (out-of-joint) dimension. This is the fundamental value of the concept of Disparity for my approach to characterization, since this cut of the Real that is also subjectivity is the very thing that distinguishes the *ontic* viewpoint (the "flat" ontology that sees all beings as objects) of all forms of New Materialism from the *uncanny ontology* of psychoanalytic materialism, which in a way separates the subject from both the object *and* the (human) person: "The dimension that resists self-objectification is not human self-experience but the 'inhuman' core of what German Idealism calls negativity, what Freud called death drive, and even what Heidegger referred to as 'ontological difference': a gap or abyss which forever precludes the exclusively ontic view of humans as just another object among objects" (Žižek, *Disparities* 27).

It is worth dwelling on the fact that this strange concept of Disparity that not only equates ontological difference with the death drive, but also elicits the "inhuman core" of the human to distinguish the status of the subject from that of the object, is thus itself rather uncanny. But at this point let us sum up that the uncanny ontology of *Disparity*, *specters*, and *the Real* allow us a means to go beyond the opposition between an *objectification of the subject*, which the structuralist view of character presupposes, and a *subjectification of the symbolic* (object), which the mimetic position effects, without actually positing some kind of third dimension, but by including the antagonism of *desubjectification* (another way of expressing this will be through Lacan's concept of symbolic castration, or as an inscription of the death drive). Desubjectification as a formal basis of character is everywhere in Dickens's new art form and is virtually nowhere in Dickens's criticism. One just has to think of the idea of the character tic and caricature from a radically different perspective (as I will argue in Chapter 1), but also, of Dickens's use of uncanny objects like dolls and effigies that haunt the difference between persons and things—all of these are not just supplements to characters but part of their very form: Tulkinghorn would not be Tulkinghorn without the Roman Allegory (an effigy central to the novel's symbolic fabric), and Esther's doll is not merely left behind when she buries it as a child, but haunts the illustrations and other liminal human figures throughout the novel.

The abundance and centrality of effigies in Dickens's novels is quite astonishing—almost as astonishing as the fact that they are so thoroughly overlooked in the criticism (except in passing or in brief speculations). Effigies, as I will argue in Chapter 2, are not props or mere effect in Dickens, but play a fundamentally formal role in his means of characterization: they are, in fact, a primary means of signifying nonmimetically and thus become a metaphor for Dickens's form of characterization itself. But the most iconic illustration I can give of this uncanny ontology of character and its desubjectifying impulse is that of Rosa Dartle, from *David Copperfield*. Rosa's scar, as I will explore in Chapter 1, forms a spectral nodal point quilting together symbolic and formal strands of the text: the sexual aggression and tension between Rosa and Steerforth, the doubling and gender play between Rosa and David, but also formal elements like Dickens's desire to subvert mimetic portraiture through the signifying free play opened by counter-representational forms like caricature and distortion. However, Rosa is a central illustration of Dickens's spectral form of characterization, perhaps above all because she so powerfully exposes how Dickens's desire to forge new nonmimetic forms of representation is inextricably bound up with his desire to disrupt ego-based models of the self in characterization, that is, to disrupt the bond between ego and mimesis forged in the concept of *identification*.

The ego in the mirror: from identification to projection and (the) beyond

Returning to Frow's articulation of this dichotomy in the approaches to characterization as "structural reduction" and "humanist plenitude" (what I have been calling simply structuralism *vs.* mimesis): I don't think the quantitative implications of "reduction" and "plenitude" are necessary for a critique of characterization, but it is interesting that, also for Frow, the position of the "schemata" opposing structuralism, that of the "humanist," is inevitably associated with both the *ego* and *mimesis* (the idea of "lifelikeness" expresses a nodal point linking all of the ideas on this pole including fullness/depth, plenitude/life, etc.). We may thus rightfully ask here why the ego is so closely linked with mimesis in this tradition, and the image of the mirror as the metaphor for mimesis is a good place to start unraveling this problem. In his chapter on "interest," in which he sets out to explain why we are affectively attached to these clusters of words and images that are characters, Frow focuses on *identification* as the primary support of ego-formation: "the identifications through which the ego is formed and which give it its imaginary unity set up a relation between inside and outside, and thus take place by means of a superimposition of the boundary of the ego on the boundary of the body" (51). I have already discussed, to some extent, the idea that the Freudian/Lacanian uncanny cuts into and ontologically *disrupts* this clear opposition between inside and outside, yet it is precisely here that Frow takes a brief detour through Lacan's mirror stage to pick up that image of the mirror as a support of *unity*, inasmuch as "Lacan's concept of the mirror stage accordingly theorizes this passage from autoeroticism to narcissism and the formation of the ego by positing a scenario of self-recognition in the bounded alterity of the body of another" (51). But taking Lacan's image of the mirror (stage) in the sense of identificatory mimesis, that is, of the mimicking or repetition of the image of the other as an image of the self, only sees part of the use of the metaphor, and especially loses sight of the context of the fundamental dynamic that gives it its place in Lacan's thought, that of the distinction between the *symbolic*, the *imaginary*, and the *Real*, which provides the basis not for a unity or identification but a radical *disjunction* found in the relation of the subject to its body.

Moreover, Lacan's essay on the mirror phase was written very early in his career and his theory of this stage was radically modified throughout his lifetime, especially as he developed and evolved his concept of the Real. First of all, it is important to realize, especially in the context of trying to theorize character, that for Lacan the ego as such exists completely in the realm of the *imaginary*, and so its link to the symbolic, not to mention the Real, is more complex than what Frow can possibly sketch out in his brief foray into Freud's concept of identification, which is a concept underlying the more conservative traditional conception of mimetic characterization (underpinning much of the bias in theories like Higbie's that evaluate subjectivity via "fullness," etc.). Yet the idea of the ego, or the conscious aspect of the I, in its relation to the symbolic, or language, must necessarily be central to the understanding of character for anyone trying to make a distinction between fictional persons and "real" persons. And for Frow there is a kind of mirroring (or doubling) between the "position" one takes in relation to an other, whether character or (real) person, since they are both formed on the same symbolic gesture: "The binding-in of the reading … subject occurs above all in its slotting into these positions which constitute it as a subject in the very process of making sense. And, conversely, 'sense' is 'made' within a textual circuit articulating positions through processes of identification" (41). Not only is character an imitation of a person, the very textual process itself mirrors (copies/reproduces) our mimetic process of ego-formation. But how does this trope hold up in the context of Lacan's thought in the broader sense?

If we are to concisely reformulate Lacan's use of the mirror (phase) in its more radical aspect, we could say here that what is in question for Lacan in the image of the mirror is more a matter of *specular projection* than of *mimetic identification*. Frow does evoke Freud's idea of the ego as a "surface" and a "projection of a surface" (51) but isn't able to make the most of this rather remarkable image, in part due to his lack of distinction between the three Lacanian registers, the symbolic, the imaginary, and the Real. We will return to this metaphor of the mirror shortly, but we can see that it functions at the heart of Frow's concept of characterization in a complex way, in a sense, in a double way:

> It is to this dispersal of ego-identifications that I wish to liken the workings of fictional character. The "recognition" or "identification" of character that forms the basis of our dealings with a fictional text would involve a mirroring of the semantic and libidinal process of "self"-construction in an imaginary construction of "other," quasi-unified selves. The character effect thus involves a kind of doubling, the shadowing of the other by myself and of my self by the figured other. (52)

The (metaphor of) the mirror forms a double bind in Frow's system, and also is itself linked to the logic of the double, since it marks a doubling between the character-as-self and the self-as-ego, which Frow calls the "character effect." The mirror stage is central to "ego-identification" that maps a surface onto the body as the cite of the self (or ego), and at the same time, the "character effect" mirrors this mirroring into the text, and out of it, in a secondary or second-order way, "binding" the reader or viewer to the character(-ego) and thereby provoking (and providing an explanation for) affective "interest" or attachment. I want to take up Frow on his idea of the character as double, insofar as it inevitably leads us to a sense of the uncanny in the very nature of character as such, although this uncanny doubleness is to a certain extent both evoked and suppressed in the *mimetic* associations of the mirror (above all in the sense of realism and immediacy or "lifelikeness") with its original/copy structure.

In other words, the mirror effect of the ego is precisely what links it to the primary concept of mimesis that for Frow, and all who fit into this tradition, is the foundational support of affect and self-formation; but at the same time, it smuggles into this schema of the self a sense of *otherness*—this sense that the ego, the self, is first of all the reflection of another and thus able to double and repeat—that haunts it with a specter of itself-as-other. This spectral/specular aspect of the ego-in-the-mirror is just what is repressed/exorcised in the ego-identification/mimesis model, and this is for Derrida, as for Lacan, precisely what reflects the ideological/ontological hierarchy as the emphasis on origin in the mimetic-identification tradition. But, as Derrida points out, once one evokes this trope, how does one distinguish an original from a reflection, a single from a double, a self from a specter of a self, and where does one halt the process? The boundaries—inside/outside, ego/body, original/copy—are all too slippery: the Ego identifies itself reflected in the bounded body of the (specular) image:

> But this Ego, this living *individual* would itself be inhabited and invaded by *its own specter*. It would be constituted by specters of which it becomes the host and which it assembles in the haunted community of a single body. Ego = ghost. Therefore "I am" would mean "I am haunted": I am haunted by myself who am (haunted by myself who am haunted by myself who am ... and so forth). Wherever there is Ego, es spukt, "it spooks." (*Specters* 166, emphasis in original)

What the image of the mirror seems to offer, by way of identification, to a concept of subjectivity grounded in the mimetically formed individual, it also threatens to unhinge in the spectral *mise en abyme* of repetition it nevertheless suggests. The image of the mirror inscribed within both the concept of the self or the ego and the idea of characterization is thus a rich and ambiguous one, as Frow's use of narcissism and ego-identification demonstrates. And Frow's concept of character, varied and nuanced as it is and ultimately resting on a foundation of mimesis and presence, also can't help but evoke these uncanny images of doubles and specters (or the act of "shadowing" as he puts it) as well.

Thus the idea of ego-identification as a basis for all characterization (the "process of narcissistic dissemination of ego-libido," which Frow takes to be "the basis of all historically specific regimes of identification

Introduction

with fictional characters" 52), reveals an ideological preconception, at bottom a kind of ontological/ideological bias, about characterization/representation/subjectivity at the heart of the concept of mimesis and therefore at the heart all mimetic theories of characterization; it is reflected above all in the primacy of what I am calling *subjectification* in mimetically informed criticism and theories of characterization not only in the novel, but in film and other art forms. For Frow, for instance, the "workings of character" is ultimately a kind of *mode of subjectification* in one form or another, even if deferred, delayed, fragmented, etc. Mimesis and the (image of the) mirror are the technological apparatus by which the subject subjectifies the self/other/world: the "reciprocal action by which the sense-making self is repeatedly constituted as unified subject in its recognition of subject positions in the text is at the heart of the process of identification of and with characters" (Frow 49). This action is consistently questioned and challenged by Frow, but nevertheless remains, as he says, "at the heart of the process," and it is very telling that for Frow this "process" is perhaps most prominent and constitutive in the case of Dickens when Frow discusses the idea of the "type." Types are impersonal or schematic tropes that are then subjectivized by an author like Dickens. Or, as Frow puts it, although there is a complex interrelation of "flows" between the certain "penumbra of virtuality" and the "'actual' that it constructs," ultimately, "[c]haracter in Dickens is a function of the thickening of these flows of language into effects of personhood and into the affective intensities it carries; into types, and into their constant transformation into selves" (148). The "flows" may be varied and diverse, but ultimately the tide sways towards subjectivized "persons" or "selves;" the purpose according to this model of the type is to "transform" impersonal forms into subjective ones, or selves. Subjectification is thus ultimately itself a process of "sense-making" that creates a Relation by imposing a meaning or unity onto a non-self-relating impersonal form, positing a Something to fill and conceal a gap, a cut of/in the Real that *is* subjectivity.

But to return to the Lacanian model of the mirror stage, Frow's conception of the ego as founded on mirroring/identification, which doesn't in this sense depart from the model of the ego in broader mimetic traditions (realism, likeness, lifelikeness, etc.), fails to make use of the full implications of the Freudian/Lacanian concept of the ego as *imaginary*—within Lacan's imaginary/symbolic/Real dynamic—or in other words, its essentially *specular* nature. The mimetic mirror model is lacking something crucial here, and what it is lacking is the essential function or structure of the *cut*—the cut of the Real that disrupts the neat opposition between reality and representation. In fact, we could say that what Frow calls *identification*, the basis of our affective investment in character that he finds most clearly set out in Freud's discussion of his theory of dreams, is *nothing other than the repression of this cut*, which in Lacan's discussion of dreams always appears in the form *the gaze*, that which situates and sustains the subject in relation to its reality in the visual sphere. As Lacan describes it,

> The reflection of the subject, its mirror image, is always found somewhere in every perceptual picture, and that is what gives it a quality, a special inertia. The image is masked, sometimes entirely so. But in the dream, because of an alleviation of the imaginary relations, it is easily revealed at every moment, all the more so to the extent that the point of anxiety where the subject encounters the experience of his being torn apart, of his isolation in relation to the world has been attained. There is something originally, inaugurally, profoundly wounded in the human relation to the world. (*Ego* 167)

This masked/missing reflection of oneself in the visual sphere is precisely what Lacan will later (in seminar XI) call the gaze, the *objet a* in the visual sphere. This *objet petit a* is the uncanny object par excellence, and the approach of this strange subject/object discussed here in the seminar on the ego in relation to dreams will be elaborated upon in his seminar on anxiety in terms of the uncanny and in *The Four Fundamental Concepts of Psychoanalysis* in terms of the gaze. This ego–reflection/uncanny–unconscious/object–gaze constellation highlights the importance of what is lacking in Frow's approach, and in the mimetic approach in general, in what, I would go so far as to say, is repressed in the very idea of mimesis—that, as Freud's remarkable discovery reveals, "beyond" the ego there must be some differentiated, inaccessible drive, a death drive:

> We are beginning to see why it is necessary that beyond the pleasure principle, which Freud introduces as being what governs the measure of the ego and installs consciousness in its relations within a world in which it finds itself, that beyond, exists the death [drive]. Beyond the homeostasis of the ego, there exists a dimension, another current, another necessity, whose plane must be differentiated. This compulsion to return to something which has been excluded by the subject, or which never entered into it, the *Verdrängt*, the repressed, we cannot bring it back within the pleasure principle. If the ego as such rediscovers and recognizes itself, it is because there is a beyond to the *ego*, an unconscious, a subject which speaks unknown to the subject. (Lacan, *Ego* 171)

Introduction

The "death drive," this repetition compulsion beyond the ego that is repressed in or "exorcised" from mimetic theories of characterization, refers not to some "deeper" sense, some "underlying" content that should be unearthed or revealed though one kind of "suspicious" critical gesture or another. It is rather a function of the Real, the lack or loss or nonrelation that characterizes the fundamental *out-of-jointness* between the order of representation and the order of reality, and indeed between reality and itself, insofar as the subject, when considered within this "order of reality" as a constituent part of it, marks a cut of the Real that throws it out of joint. "There is something originally, inaugurally, profoundly wounded in the human relation to the world" (Lacan, *Ego* 167)—this is what the mimetic tradition of realism must always miss, that there is "a subject which speaks unknown to the subject" (171) from a (non) space that haunts the ego/reality from within/beyond. As Rosa's scar, with its uncanny temporality returning from beyond her self-presence and beyond Dickens's authority, bears witness, it is from this (non)place of the subject as haunted, as a cut in the Real, that Dickens's characters both appeal to and elude us.

The subject–mimesis/object–structure opposition is haunted by the extimate

With all of this in mind we can return to the moment when Frow appeals to Freud's pregnant image of the ego as "surface" or "projection of a surface," but this time with a focus on *spectrality/specularity* (a projection of specters) rather than on identification, which seems by definition to presuppose a kind of subjectivization of the other. It is within Lacan's imaginary/symbolic/Real dynamic that the ego reveals its strangely virtual and projected structure, which Lacan likens to the structure of the Mobius strip or the cross-cap: "The ego is not only a surface but, so [Freud] says, the projection of a surface. In relation to what it duplicates, the specular image is exactly a right glove becoming a left glove, which one can obtain on a single surface by turning the rim inside out" (*Anxiety* 96). When the surface is turned inside out to form a specular image, as in the Mobius strip, something is lost—not being, but a part of itself making it complete and self-contained, in Lacanian terms, an uncanny object that is *neither* pure object nor pure subject, but is rather the potentiation of the *cut* or nonrelation between the two: the *objet a*, the partial object of desire that introduces the impossible nonspace of the Real into the symbolic/

imaginary structure of the realm of subjects and objects. It is therefore this object that allows us to appreciate the "extimate" dimension of the uncanny—the fact that, to quote Mladen Dolar, in the uncanny we "can speak of the emergence of something that shatters well-known [metaphysical] divisions [such as subject/object, interior/exterior] and which cannot be situated within them" (6). When Freud stumbles upon the idea of the uncanny, the ego becomes haunted by a sense of an underlying *automatism* of the subject due to the insistent presence of what he calls a "compulsion to repeat" or a return of the repressed past (both of the individual and of the species, and even encoded within the organism itself). This strange "invisible" force of repetition that puts the subject's capacity for free will into question is what Freud ultimately names the death drive—this drive that lies "beyond" the interests of the ego, consciousness, and even life, steering the subject from within but that is itself radically Other, in some strange way foreign or prior to its subjectivity—the "inhuman core," as Žižek says, that makes it a (human) subject. It is this dimension of the *extimate*, to use Lacan's name for the uncanny insofar as it evokes this inhuman core of the subject, that disrupts the objective structure versus subjective mimesis dichotomy that has defined the study of character by (re)introducing an unassailable otherness or subjectifying distortion into the picture, opening the space for a hauntology, or uncanny ontology, of characterization.

Thus the recent trend in the study of characterization—tending overall to frame the question of character in terms of how "fictional characters" are similar to or different from "real persons"—frames the problem in a completely *ontic* way, as it is oriented and delimited by this (mimetic) original/copy ideology. This *ontic* perspective (since characters are merely persons without presence), relies on an ideological displacement of ontology by a subjectivizing psychology, making many of Dickens's characters appear "flat" or "one-dimensional" (or "unresolved") according to an incompatible model—but we need only observe how uncannily ontological even the most caricatural characters can become when considered in terms of an intensely de-psychologized, or desubjectivized, criteria. For example, Mr. and Mrs. Smallweed from *Bleak House* seem to me to be the unmistakable literary forbears of Nagg and Nell from Beckett's *End Game*, but few critics would fail to see these latter characters' radical potential for ontological critique of psychological innerness, whereas far too many see the former as caricatures in the "flattest" sense. Is not this discrepancy, this critical unwillingness, the symptom of an ideological

Introduction

framework that presents the framework of historicism as "objective," as somehow external to any subjective position?

Perhaps we should start not from the question, "what *is* a character?" but from the question "*what do fictional characters as such do?*"—thus rather than positing a fixed being-present to (mimetically) measure up to, we would attend to the processes or forces that the literary character draws on, as much as do the "real" person and perhaps other or all beings as well. In this way I am proposing to do away with the implicit ontological opposition between imitative-value and presence-value, where one "order" is the "analogue" of another (to paraphrase Frow), and instead suggesting that we "[introduce] haunting" as Derrida says, "into the very construct of" the concepts of reality, real person, character, even the material body, etc. This is why, as John O. Jordan points out in his discussion of specters in *Supposing Bleak House*, hauntology for Derrida always highlights the question of *justice* (131 ff.). For me this is a question that bears profoundly on the problem of realism: character can be said to stage not an *encounter with a simulacrum* of a "real person," but an *encounter with the Real*, which is as such a distinct kind of *encounter with otherness/impossibility*. This encounter with the Real, precisely what is conjured away in the idea of mimetic realism, is what gives literary character not only its ontological but also its ethical force. Or as Anna Kornbluh puts it, "[r]eading literary ethics, reading impossible symbolizations, reading the Real: these critical practices would all take for their horizon not a given set of meanings, nor even a given aesthetic, but simply an ontology of literature that privileges its capacity for grappling with the Real" (51), making literature appear "less as a representation than as a creative formalization of something properly unrepresentable" ("Reading the Real" 53). The Real, then, as the embodiment of these impossibilities, these unrepresentable gaps in the symbolic, also marks the literary text's potential for revolutionary disputations of ideology and its historicity, or as Todd McGowan puts it, "the text's ability to act as a traumatic disruption to its context" ("Bankruptcy" 92). This is why, as McGowan argues, we "must retain the category of the masterpiece despite the ideological uses that critics have made of it because it provides a name for the power of the literary work to change our symbolic coordinates … One reads for the possibility of an impossible occurrence. This is a revolutionary power that historicism refuses to grant the literary work" ("Bankruptcy" 101). There is therefore a kind of potential (revolutionary) eruption of freedom in the encounter with the Real, and therefore in the encounter with the literary text, which is also a kind of "trauma" (hence the drive to exorcise or contain it)—the trauma, we could also say, of the encounter with specters.

Victorian specters

Character is specter—that which ultimately cannot be bound to, nor escape from, an ontology—just as is ego, or "I." Thus, characterization is not limited to subjectivity or interiority, in a mimetic sense, nor to clusters of words or images, in the structural sense. It is frequently, and often in the most powerful and complex of instances, especially in the case Dickens, made of various forces, some subjectivizing and some desubjectivizing—which is not the same as a hybridity between objective and subjective approaches to representation, but the introduction of an-*other* mode of the nonrelation, the *uncanny* or extimate, into this dichotomy. My point here is that this is what is generally forgotten, repressed, exorcised, silenced, or otherwise edited out of recent theories of characterization and even generally in our critical assumptions about character. And this not only in the novel, but in other art forms as well, especially film, as Nicholas Royle suggests in his observation that the "entire [film] 'industry' might be defined as a palliative working to repress the uncanniness of film" (75). Moreover, it has become more and more an open stance today for Victorianists to be "opposed" to theory, whatever that might actually mean (as if it were running for office), and more and more of an open secret that this antipathy expresses a certain fear of theory—and in particular, I would go so far as to suggest, of psychoanalysis of the Lacanian school. Yet one of the tenets of contemporary Victorian scholarship on character is that the subject is "embodied" (consider for instance the whole range of affect theory scholarship on the Victorian novel), and that this fact of being embodied grounds the "real" of the person as distinct from that of the character that, of course, can only reflect embodiedness through the text, or mimetically—a phenomenon that in itself illustrates that Daniel Novak's *Realism, Photography, and Nineteenth-Century Fiction* has not been fully appreciated for its potential ontological critique of our traditional historical understanding of the rise of realism and (supposedly) mimetic technology like photography. Lacanian psychoanalysis, on the other hand, completely upsets this all-too-comfortable distinction between a "real" body and a representational body. It tells us that the body (the "actual" body) is *always already a text*, always already inscribed with and by signifiers—Rosa Dartle with her character-defining scar is only one of the most salient examples of this in Dickens's works. If the body

Introduction

is a text, and the ego is imaginary/specular, then we should find it harder and harder to ground our definition of character in supplementarity or even ontological "hybridity." For the "real" or "nonrepresentational" body is always already hybrid, part flesh and part signifier—making the opposition between a "material" body in reality and a textual body in a fiction far from self-evident. So what do we do with this place of the Real in relation to representation?

Audrey Jaffe makes the point in her recent study *The Victorian Novel Dreams of the Real*, that, although it has become a "post-structuralist truism to say that realism can only gesture towards the real," nevertheless, "criticism of the Victorian realist novel remains, and, indeed, has in recent years become increasingly attached to, the idea of a real behind realism, as attested to by recent methodological turns, including New Historicism … thing theory, and surface reading" (2). It thus demonstrates an important and much needed (however admittedly belated) paradigm shift that Jaffe convincingly argues for a restructuring of the realism versus fantasy dichotomy, such that realism and fantasy are shown to be on the same side of the dichotomy, both opposing the Real (the "traumatic Real," as she quotes Žižek in the chapter's epigraph). "Realist novels" she thus concludes, "represent not the real but the desire for it" (5), the fantasy that it can be attained or captured in representational form. While Jaffe does not make characterization a central concern, at least not explicitly, the way in which her thesis effects character is quite revealing here. It is telling that this reconfiguring of oppositions takes on a more precarious nature when Jaffe applies it specifically to characterization. As she describes it:

> These novels [examples by Hardy, Eliot, and others] also stage a tension between traditional realist character—possessing the effects of depth, interiority, and individuality that are conventional in realist fiction—and a fungibility or positionality more typical of sensation fiction: that is, the recognition or awareness that a social role (mayor, mother, or orphan boy, for instance) may be held by more than one person, and indeed what often seems to be the necessary priority, in plots frequently implying doubling and duplicity, of position over person. (13)

In these latter cases, character is "perhaps something more like a frame for a certain kind of content" (14). It is not difficult to see that, although Jaffe has made the first step towards shifting the paradigm, she still reverts back to a version of the mimesis/structure dichotomy when she addresses character specifically; and when attempting to articulate an opposite pole to mimetic characters she seems at a loss for concepts and terms. The example of "sensation fiction" seems to offer only exchangeability or "positionality" as an alternative to "depth" and "innerness," not to mention the implicit downgrade in literary "status" in relegating the genre from realist "novel" to "sensation fiction."

To me this seems dissatisfying and partial at best. Again, the symmetry is out of whack, the shift from innerness to plot does not offer two forms of representing subjects, but more or less incommensurate concepts, except insofar as we are still embedded in the subject/object opposition. More broadly, it is not difficult to see what restricts Jaffe in her approach here. At the very outset of the study she introduces Žižek and Lacan's concept of the Real as the source of her inspiration for the paradigm shift regarding the reality/representation dichotomy—indeed, for the very title of her book. The point of inspiration for Jaffe is the idea that in the Lacanian model, developed further by Žižek, reality is not opposed to fantasy, but *aligned* with it in opposition to the Real. While this concept in itself proves fruitful for Jaffe, she completely dispenses with the whole context of the Lacanian/Žižekian theoretical apparatus from which this concept came, sweeping it under the carpet, after the first mention, for the rest her entire book. Crucial for understanding this new dynamic according to which reality and fantasy are on the same side in an opposition with the Real is Lacan's famous symbolic/imaginary/Real dynamic.

The psychoanalytic symbolic/imaginary/Real dynamic should radically change the way we think about characterization and the mimesis/structure dichotomy that has always framed it, as it alters many of our reference points and limit-concepts when we engage in literary criticism. According to this dynamic, for instance, the ego is imaginary, the body is a text (symbolic), and subject (or unconscious) is the cut of the Real. This is what is at stake in the recent trend towards "psychoanalytic materialism" because it reframes social/ideological antagonisms in ontological terms. By expanding the use of contemporary critical theory in relation to the study of characterization and representation in the nineteenth-century novel, especially in terms of these three concepts of the Freudian *uncanny*, Derridean *specters*, and the Lacanian *Real*, I hope to bring the study of novelistic characterization beyond the impasse of the structure/mimesis dichotomy. While Jaffe, Dever, and Jordan, for instance, all draw on psychoanalytic theory in some way, their work draws primarily on Freud, post-Freudian criticism, and affect theory, whereas this volume sees Freud through contemporary psychoanalysis, especially Lacan, Dolar, Žižek, and Zupančič, and draws on the recent development of

Introduction

"psychoanalytic materialism" in literary criticism of the past several years. This volume thus sets out to develop some spectral concepts that offer a new language to discuss nonmimetic characterization, drawing on this psychoanalytic materialism insofar as they comprise the desubjectifying counterflows to subjectification. These concepts include: *distortion*, *effigy*, *anamorphosis*, *dream representation*, *caricature*, *spectral mimesis*, and *spectral materiality*. These spectral forms of representation are characterized by their *otherness* to, or doubling of, mimesis, marking an uncanny ontology, or hauntology, that doubles the "ontologically" "real" and "present" idea of the subject/character.

Part I

Spectral mimesis: portraits, caricature, and character

1

Mimesis's ghosts: caricature and anamorphosis

> The standard realist approach aims at describing the world, reality, the way it exists out there, independently of us, observing subjects. But we, subjects, are ourselves part of the world, so the consequent realism should include us in the reality we are describing, so that our realist approach should include us describing ourselves "from the outside," independently of ourselves, as if we are observing ourselves through inhuman eyes. What this inclusion-of-ourselves amounts to is not naïve realism but something much more uncanny, a radical shift in the subjective attitude by means of which we become strangers to ourselves. (Žižek, *Disparities* 328–9)

Since the very beginning of his career there has been trouble placing Dickens squarely in the tradition of mimetic characterization in which other Victorian novelists became so deeply entrenched over the course of the century. In fact, in some ways (and especially in terms of character) it is difficult to situate Dickens within the tradition of Victorian realism at all; and this tension between Dickens's style of representing character and the tenets of realist representation, which became increasingly institutionalized and technologized in forms like portraiture and eventually photography and other means of mechanical reproduction, was not infrequently the source of harsh criticism for Dickens. One response to this tension, for instance, has long been and remains to be to "accuse" Dickens of being a "caricaturist" as opposed to a realist. A central implication of this claim (which is of course typically a means of diminishing or dismissing a certain kind of characterization) is that his characters give us an "external" or even surface or superficial image of character rather than the "innerness" and psychological "depth" valued by mimetic realism. But it is perhaps only Chesterton who, rather than defend Dickens against this claim of being a caricaturist, truly reconsiders and revaluates the term itself:

> Caricature is not merely an important form of art; it is a form of art which is often most useful for purposes of profound philosophy and powerful symbolism ... One extraordinary idea has been constantly repeated, the idea that it is very easy to make a caricature of anything. As a matter of fact it is extraordinarily difficult, for it implies a knowledge of what part of a thing to caricature. To reproduce the proportions of a face exactly as they are, is a comparatively safe adventure; to arrange those features in an entirely new proportion, and yet retain a resemblance, argues a very delicate instinct for what features are really the characteristic and essential ones. (Chesterton, *Charles Dickens* 27)

The common claim that Dickens's characters are caricatures, we can say, derives largely from his ability to capture "the essence" of a character in "a few strokes," a few key features uniquely capable of being "profound[ly]" and "powerful[ly]" symbolic, such as verbal tics, bodily gestures, personal mannerisms, or even objects (as in the eternally animated butterflies on Mrs. Markleham's hat), which are distorted or overdetermined. The "resemblance," or "essential characteristic" that makes a caricature effective or convincing, is not based on a skill for recreating likeness at all, but on some more elusive understanding or "delicate instinct" of "what part of a thing" captures its identity or its potential for symbolic expression. T. S. Eliot, for example, said that "Dickens' figures belong to poetry, like figures of Dante or Shakespeare, in that a single phrase, either by them or about them, may be enough to set them wholly before us" (411). Thus we can make an important distinction at this point, and recognize that Dickens's characters are not, *stricto senso*, caricatures (aggressively transformed likenesses directed at individuals or types) but *are* structured on the same nonmimetic principle as caricatures; that is, they are not caricatures in a generic sense, but they share a similar *formal aspect of representation*, which *locates "essence," or being, not in likeness but in distortion.*

The idea of "charging" a particular feature or a particular group of features with the essence of the whole is, as Ernst Kris tells us, inherent in the very word "caricature": "The Italian *caricare* and the French *charger* (*charge* = caricature) convey the same idea: to charge or overcharge; we would add, with distinctive features. Thus a human countenance may have a single trait accentuated so that the representation is 'overcharged' with it" (Kris 174). Mimetic likeness is therefore not the basis for caricatural representation but in fact part of the representation material, an aspect of content not form: caricature is a "playful transformation of [a] likeness," as Kris puts it (192). Thus instead of mimesis or imitation, Kris sees at the heart of caricature a representational method analogous to that of wit and dreams according to Freud: "The psychologist has no difficulty in defining what the caricaturist has done. He is well acquainted with this double meaning, this transformation, ambiguity, and condensation. It is the *primary process* used in caricatures in the same way that Freud has demonstrated it to be used in 'wit'" (196).

Ernst Kris frames his famous essay on caricature (written in collaboration with E. H. Gombrich, though later published separately after some differences of opinion) with the question of why "portrait caricature was not known to the world before the end of the sixteenth century" (189). His answer draws on the now more familiar narrative that, historically, art of the modern era tends to move away from the emphasis on imitation seen in classical art and towards imaginative invention or play. But it also uses this narrative to tap into some less familiar ideas about the image as such, and particularly visual images, that, though only adumbrated here, could be compared with more theoretically nuanced arguments in recent criticism, like that of Garrett Stewart (*Between Film and Screen*), about the nineteenth-century novel prefiguring the imagistic or specular expressiveness of modern cinema: as Kris puts it, "[t]he work of art is—for the first time in European history—considered as projection of an inner image. It is not its proximity to reality that proves its value but its nearness to the artist's psychic life" (198–9). As in Chesterton's comments on caricature (as a means of "profound philosophy and powerful symbolism"), this formulation of modern art (though perhaps a bit schematic) stages an implicit opposition between mimetic representation and artistic vision: "The successful caricature distorts appearances but only for the sake of a deeper truth. In refusing to be satisfied with a slavish 'photographic' likeness the artist penetrates to the essence of a person's character" (Kris 198). For Kris and Gombrich, this "playful transformation of a likeness" appeared so late in the course of the history of the visual arts, as opposed to the linguistic arts, because "the visual image has deeper roots, is more primitive," and thus to *play* with visual images presupposed "a degree of security" about the mutual independence of the two orders, representation and reality. This is why "the birth of caricature as an institution marks a conquest of a new dimension of freedom of the human mind, no more, but perhaps no less, than the birth of rational science in the work of Galileo Galilei, the great contemporary of the Carraccis," who were, according to Kris and Gombrich, history's first real portrait caricaturists (Kris 202).

Spectral mimesis

While Kris's conclusions become more difficult to sustain the more literally (including a certain kind of historicity under this label here) one tries to take them, I *am* suggesting that there is something profoundly useful in his intuition here linking the visual image, in a preconscious way, with the ideological force of mimesis as a means of grounding the "real" in a sense of presence, and representation in simulation, so that distorting, or as it were scarring, the sacred surface of mimesis is perceived as dangerous to the "objective" ground of this reality itself. Whatever historical narrative we do or don't give it, caricature plays with the opposition between the two realms (representation and the real) in way that specifically haunts the mimetic exhibition of individuality embodied in nineteenth-century portraiture, giving caricature a certain spectral dimension. And we can add here that where mimesis posits a seamless presence in the order of the real reflected in the sense of completeness mimesis generates, caricature opens a Disparity or "bar" within the real itself by maintaining, as I will discuss presently, a certain doubleness or gap in itself and a certain representational materiality of the real: as Agamben puts it, "with apparent frivolity, caricature separated the human figure from its signified; but … only by twisting and altering its proper lineaments could it acquire new emblematic status" (144) and thus "[m]etaphor, caricature, emblem, and fetish point toward that 'barrier resistant to signification' in which is guarded the original enigma of every signifying act" (149). In this sense, caricature, as a *form* of (nonmimetic) representation comparable to dreams and jokes, is disruptive and subversive in a more ontological sense than is generally accepted: it embodies a breakthrough that marks a "new dimension of freedom" from the grasp ideology has over the order of the real.

To illustrate this "breakthrough" caricature achieves with respect to the kind of authority the mimetic image holds in the visual sphere, Kris gives the example of "Les Poires," Charles Philipon's famous caricature of King Louis-Philippe as a pear (Figure 1).[1] This legendary caricature gives us an excellent example of the form's potential for overdetermination and even captures the process of distortion that allows for its transformation of mimesis into symbolic material. "The Pear" originated in the trial against Philipon who was charged—as well as heavily fined and faced with imprisonment—with slander for claiming Louis-Philippe was a "fat head" (or in the French expression, a "pear"); as the story goes, Philipon sketched it off the cuff to demonstrate to the court the natural relationship between the king and a pear, as if he were merely bearing witness to an objective discovery, as the illustration proved. This partly anecdotal context thus captures well the kind of playful but effective subversion of

1 Honoré Daumier, "Les Poires" (The Pears), lithograph published in *La Caricature*, 1831.

established law and logic that is latent in the caricatural form as such. Wielded effectively and in the right context, as demonstrated here, caricature can distort the laws of the signifier, so that "conscious logic is out of action, its rules have lost their force" as Kris puts it, revealing a kind of underlying dream logic that rearranges the structure between words and images through a nonmimetic link: here, for instance, "one of the mechanisms now in action [condensation] can cause, as in a dream, two words to become one, or merge two figures into one" (196), so that king and pear become "Les Poires."

Neither Kris nor Gombrich give a truly detailed visual analysis of "Les Poires," and in fact both of them seem to attribute it to Philipon alone, whereas it was at first conceived and sketched out by Philipon (Figure 2) but was later refined and executed as a lithograph for *La Caricature* by Daumier (Figure 1). Yet a close visual analysis of Daumier's/Philipon's "Les Poires" would be as good a place as any to begin formulating this idea of a breakthrough in the visual image, not least of all because Kris attributes the subversive and revolutionary power of this image to a kind of cultural return of the repressed that structurally resembles the repetition compulsion of Freud's uncanny—where magical thoughts that were supposed to be "surmounted" return in objective form—when he says that, "under the surface of fun and play the old image magic is still at work ... if the caricature fits, as Philipon's *Poire* obviously did, the victim really does become transformed in our eyes" (Kris 199). As is the case with the uncanny, the very affect produced by caricature haunts us with our own spectrality: we imagine the *real king* differently after seeing this caricature because, after all and despite our own logical "knowledge," we can't dismiss the image as merely a neutral copy detached from the real person, or shake a belief in the image's ability to transgress that strict opposition. Indeed, the idea of "image magic" here can thus be thought of in terms, again like the uncanny, of an approach to the desubjectifying Real that transgresses the reality/representation and internal/external oppositions. I will develop the onto-political aspect of this idea in the next chapter in relation to the revolutionary and polysemic nature of effigy, but here it is important to note the revolutionary nature of the caricatures themselves as developed by the French lithographic caricaturists of the 1830s and 1840s: these images not only represent revolutionary views in content, they were the focal point of a kind of antagonism inherent to representation. Philipon, Daumier, and others were fined, and even sentenced to imprisonment, for caricatures they published in Philipon's two publications, *Caricature* and *Charivari*. This creative explosion of

Mimesis's ghosts

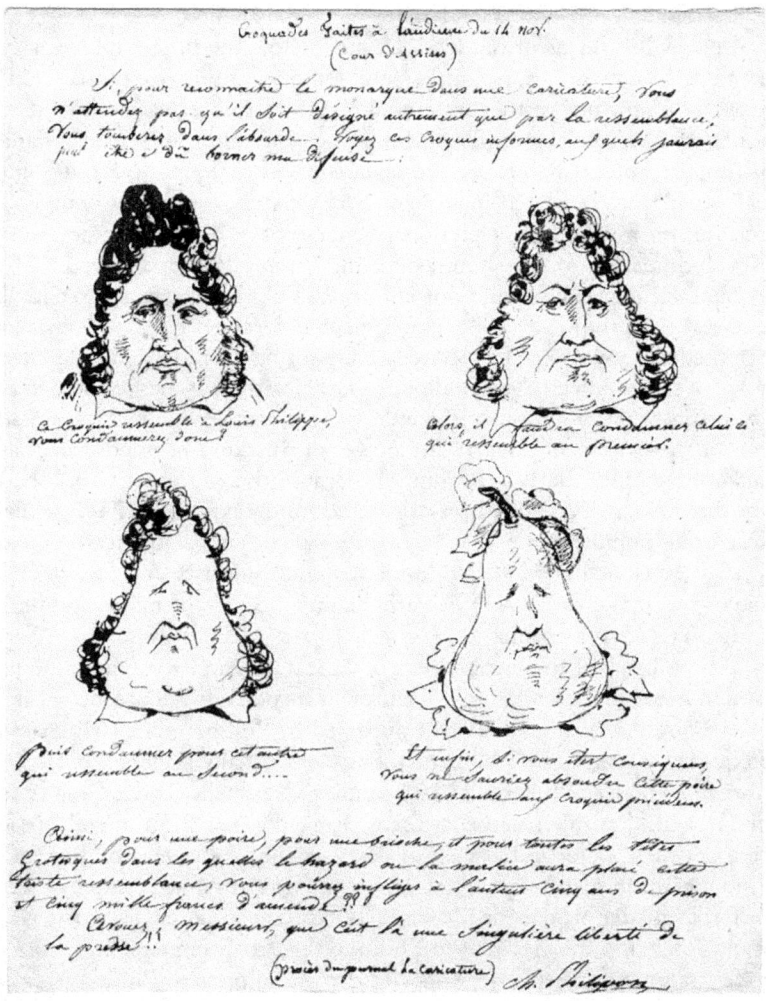

2 Charles Philipon, "Croquades faites à l'audience du 14 nov."
(Jibes Made at the Hearing of 14 Nov.), sketch, 1831.

caricature as an art form, so fertile for the developments in the visual arts throughout the nineteenth and twentieth centuries, was engendered in Paris in the 1830s and 1840s as part of a brand new medium, the first illustrated journals to use lithography to mass produce images—images that were at once darker and more playfully nuanced and tonal than most previous forms of production allowed for. The lithographic image lent itself to distortion, visual play, and reproduction in a way that etching and engraving at this scale couldn't; it therefore readily served as a perfect medium for the breakthrough of the nonmimetic image and its unique potential to express antagonisms—social, political, ontological—that were repressed in realism, for instance in the very bourgeois form of portraiture. Its revolutionary energy originated in the post-July Revolution reign of the "Bourgeois King," Louis-Philippe, as soon as it became clear that he would not enforce the Charter granting freedoms and rights to the masses, but had "quickly adopted a policy of stasis as opposed to movement" (Vincent 13). Opposing this more middle-class force of status quo charged Philipon's journal with new energy and determination, which found a particularly fraught battleground in the *visual* image, or as Vincent put it: "The power of this kind of opposition was unknown before the July Revolution because the censorship, abolished for the press, still remained for prints and lithographs" (18). Meanwhile, true to his popular name, the *Roi Bourgeois* made status quo his foremost goal in every matter of state despite persistent injustice and unrest, and his own expression, "*juste milieu*," the happy medium or middle ground, came to typify his regime.

At the heart of the uncanniness of caricature and its overdetermination in nineteenth-century visual culture is its pervasive doubleness. Like "Les Poires," the caricatures that appeared in Philipon's magazine were frequently *conceived* by Philipon (though not usually sketched out) and *drawn* by more skillful artists like Daumier, Grandville, Traviés, and others. In a kind of micro sense, caricature staged a new form of collaboration between writer and visual artist. The relation between Philipon and Daumier in particular grew out of a mutual relation structured by the different media, where for instance, "[t]he Rabelaisian style of wit was more congenial and habitual to Philipon than to Daumier, all of whose independent satire—that is, work not in association with Philipon—had compassion and, in general, was unliterary and un-allusive to fiction" (27), as Vincent points out. And on the writer's side "[i]t was fortunate for Philipon that he had an artist who could carry out his ideas with such skill, just as it was providential for Daumier that he had a director with such fertile ideas and such infectious enthusiasm" (43). This underscores the uniquely dualistic relationship between word and image embodied in caricature in general: "Caricature is a double thing," says Baudelaire, "it is both drawing and idea—the drawing violent, the idea caustic and veiled" ("On the Essence of Laughter" 151). As the term "visual pun" suggests, caricature is not a "translation" of ideas or words into images, but rather a kind of disjunctive, material antagonism and prolific tension between word and image, each somehow containing and obstructing and the other beneath or within itself. "Grandville's hybrid form," says Wettlaufer, "combining words and images, visual and verbal tropes, and multiple levels of meaning, resists the fetters of imitation and the identity of the *artiste singe* for a new conception of art based in a more modern self-referentiality that destabilizes and problematizes the very concepts of representation, reality, and meaning" (485). In this sense, caricature (and lithography) should be included in theoretical narratives that articulate a kind of prehistory to cinema in the Victorian novel along with other nineteenth-century visual technology (from the magic lantern to panoramas, camera obscuras, photography, etc.), such as Garrett Stewart's.

Comparing Philipon's sketch with Daumier's final product helps illustrate this unique disjunctive relation between word and image in caricature. Philipon's sketch gives us the inspirational material, the *idea* for the caricature's visual pun, but it does not fully capture it *visually*. It is only in Daumier's image that we see the magic happen, the delightfully convincing transformation that strikes us as a sleight of hand or conjurer's trick. What Daumier manages to convey visually is a sense of this transformation in process, in time, which comes with a kind of logic of the signifier, like "logical" stages in a metamorphosis, each one "naturally" leading to the next. That is why this caricature is much more complex than it at first seems. It conveys visually, with incredibly elegance of efficiency, the ideas that make it effective: that what is "happening" is that the mimetic image of the king is not being changed at all, but whittled down, as it were, to its underlying essence, as if the excess (mimetic) surface of the face is being erased bit by bit to expertly reveal an underlying, ghostly essence. Thus the final image appears spectral, ghostly. In fact, what remains is the essence, the spirit of the king, his core: a pear! The idea is not to change the image, but to transfer a signifier, that of King Louis-Philippe, to another image, the pear. It works, and King Louis-Philippe's self is now trapped in a pear; he *is* a pear. The crisscross in the center acts exactly like phonemes in a pun: like the shared phonemes in Freud's examples of condensation in jokes, such as "alcoholidays," the crisscross lines are at once the contours of a pear and Louis-Philippe's sad frown. The distortion that makes this "sliding" or transformation possible enters into the mimetic image precisely by way of caricature's disjunctive doubleness between word and image.

Vincent describes "The Pear" as "a 'metamorphosis' in the manner of his artist friend Grandville" (20), who was fond of transforming human faces into animal faces by a chain of graphic associations (Figure 3). But Grandville also engaged flights of logic and visual metaphors that were much more imaginative and comprehensive, at once dreamlike and cosmic (Figures 4 and 5). In the case of Figure 3, "Man and Animal Portraits Compared," we note that although the same principle of transformation is at work as in Philipon's and Daumier's "Les Poires," the last image does not contain two figures as it does in Philipon's example. Figures 4 and 5, however, show a complex use of dreamlike allusion and metaphor, both linguistic and graphic. In "Premier Rêve: Crime et expiation" (Figure 4) the theme of guilty flight from the law—containing biblical allusions ranging from Cain and Abel to Jonah—is paralleled visually in the wild flight of graphic associations by the artist. In this visual transcription of a "dream," an omniscient eye, emerging from the scales of justice, pursues a fleeing man at every stage of associative transformation while an image of the cross reappears as lantern, sword, scales of justice, and precarious pillar at different points of the journey. Although we can only touch upon the complexity of this illustration, it provides an excellent example of the associative links generated in caricature by the dreamlike play

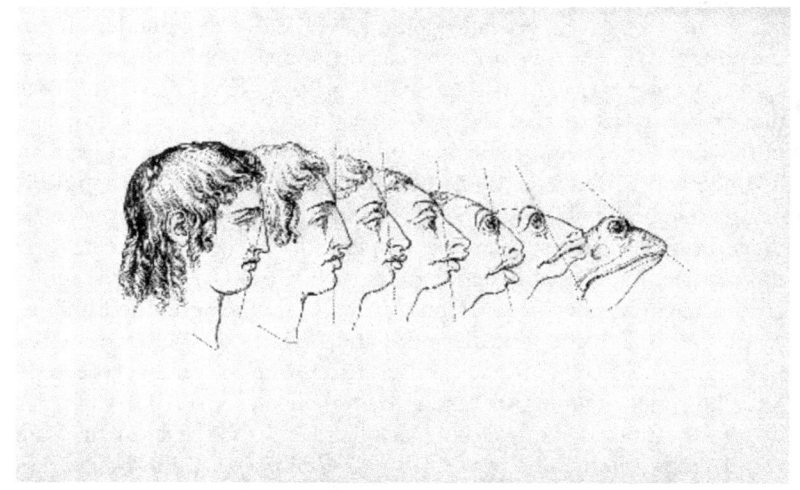

3 J.J. Grandville, "Man and Animal Portraits Compared," lithograph in *Le Magasin pittoresque*, 1844.

4 J.J. Grandville, "Premier Rêve, Crime et expiation" (First Dream: Crime and Atonement), wood engraving illustration (from lithograph on wove paper) in *Le Magasin pittoresque*, July 1847.

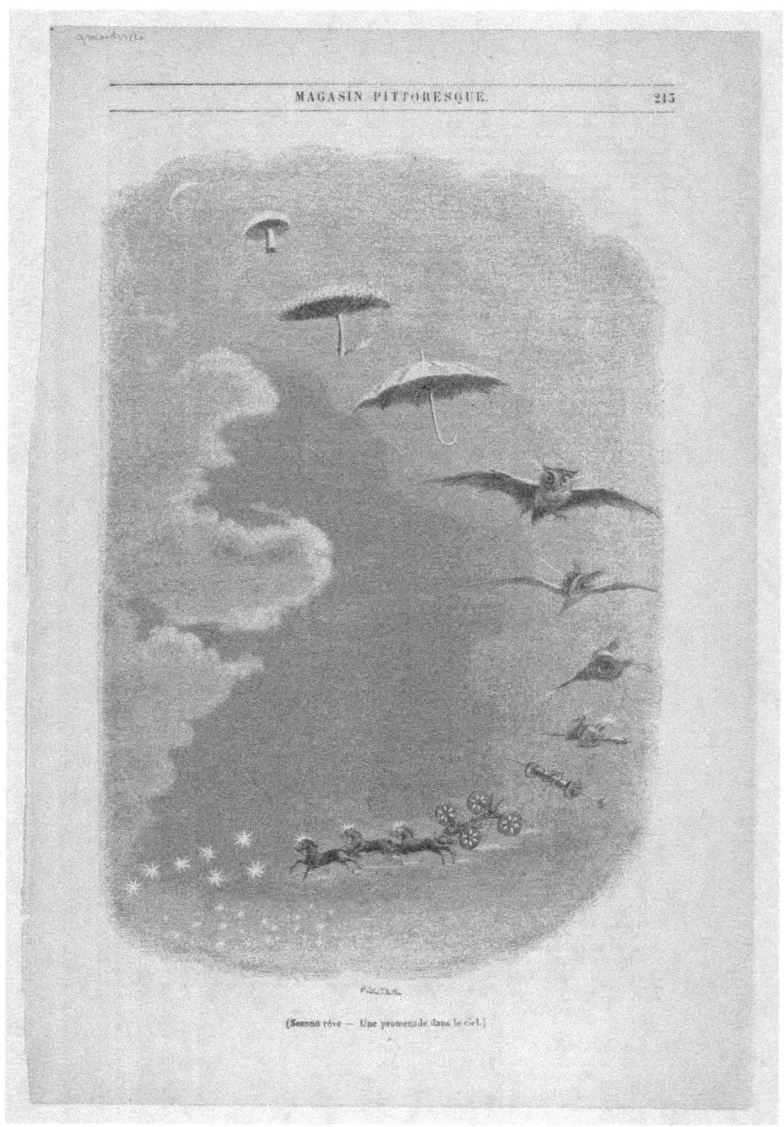

5 J. J. Grandville, "Second Rêve, Une promenade dans le ciel" (Second Dream: A Promenade Through the Sky), engraving (from lithograph on wove paper) in *Le Magasin pittoresque*, 1847.

between word and image and yet in antagonism with the traditionally restrictive dictates of the logos. Such imagistic links often form nodal points that drive a kind of specular narrative: the upper right-side image of the scales, for instance, condense in a single graphic nodal point a pointing finger (suggesting accusation and crime), the tilted or shaken scales of justice, the cross (religion), the eye of God that sees all, and a pen that forges the next link by tracing an eyebrow for the disembodied eye that detaches itself from the scales to pursue the criminal and will finally appear re-embodied in the fish that threatens to swallow the fleeing man. There is a kind of manic, unrestricted energy of association in these prints that almost reminds one of William Blake. In these examples, Grandville sheds light on an important aspect of caricature: its essential power to loosen and transform the rigid traditional ideas of perspective, shape, physiognomy, and association, all of which Grandville was very interested in exploring for their own sake and also as phenomena representative of the experience of dreams. But, as we see here, he is also conscious of the cosmic scope of caricature, drawing on a traditional association between perspective and cosmology. Baltrušaitis observes, in his book on anamorphosis, that Agrippa places perspective in a hierarchy of sciences in which "optics, also called perspective, directly follows geometry, and (after painting and engraving) is succeeded by cosmography: thus perspective is one of the geometrical measures of the world" (98). Grandville could thus be said to be one of the first artists to turn this "geometrical measure of the world" around to discover the "inner" perspective of the psyche, of dream logic, of the unconscious. In fact, we could call this obverse "perspective" of the unconscious—absurd, nonlogical, and distorted in itself by its very nature—*anamorphosis*.

Though Grandville occasionally distorts the perspective of forms anamorphically, however, it should be noted that these are not strictly cases of anamorphosis, since there is no privileged point from which the image acquires its "true" perspective; rather, anamorphosis is inscribed onto the forms themselves, and there is no longer a position from which things would appear *un*distorted. But in these examples, the medium's deficiency for recreating the characteristic mechanism of anamorphosis—the contrast of two separate perspectives from which a fixed image such as a painting would appear alternately realistic or distorted—is compensated for by a *distorting idea*, as it were, an allusion or joke that plays a distorting or self-transforming role *within* the image. In "Duel Between a High and Low Soldier," for instance, the high-status officers are not simply depicted from beneath to reflect their intimidating "high" status; though the dueling officer is tilted back in such a way as to suggest that the distortion is a function of perspective, the other high-status officers standing around are similarly warped so that from no perspective would they appear proportionate; the pun on "high" sticks to them not just in size, but in the literalization or embodiment of the inherently distorted social perspective. There is thus a comic element in the very limitation of the medium itself, which lacks the temporal element provided by the relation between a fixed painting and a mobile viewer (allowing for sequential perspectives) to express anamorphic distortion; we laugh at the way in which the picture has found such a "silly," simple, and yet concise, way to at once include and circumvent its own limitations. Details such as the tall, slim, and short squat glasses reinforce the absurd/symbolic conclusion that this metaphoric expression for social structures is inscribed into reality itself. In "Poachers of Small Stature" the dachshunds are included as play on the expression "to put something into perspective" (in the sense of being able to situate it in reality); the only "undistorted" detail that might give us a sense of the distortion of the scene are in fact dogs that in reality are absurdly short and long, so that instead of placing the distortion in relation to reality, they find their proper proportions in this distorted representation. This type of complex play with perspective translated into simple expressions, like jokes, should be distinguished from what Hogarth had done nearly a century earlier in his illustration "False Perspective" (1754), in which everything seems proportionate in itself, but the relations between the objects are distorted and comic. Hogarth's illustration plays with *rules* of perspective, exposing them in a playful way as mere formal conventions, but in Grandville's caricatures, the distortion of perspective is *inscribed into the images themselves as a potential point of ambiguous transformation, a point of absurd (non)relation between representation and the Real.* The result is not merely self-referential as in Hogarth's engraving, but, even if in a very simplified and at times frivolous way, suggestive of the ontological distortion that Lacan terms "the gaze."

What makes Grandville and Daumier so important in this context is that they were already aware of and expressing in their artwork the representational breakthroughs they were ushering in. In "Man and Animal Portraits Compared" (Figure 3), for instance, Grandville is implicitly satirizing the historical alliance traditionally established between the arts and sciences: the first head is clearly meant to evoke a classical model and the lines drawn in slightly increasing angles across the profiles allude to the formal systems for establishing ratios of the human form common in the Renaissance development and technologizing of the arts. But under Grandville's hand the image undergoes a kind of reverse evolution from a classical human form into a reptile and what as a system of representation is meant to typify the height of human knowledge, unifying science and art, reduces the likeness of man to an image of the lowest life form. Anamorphosis, Grandville suggests in this and other similar caricatures, has the subversive potential to expose something ideologically questionable underlying the established role of geometric perspective in scientific and technological "progress." This potential stems in part from the fact that anamorphosis, involved as it is in the search for and development of systems of perspective, was born from the collaboration between science and art as a strange and "dreamlike" counterpart to a "serious" and progressive technology for representing nature: "The perspective of dreamers distorting the truth is built up, paradoxically, by the system which describes it," says Baltrušaitis in his book *Anamorphic Art* (4). Baltrušaitis explains, for instance, how Dürer's "window" (the very typification of the perspective device) was recreated in manifold variations that actually *reversed* its proper structure for experimental purposes by Maignan (1648), Gasper Schott (1657) and others: "One is surprised to recognize in [Maignan's apparatus] Dürer's 'window,' and even more to see the use to which the device is put, serving not to arrange but to distort perspective. The mechanics are the same ... However the apparatus works in reverse" (55). Anamorphosis may have sprung from those same scientific mechanisms and formulae invented to technologize mimesis, to scientifically formalize a means to represent reality, but it was conceived in the artist's impulse to disrupt and desubjectivize these forms of *techné*, thus countering the powerful lure of mastery with the liberating force of play.

The playful reversal of perspective of anamorphosis, as I will expand upon later in the chapter, has everything to do with disrupting the nineteenth-century tendency to subjectify historical forces, itself a means of adopting a position of mastery in relation to vast world-historical and technological changes,[2] for anamorphosis introduces distortion into the objective image precisely by inverting, in mechanisms such as Dürer's Window, the positions of the subject and that of the object, the perceiver and thing perceived. It is historically overdetermined, then, that these late medieval and early renaissance perspective devices, contrived to formalize or reify the subject/object relation in perspective in order to technologize representation, reappear in the subject matter of many of Grandville's works at a time when caricature is radically altering the mimetic representation of the subject. For instance, in the background of "Un peintre, à cheval sur son dada raphaélique" (Figure 6), a copying apparatus of this type, a kind of profile machine, is brought to life, and, clinging to a canvas with one "claw," traces of its own accord an eye from a face in profile. The image of an eye often appeared in instructional diagrams illustrating perspective techniques; it indicated the perspective "point," or the position, occupied by the subject, from which the "visual rays" connecting the seer to an object may be mapped onto a flat surface, thereby reproducing the image realistically and with mathematical precision. Grandville often uses the eye, as he does here, to allude to these instructional diagrams, and the face being traced is again a classical profile like the one transformed in "Man and Animal Portraits Compared" (Figure 3). We thus find a much more complex and elaborate play with the same themes of technological progress (in representational methods) and evolution: the "apprentices" transform progressively from small mouse to rodent to monkey to a Raphael-ape composite upon a wooden hobby horse with the wooden head of Raphael. The theme of the monkey-artist is common in Grandville as a satire upon mimetic representation that (unlike Grandville's art) slavishly, mechanically copies its object, "apes" it, so to speak. As Wettlaufer points out, for instance, "[t]urning the tables on the generic hierarchies, Grandville highlights the difference between the painter's art and his own by demonstrating the ways in which the caricaturist transcends mere imitation with invention, transforming the humans into their simian counterparts to impart a meaning beyond the surface mimesis" (477). If we take a global perspective of this composition, moreover, we see that the lines of the string that manipulates the perspective device and the tail and back of the hobby horse form the shape of a pair of compasses with a tracing pencil on one end and a needle point on the other, a mechanical means of mimetic reproduction; and in this illustration the classical artist, in a kind of distorted dream allegory, is visually condensed with an ape and anamorphically transformed into a cog in a mechanical perspective device. The reversal here is not only evolutionary, however, since the leg sketched out on the canvas may belong to the same image as the head and eye on the wall, the only human images along with the wooden head of Raphael, so that the human exists only in scattered fragments of representation while animals and mechanical devices claim ontological autonomy for themselves. All of the ideas expressed in this plate, therefore, are subjected to dreamlike transformations from familiar linguistic expressions—such as

Mimesis's ghosts

6 J. J. Grandville, "Un peintre, à cheval sur son dada raphaélique" (A Painter Astride His Raphael Hobby Horse), lithograph illustration in *Un Autre Monde*, 1843.

"aping," "riding on the shoulders" of a master, and even "hobby horse" (imitation is a favorite theme of Grandville)—into visual images with an uncanny and spectral "perspective" of their own (the object's perspective or gaze). This is because these images comprise more than just a play on words; they realize a kind of ontological distortion in the visual sphere theorized by Lacan as anamorphosis.

Lacanian anamorphosis and the object (a's) perspective

Lacan first really develops the idea of anamorphosis as a psychoanalytic concept in his seminar *The Four Fundamental Concepts of Psychoanalysis*,[3] though it was an integral part of his previous year's seminar on *Anxiety*, during his discussion of the uncanny and the gaze as the "object petit a" that structures being in the visual sphere. Lacan discovers what I'm calling the ontological distortion at the heart of anamorphosis by linking it to the Cartesian cogito in its origin. Starting from the point of view of the Cartesian cogito as designating the philosophic search for certainty and its foundation upon "methodological doubt, which concerns whatever might give support to thought in representation" (Lacan, *FFC* 80), Lacan sees anamorphosis as a means to expose the structure of the post-Cartesian subject's being as a mapping of oneself in the visual field. In the visual sphere, what grounds the certainty of the cogito is the self-reflexiveness of consciousness in the phenomenological structure of "I see myself seeing myself." "How is it," Lacan asks, "that the *I see myself seeing myself* remains [the cogito's] envelope and base, and, perhaps more than one thinks, grounds its certainty?" (*FFC* 80). The answer to this question relates to its structure, according to which subject and object are not simply split, but set in a "bipolar reflexive" relation: "the phenomenologists have succeeded in articulating with precision that ... I see outside, that perception is not in me, that it is on the object that I apprehend" (*FFC* 80). Of course, though perception is projected onto the object, the privileged position in this opposition is that of the subject, who lays claim to this perception of the object in the very act of perceiving: "the privilege of the subject seems to be established here from the bipolar reflexive relation by which, as soon as I perceive, my representations belong to me" (*FFC* 81). It is this (seemingly) inescapable trap of understanding the subject and object relation in terms of a mutual opposition (here, in the field of vision) of self-presence that ends up robbing the object of its presence and that thus leads to the philosophy of Idealism, or the "suspicion of [the world] yielding me only my representations" (*FFC* 81). Lacan concisely articulates the paradoxical situation into which this path to certainty—according to which as one position grows stronger in certainty the other diminishes—leads: "The mode of my presence in the world is the subject in so far as by reducing itself solely to this certainty of being a subject, it becomes active annihilation" (*FFC* 81) (i.e., annihilation of the object's certainty and thus of the certainty of the world that situates the subject as subject).

It is at this point, at this philosophic impasse, that Lacan establishes a "break" with traditional philosophy, breaking from the subject/object relation by introducing an uncanny (non)object, the *objet a*, that is also the most "intimate" part of the subject, paving the way for his (later) concept of the "extimate": "It is here that the interest the subject takes in his own split is bound up with that which determines it—namely, a privileged object, which has emerged from some primal separation, from some self-mutilation induced by the very approach of the real, whose name, in our algebra, is the *objet a*" (*FFC* 83). It is, then, the extimacy with respect to consciousness of this formative subjective lack, the *objet petit a*, or the gaze of the Other, that founds the very structure of the self-conscious subject, or the subject's sense of self-presence; but it is the function of anamorphosis to confront the subject with this symbolic lack as a repetition of its own ontological contingency, its spectrality or decenteredness, which in the visual register takes the form of the Gaze (of the Other). Another way to think about this is that just as the subject must repress that lost object (or desubjectivized part of itself) in order to apprehend itself as a grounded/grounding point of view in conscious thought, *Realism*, as a technology of objective reproduction of reality, must repress the ontological implications of anamorphosis in order to sustain its claim to objectivity.

Thus Žižek describes anamorphosis in *The Ticklish Subject* as a kind of uncanny moment of decentering when "we ... become aware that reality already involves our gaze, that this gaze is included in the scene we are observing, that this scene already 'regards us'" (78). And when Žižek further explains, responding to the *being-is-being-perceived* formula of the Idealists, that "the fact that reality is there for the subject only *must be inscribed in reality itself in the guise of an anamorphic stain*—this stain stands for the gaze of the Other, for the gaze qua object" (79, emphasis in original), he touches upon the radically ontological role anamorphosis assumes in its historical link with Descartes, as I will discuss presently.

The power of Lacan's historical reading of anamorphosis lies partly in the analogy he discovers between the geometral optics in the era of Descartes (in the development of which Descartes played an important role) and "the Cartesian subject, which is itself a kind of geometral point, a point of perspective" (*FFC* 86). Baltrušaitis himself, in his seminal book *Anamorphic Art*, notes the historical relevance of this connection: "By a curious coincidence," he says, "all the men who were concerned with paradoxical perspective systems found themselves to some extent linked to Descartes" (62). The development of and experiments in the science of perspective was by no means unrelated or even marginally related to Descartes's philosophy of knowledge and epistemology; as Baltrušaitis points out:

> All Descartes's demonstrations of the unreliability of our organs of perception reflect that concern which, in his *Meditations* (1641), he formulated as a doctrine of knowledge in which considerations also intervene on the vision of things and on artists' pictures—the real and the imaginary. The same teaching emerges spontaneously from the experiments of the perspective specialists of the time. (69)

This historical and epistemological parallel between the invention of perspective systems and the emergence of metaphysical doubt puts the seemingly aesthetic phenomenon of anamorphosis into its proper context. As the obverse of both mimetic reproduction (realism) and metaphysical certainty (*cogito ergo sum*), anamorphosis marks the artist's ability to reassert a disruption or *distortion*, a spectral noncertainty or play, at the heart of the geometrical rules and subjective self-presence that give being its objective reference points in the visual field. In other words, the anamorphic stain, standing "for the gaze of the Other, for the gaze qua object" inscribed into reality itself, is the vanishing point between optics and ontology, as well as between subject and object—a *spectral distortion* of subjectivizing vision/consciousness in the Cartesian sense.

An important factor in this ability to play with the metaphysical link between geometrical science and sense perception is that anamorphosis *applies* the very geometrical laws that it distorts, but in reverse. In his treatise on perspective, Gasper Schott describes a perspective device exactly like Dürer's "window" but inverted: "It is no longer a matter of establishing 'normal' perspective. From now on the 'window' also becomes a magical instrument which can be used for anamorphosis" (cited in Baltrušaitis 88).[4] Since, as Lacan points out, "what is at issue in geometral perspective is simply the mapping of space, not sight" (*FFC* 86), the *visual* as such—sight, light, *being in the visual sphere*—is thereby eluded, excluded from the structure of the visual dimension, like the *Being* (God) that granted and guaranteed the subject's metaphysical certainty from without before the Enlightenment, which is what makes geometral perspective for Lacan a metaphor for the Cartesian reification of the subject apprehended in the punctiform "I think": the schematization of perspective systems as a basis for transforming the unreliability of perceptual systems into technological reproducibility is analogous to Descartes's *cogito ergo sum*, which compensates for the loss of absolute/universal (external) *Being* by granting certainty to (subjective) *being* (in the I of I think) but only by excluding/repressing part of itself. Anamorphosis, therefore, which inverts this reification on itself—the "inverted use of the window"—is experienced as an uncanny return of the repressed/lost object in the visual sphere that destabilizes both its scientific and ontological (conscious) certainty or presence. For the artist it is the "magical instrument" that, subverting science's grasp on the calculability of the real, reinscribes desire or the gaze into that reality itself (as opposed to something that is added to or subtracted from it in the form of the subjective), and serves as an image of the decentering of the post-Cartesian subject, suggesting a subject supported by unconscious desire or (death) drive rather than thought—a subject contingent upon being's repressed spectral lack or uncanny surplus (which are the same thing, the *object a*).

Lacan's distinction between "the line and the light," between reified matter under the mastery of mathematics (line) and the return of the repressed of its elusive, ungraspable, unrepresentable being (light), exemplifies this dialectic between science and art whereby as scientific and technological thought reify the visual in the *line* (eliding light) and the subject in the certainty of the *cogito* (eliding the unconscious, or non-subjectivity of the subject), counter-realist art of all kinds reinscribes what has been rejected by means of the dreamlike, even psychotic work of distortion: "Distortion may lend itself ... to all the paranoiac ambiguities, and every possible use has been made of it, from Arcimboldo to Salvador Dalí. I will go so far as to say that this fascination complements what geometral researches into perspective allow to escape from vision" (*FFC* 87). Thus, as Žižek puts it, anamorphosis discloses the "gaze of the Other" in the visual sphere (the gaze here being unrepresentable *light-being*), inasmuch as it is always already "inscribed in the world" as the point at which this gaze manifests itself, but this point, this gaze, is never visible as such from the logical/self-present perspective of the conscious (Cartesian) I, only from *the decentering of that position*, which is why Lacan says that only in the dream "it shows."

Lacan makes the contrast between the questioning of the ontological status of the "real" in psychoanalysis and that of Idealism (especially Bishop Berkeley) even more explicit in his seminar on ethics:

> Compared to Freud, the idealists of the philosophical tradition are small beer indeed, for in the last analysis they don't really contest that famous reality, they merely tame it. Idealism consists in affirming that we are the ones who give shape to reality, and that there is no point in looking any

further. It is a comfortable position. Freud's position, and that of any sensible man for that matter, is something very different. (*Ethics* 30)

Freud's ontology is, in fact, the reverse. "Reality" is not, as in the Idealists, contained by the subject and supported by its being (in the form of an object of consciousness), but takes the form of an unconscious "detour" for the subject that must be mediated (symbolically) and regulated in relation to drives that oppose it: "[The reality principle] operates in the mode of detour, precaution, touching up, restraint. It corrects and compensates for that which seems to be the natural inclination of the psychic apparatus, and it radically opposes it" (Lacan, *Ethics* 28). As Žižek explains, the "anamorphic stain" necessarily repressed in this reality-construction (as a "blind spot") allows us to glimpse the

> imperceptible, but none the less crucial gap that forever separates Lacan from the standard Idealist notion of "subjective constitution" (according to which reality as such, the whole of it, is anamorphic in the general sense of esse = percipi, of "being there" only for the subject's gaze): Lacan's notion of the blind spot in reality *introduces anamorphic distortion into reality itself.* (*Ticklish Subject* 78–9)

Lacan uses the well-known example of anamorphosis in Holbein's "Ambassadors" to illustrate how the subject, in this radical decentering of the *esse est principi* model, is thus "annihilated" (precisely as that grounding ontological reference point) in its encounter with the "gaze of the Other" that locates it at the place of pure lack as a subject of desire:

> All this shows that at the very heart of the period in which the subject emerged and geometral optics was an object of research, Holbein makes visible for us something that is simply the subject as annihilated—annihilated in the form that is, strictly speaking, of the imaged embodiment of the *minus-phi* of castration, which for us, centers the whole organization of desires through the framework of the fundamental drives. (*FFC* 88–9)

Lacan's metaphor of *the line and the light* thus rearticulates the anamorphic reversal of perspective systems in psychoanalytic/ontological terms: the subject of Durer's window "maps" the object according to the logic of "the line," imaginary geometrical "visual rays" that center the (re)construction of reality on the conscious subject's viewpoint and place it in the position of (illusory) mastery and control, but only while the uncontainable and ungraspable dimension of "light" (*being* in the visual sphere, or the omnipresence of the gaze, or even what Lacan's friend Merleau-Ponty means by "depth of field") is excluded from the system. Once the apparatus is reversed, the elusive surplus, the "in itself" or recalcitrant materiality of being of the object that already assumes the subject's perspective in itself, returns in *the form of the gaze (as object)*, an anamorphic stain in reality: the objective embodiment of this light-being-desire that *maps the subject* into the "grid of desire" and the "framework of the drives" (the subject is "photo-graphed," to use Lacan's pun, by "the gaze as such, in its pulsatile, dazzling and spread out function," *FFC* 89), revealing the subject as contingent, symbolically castrated. In short, anamorphosis enacts this ontological disruption of the subject/object structure that supports scientific realism such that the subject position is literally displaced, distorted, and desubjectified by the gaze of the Other: the uncanny stretching out of the object by means of which the anamorphic structure distorts human perspective exposes the dreamlike "phallic ghost" concealed within the Realist schema. This is the reason that the death's head, or skull, as in Holbein's "Ambassadors," is the most frequent image concealed at the center of the unexpected anamorphic transformation: the "magic" stretching of the mimetic object in anamorphic distortion that changes a blind spot into a *memento mori* exposes subject's *extimacy*, the inhuman "core" or Disparity that, as symbolic castration, gives the subject its ontological status as speaking being and mars its relation to the Real.

Notes

1 Agamben too points to Daumier, and specifically Daumier's "The Pear," as an example of caricature's "emblematic status," which emphasizes the specific historicity of the caricature in question here (see Agamben 148).
2 See, for example, Anna Kornbluh's *Realizing Capital: Financial and Psychic Economies in Victorian Form* for the ways in which capitalism's speculative economic forces were subjectified as the "psychic economy" of "finance."
3 Abbreviated hereafter as *FFC*.
4 The frequent use of the term "magic" to describe the inverted use of this otherwise (or "properly") scientific device will remind us of the transformative power of caricature, especially in the Part II on effigy, as if magic were the inverse of science, or, as Adorno would, the return of the repressed of science.

2

Spectral character: dreams, distortion, and the (cut of the) Real

The structure of anamorphosis and its emergence, historically speaking, thus provide a key to the whole concept of spectral forms of representation. Anamorphosis's ability to unlock the ontological gap, the Disparity or as Žižek says, "what German Idealism calls negativity, what Freud called death drive" (*Disparities* 27) suppressed in mimetic representation is precisely what gives it its critical dimension, its means of representing social antagonisms necessarily smoothed over, touched up, or elided in forms of realism. The lithographic artwork of Philipon, Daumier, and Grandville first really tapped into this ontological spectrality in the visual medium in their political attacks on the *Roi Bourgeois* as a symbol of bourgeois ideology, specifically its influence over forms of representation and their technologization. "Les Poires" is a case in point here; but perhaps the best illustration of the way in which these French caricatural artists directed the critical (and spectral) force of their new art form towards the socio-ideological implications of mimetic representation can be found in Grandville's "Il a beau faire" (Figure 7). This is just one of Grandville's many allusions to Daumier's "The Pears," but on first sight it seems that he has, at least on the surface, removed the pear image from its political context (since Louis-Philippe is literally only present as a trace of a trace here) and placed it in a kind of arcane and dreamlike allegory about artistic practices. In this remarkable illustration, a monkey in the role of an artist is using some kind of perspective device, which also looks like a scepter or a magic wand, to copy out an image on an oversized canvas. He paints perched on a high stool that in order to reach he has had to climb up on a ladder (figuratively not unlike the apes upon the back of the Raphael horse). The pear on this canvas is not simply a generic image or allusion, but in fact a carefully deliberate echo or repetition of the last pear in Daumier's "The Pears," with its crisscross mouth and

Spectral character

7 J. J. Grandville, "Il a beau faire, il n'aura pas la croix" (No Matter How Hard He Tries, He Will Not Find the Cross), lithograph illustration in *La Caricature*, 1832.

askew eyes doubling as contours of the pear—here traced out in grand dimensions upon a massive canvas in the manner of royal portraiture. The image of Daumier's pear, itself implicitly phallic (a visual pun played upon endlessly by the caricaturists in Philipon's publications, as I will discuss later) is here distorted such that it appears stretched out, elongated, and ghostlike (it could even be seen to be rising out of the chest placed below the canvas, like an unleashed apparition). One could almost read an allegory of the Lacanian formula for anamorphosis in this image of magically unleashing the "phallic ghost" (as Lacan calls the anamorphic mage), which stands for "the gaze that is beyond," captured in the giant surreally disembodied eye on the wall behind the canvas. We can read part of this "allegory" in terms of Grandville's fascination with perspective and profile devices: the eye on the wall stands for the subject of geometric perspective from which the perspective device takes its laws in order to technologically reproduce the mimetic image on the canvas, operated mechanically by the apelike artist; except that under Grandville's pen, what emerges on the canvas instead of a mimetic reproduction is an anamorphic ghost, a revenant of Louis-Philippe, the *Roi Bourgeois*, as a sad spectral pear, symbolically castrated by the very process of anamorphic distortion.

It is remarkable, to me at least, how explicitly Grandville and Daumier pursue in their art these themes and images linking forms of representation—especially contrasting the entrenched-ness of mimesis to the playfulness of caricature—to sociopolitical and ideological antagonisms hinging on the idea of the person or subject. If there is a kind of dreamlike "allegory" in this last illustration, for instance, it clearly bears on an uncanny intuition that there is a powerful political force to the very nature of *dreamlike* representation itself ... and to the role caricature seems to play in bringing about a return of the repressed of bourgeois realism (as in, for instance, portraiture). Moreover, Grandville's image seems to enact this unexpected return in another anamorphic way. In most cases of anamorphosis the images on a canvas (or in other media) can mysteriously transform from one signified to another right before the viewer's eyes: a landscape seen from one angle becomes a monk in prayer from another, for instance. Analogously, if we take a "global" perspective of "Il a beau faire" ("step back" mentally rather than physically, as it were), we realize that the ladder leading up to the oddly tall stool set like scaffolding on the wooden platform and the long rod in the monkey-artist's hand used for a perspective device transform into the shape of a gallows *hanging the pear as an effigy of the king's head*, and the monkey-artist's noose-like tail contributes to this impression. (I will return to this image of hanging the pear or otherwise using it as an effigy in order to show how much Dickens uses this motif in his own characterization.)

The allegory? The caricatural artist symbolically castrates the bourgeois subject (as an ideal, or ideal image), in effigy, through the very process of distorting mimesis; or, put another way, precisely what the portraitist *obfuscates* by exhibiting the ego's ideal image "objectively" on the canvas, the caricaturist *conjures up* in the image as a distorted anamorphic ghost, revealing the gaze of the Other that symbolically structures the image in the first place.

This dreamlike quality of Grandville's work was noted by Baudelaire, not simply as surrealist visions, but as an earnest means of grasping the system of unconscious associations that make up the phenomenology of dreams that underlies the primary workings of the human mind: "Before his death, he applied his always stubborn will to the noting of his successive dreams and nightmares in plastic form, with all the precision of a stenographer writing down an orator's speech. Grandville wanted—he really wanted—his pencil to explain the law of the association of ideas!" ("Some French Caricaturists" 172). But it is not necessarily the "law of association of ideas" that makes Grandville's artwork so powerfully dreamlike (giving it the subversive potential I have just described). What Grandville seems to touch upon is that the structure of the image in anamorphosis (and in this respect in caricature) is like that of the image in the dream in that it *unmasks what is normally elided in waking perception*: the fact that the subject-position is already inscribed into objective reality. In other words, the subjective phenomenology of dreams differs in one crucial way from that of consciousness, and this way is analogous to anamorphosis. Where in waking life, as Descartes found, the subject can apprehend himself in thought, the dream denies the subject this subjectifying position: "[In the dream] the subject does not see where it is leading, he follows. He may even on occasion detach himself, tell himself *it is only a dream*, but in no case will he be able to apprehend himself in the dream in the way in which, in the Cartesian cogito, he apprehends himself in thought" (Lacan, *FFC* 136). But it is in this way that "in the field of the dream what characterizes the image is that *it shows*" ("it" alluding to the French *"Es,"* both the Id and the subject of the unconscious formalized *S*). But what does it show? Precisely that the position of apprehending oneself in the "I think" is already inscribed in reality itself, a position that lures us into our ideological assumption of mastery over the Real. The dream image, as in Lacan's example of the patient Chuang-tsu dreaming he is a butterfly, does not obfuscate the way we must internalize this imaginary image of the self (the ego) as a "natural" ontological presence before the gaze of the Other, but lets *it show*, opens us up to its play: "In fact, it is when he is a butterfly that he apprehended one of the roots of his identity—that he was, and is, in his essence, that butterfly who paints himself with his own colours—and it is because of this that, in the last resort, he is Chuang-tsu" (*FFC* 76). Similarly, by shifting the perceiver out of his "proper" perspective point, which is also the Cartesian "I think," anamorphosis makes it apparent that this point is supported by a lack or gap that the subject must fill (occupy) in the eyes of the Other.

In a sense, this gesture of placing and apprehending oneself in this position of self-identity before the gaze of the Other is captured visually and metaphorically in the genre of portraiture. It is for this reason that I would like to think about caricature as a kind of overdetermined counterpart to portraiture in the nineteenth century, and in order to do so the character of Rosa Dartle, from *David Copperfield*, who appears in an important portrait scene, is very useful. In a fascinating essay on *David Copperfield* and film, John Bowen suggests that "Rosa, the most persistently eroticized, fetishized and perverse figure in the novel, has a profoundly disturbing, not to say castrating, effect on David's psyche" (*Other Dickens* 35). Bowen is certainly right to see that there is an overdetermined element of sexual fantasy in Rosa's character, although voyeurism or perversity doesn't seem to capture the complex imagery here; rather there is something elusively uncanny and spectral about Rosa's character, something that remains insistently latent or beyond signification, like her "unearthly" signing that sounded "as if it had never been written, or set to music, but sprung out of the passion within her; which found imperfect utterance in the low sounds of her voice" (*David Copperfield* 369). Moreover, at the core of her character are two hauntingly symbolic, distinguishing character traits or tics, like a caricature: her cutting irony and the scar cut across her mouth, inflicted by Steerforth's having thrown a hammer at her as a child, which fades and flares with her passionate outbursts. Rosa's irony, her constant probing of seemingly ingenuous statements with cutting questions—"but isn't it, though ... isn't it, really?" (251)—destabilizes discourse in that it evokes unspoken ideologies or prejudices beneath the surface of seemingly "neutral" language, without naming what they are. And the first visualization we get of Rosa in the novel is sparked by a rather uncanny simile when David tells us that "she was a little dilapidated—like a house—with having been so long to let; yet had ... an appearance of good looks" (251). Both Freud and Jung tell us that the image of the house often stands in dreams as a metaphor for the self or psyche (the self as a house to let, in a very strict sense *unheimlich*), and the image of the dilapidated house to let adds a sense of memory, past childhood, and loss. These associations run deep in the case of David's childhood home that was imbued with a sense of loss from the start—both Rosa and David are orphaned—and that we later find has been put to let since soon after his mother's death, so the unsettling splicing together of Rosa and a dilapidated house from the beginning suggests a kind of overdetermined projection, or dreamlike condensation that distorts mimetic expectations.

The scene when David confronts Rosa Dartle's portrait in the guest bedroom on a visit to the Steerforth household, however, captures this disjunction between mimesis and spectral representation in an even more explicit and suggestive image. While the portrait itself notably omits Rosa's most strikingly visual character trait, the scar, the portrait scene as David narrates it revolves around her two distinctive traits, the scar and the irony, as being beyond the representational capacity of the portrait. While a guest at Steerforth's house, David gazes at the portrait of Rosa in his room before he retires to bed, which he describes thus: "It was a startling likeness, and necessarily had a startling look. The painter hadn't made the scar, but I made it; and there it was, coming and going; now confined to the upper lip as I had seen it at dinner, and now showing the whole extent of the wound inflicted by the hammer, as I had seen it when she was passionate" (255). The moment of gazing at Rosa's portrait seems to spark a kind of splitting or doubling of the narrator, revolving around the "I" of the speaker" and reflected in the split between the Rosa of the portrait and the Rosa of the text: the subject of the portrait, "it," splits between the portrait's "startling likeness" (a representation passively gazed at) and its subject's "startling look" (the character actively gazing); and from David's doubling between the artist and himself ("the painter hadn't made [it]" / "I made it") to the doubled "now" ("now confined"/ "now showing") that splits Rosa of the portrait from David's memory of her, revealing or concealing the original childhood trauma inflicted by Steerforth's phallic "hammer"; to the flickering of Rosa's passion in the presence/absence of the scar. The splitting/doubling of the artist between David and the portraitist through the verb *to make*, revolving around the scar, in particular, marks a distinction between the selective omissions of mimesis and the expressive distortion of the narrator. This tension between doubles only increases, moreover, once David tears himself away from the portrait and goes to sleep, but without being able to shake her now eroticized gaze: "To get rid of her, I undressed quickly, extinguished my light, and went to bed. But, as I fell asleep, I could not forget that she was still there looking, 'Is it really though? I want to know'; and when

I awoke in the night, I found that I was uneasily asking all sorts of people in my dreams whether it really was or not—without knowing what I meant" (255). In David's unconscious, the moment of gazing at the portrait is reversed and it is Rosa's ghostly image that is "still there looking" at him, subjecting him to a gaze and irony that seem to elude to the subjectivity of either subject. The struggle over the "I" of the sentence reflects this ambiguity of subjectivity, as the unconscious David's "I" is in fact *possessed by Rosa*, asking, ventriloquized by *her* ironic voice, "whether it really was or not," without self-possession, not "knowing what I meant." in his dream, David speaks from the place of the other; like Chuang-tsu dreaming he is a butterfly, he sees that in the dream, *the gaze shows*.

Rosa is therefore not just a coincidental choice for the portrait scene: she signifies quite strikingly the potential for David's subjectivity to split and double into disjunctive but parallel versions. Rosa's scar quite literally inscribes this symbolic function into her flesh, as if an instance of natural mimicry: the scar is at first described as a "seam," as if her face were liable, as it were, to come apart at the seams, or as David describes it: "It was an old scar—I should rather call it, seam, for it was not discolored, and had healed years ago—which had once cut through her mouth, downward towards the chin, but was now barely visible" (251). And in spells of intense passion the split seems to threaten to return and tear her very face in two: as David says, "As she looked full at me, I saw her face grow sharper and paler, and the marks of the old wound lengthen out until it cut through the disfigured lip, and deep into the nether lip, and slanted down the face" (366).

The scar across Rosa's mouth has an archetypal force when we consider Lévi-Strauss's discussion of the deep-seated mythological association between "harelips," doubles, and twins with an ancient story of a girl who hits the mythic figure Rabbit on the mouth with a stick (compare Steerforth's hammer) and "begins a cleavage that, if completed, would split the animal's body and turn the animal into twins" (205). "Now if twins result from a child, an embryo, or an animal that has split or is about to split," Lévi-Strauss continues, "the myths attest that a rabbit and a harelipped human being are themselves the splitters" (205). Rosa herself can be seen then as a kind of feminine double of David, perhaps even a kind of uncanny female twin, if we recall David's fictional female twin since birth, Betsy Trotwood ("conceived" by his Aunt Betsy, who had wanted and predicted a girl), whose name, cut down to Trotwood and later Trot, David adopts for a period of his life, as if illustrating or projecting the potential to have become a feminine double of himself, or the potential of a totally different narrative (fantasy) of himself externally existing alongside his own. Rosa is then both an alternative or displaced projection of David's subjectivity and the unconscious force (or drive) that splits his subjectivity into self and other. As a "splitter" (she is repeatedly described as "sharp" or as one who "sharpens" (*David Copperfield* 253, 366, 370), therefore, Rosa is not so much a "castrating" force (as Bowen claims) as an uncannily proliferating or spectral one, disrupting the tendency to unity, bourgeois normalcy, and mastery of David's narrative telos. As Rosa's cutting irony illustrates, what she conjures exposes something that should have remained hidden, like the uncanny, like a dream. As both spectral other and displaced desire, Rosa splices into David's/Daisy's/Trot's narrative an uncontainable sense of extimacy, of a sense that his I, to quote Lévi-Strauss again, "would split ... has split or is about to split" (205).

Dickens's working notes for the novel give us a glimpse of the author conceiving Rosa in her two overdetermined character traits, the scar and the irony, as if the germs cells of her character were planted in his mind, or like a caricaturist seeing the essential traits: "Miss Dartle. 'Threw a hammer at her?' / 'Eh? But is it really though? I want to know?'" (*David Copperfield* 748). In that obscure, subject-less question about her origin—"threw a hammer at her?"—just beyond the frame of the narrative, just as the origin of the scar remains at the obscure margins of the plot, we get a sense of the elusiveness of Rosa's character to mimetic realism. She belongs much more to what Chesterton felt compelled to term Dickens's "unbearable realism of a dream" (*Charles Dickens* 65). The only features of Rosa's character capable of constituting her subjectivity—her scar and her irony—are isolated in the portrait scene as being *outside the representational capabilities of mimesis as such*. If the complicity between mimesis and bourgeois subjectivity is ineluctable, mimesis is unmasked in the disruptions and distortions of the "surface" of the portrait, its illusive claim to a totality of appearance, a complete and representable reality. Rosa, especially when we consider Dickens's gesture of scarring mimesis itself in her portrait scene, embodies this cut of the Real, this essential point of spectral characterization that, according to Lacan, "[t]here is something originally, inaugurally, profoundly wounded in the human relation to the world" (*Ego* 167). And nowhere is it so evident in Dickens's writing that this inaugural wound is a function of the signifier, as Rosa's scar is itself a kind of writing, a signifier, like the symptom, as Lacan says, which is "a metaphor in which flesh or function is taken as a signifying element" ("Agency of the Letter" 518).[1]

Rosa's relation to the cut of the Real, then, illustrates particularly well the complex relation of the body to language, which I discussed in the Introduction. Rosa's scar is truly a metaphor that takes flesh as its signifying element; but it is in the end a metaphor for a certain kind of *writing*, a writing that seems to be of its very nature liminal, to oscillate between presence and absence, the visible and invisible, like "a mark in invisible ink brought to the fire," says David of Rosa's scar, which when he sees "start forth" he likens to "the old writing on the wall" in *The Book of Daniel* (*David Copperfield* 253)[2] that seems to write itself. This form of writing touches upon the primal relation between the signifier and *jouissance* that marks the essence of engendering itself, as Leclaire explains: "The transmission of erotogeneity, which is a body of *jouissance* as much as it is a letter, cannot in fact be carried out except by a mark made on a body with another body, except by a trait inscribed directly by one body on another body" (122). This writing in *jouissance*, in other words, is inextricably linked with the very possibility of writing itself, for "it is … as bound to the very origin of the signifier's coming into play that it is possible to speak of *jouissance*" (Leclaire 177).

"Pickwick Sits for His Portrait": the gaze as spectral inscription

The illustrations of Hablot Browne, or Phiz, have been considered primarily in the English iconological tradition of Hogarth, Gilray, and Cruikshank since the foundational studies by Harvey and Steig, but, to my knowledge, no one has given significant consideration to the influence on their work of Dickens's and Phiz's contemporaries in France. Daumier's influence on Phiz has been very briefly mentioned by both John Harvey, who shows that Phiz uses Daumier's "Sick Nurse" as a model for Mrs. Gamp from *Martin Chuzzlewit* (132–3), and Steig, who (most notably here) notes Phiz's allusion to Daumier's "The Pears" in his satire on the pompous Pecksniff, again in *Martin Chuzzlewit*, whose head, in one illustration, appears three times in various distortions suggestive of a pear. And yet even though Thackeray famously told Phiz in the beginning of his career that he would benefit from studying the technique of Daumier, this influence is left astonishingly underdeveloped and underexplored. So how *did* this very different form of caricature, less iconological and more surreal and dreamlike, influence Phiz's and Dickens's art of *characterization*?

Spectral character

One of the fundamental representational techniques of Philipon, Daumier, and Grandville that influenced Dickens and Phiz was the use of expressive distortion—the use of distortion, that is, for the sake of its own intrinsic subversive and signifying potential, as in anamorphosis—we could say, as a key aspect of spectral representation. Phiz never, to my knowledge, made anamorphic references as explicitly as Grandville did, but he does allude, as it were, to anamorphosis and incorporate it in subtle ways. In one of Phiz's greatest early illustrations, for instance, "The Valentine" (Figure 8), depicting Sam Weller and his father Tony in a pub discussing Sam's valentine letter, we find an example of this Grandville-type anamorphosis in Tony Weller's "overcharged" and almost surreally spherical belly, which so obviously inscribes distortion into the center of perspective of the illustration. Tony Weller is anamorphically expanded to make him bulge at the belly and tower over Sam, comparable to Grandville's high and low soldiers, but his belly also appears like a gleaming grid that, in a very geometrical, almost abstract manner, seems to reflect the composition of the picture itself. The composition, for instance, is structured according to various configurations of circles and squares, in fairly neat rows, from the three large rounded central figures on the bottom to the two rows of square frames, three in each, over the mantelpiece, like tiers, at the center of which, framed by the square hearth, is Tony's spherical belly girded by grids. The three central figures of the plate are, from left to right, Sam Weller, Tony Weller, and, strangely enough, a cat (never even alluded to in the text) sitting like a person in a chair with an overcoat draped over it. Although I have yet to come across an attempt to explain the cat, one wonders if Phiz isn't toying with a Grandville/Daumier-type game of surreal metamorphosis here in the symmetry between the coy waitress peeking in from behind the door on the left and the feminine feline gazing up at Tony Weller on the right, perhaps as commentary on the ludicrous romanticism of the Wellers.

This illustration, moreover, gains a new complexity when read in the context of Dickens's dramatization of the relation between word and image throughout this chapter and throughout much of the novel. The whole scene, of course, dramatizes an act of writing as Sam writes a valentine letter to his love interest in a pub with his father, Tony Weller, assisting in the "composition." On the way to the pub, just before the scene illustrated, Sam stops in front of "a small stationer's and print-sellers window" where he sees the valentine card that inspires him to write his own, and of which Dickens gives the following brilliantly comic ekphrastic description: "a highly coloured representation of a couple of human

8 Phiz (Hablot K. Browne), "The Valentine," etching for *The Pickwick Papers*, 1837.

hearts skewered together with an arrow, cooking before a cheerful fire, while a male and female cannibal in modern attire ... were approaching the meal with hungry eyes, up a serpentine gravel path leading thereunto" (*Pickwick Papers* 536–7). Steven Marcus rightly points out that Dickens is "implicitly and covertly asserting" that "he can turn pictures into writing which is more vivid, more graphic, more representational than the pictures themselves" ("Language into Structure" 148), but he doesn't seem to consider that just as Dickens is turning pictures into writing, Phiz is turning Dickens's writing back into pictures, and, moreover, that this competitive/prolific relationship itself is nowhere so near the surface as in this number (including this and the next chapter). The chapter and the illustration "The Valentine," that is, depict a scene of writing and reading both visually and verbally; as Sam reads his letter aloud, his father Tony makes observations concerning "literary composition" (as the title of the chapter has it) and their dialogue abounds in puns, playful misreadings, and, especially, a play on the word "letter." The separation into the competitive and complementary representational forms, text and image, here generates a new level of symbolic exchanges and self-reflexivity: we witness not a translation from text into image (typical of illustrated texts), but a furtive play between images, writing about images, and images of writing. After several interruptions to comment on "literary" style, for instance, Tony listens with "critical solemnity" to more of Sam reading his letter aloud and again intercedes, hearing some hesitancy:

> "Werry good," said Mr Weller. "Go on."
> "Feel myself ashamed, and completely cir-, I forget what this here word is," said Sam, scratching his head with the pen, in vain attempts to remember.
> "Why don't you look at it, then?" inquired Mr Weller.
> "So I *am* a lookin' at it," replied Sam, "but there's another blot. Here's a 'c,' and a 'i,' and a 'd.'"
> "circumwented, p'haps," suggested Mr Weller.
> "No, it ain't that," said Sam, "circumscribed; that's it."
> "That ain't a good a word as circumwented, Sammy," said Mr Weller, gravely.
> "Think not?" said Sam.
> "Nothin' like it," replied his father.
> "But don't you think it means more?" inquired Sam. (540)

Mirroring the dialogue between Sam and his father in this pub scene, the symbolic exchanges between word and image in Dickens's and Phiz's new art form generate overdetermined signifying play in slips, distortions, representational material, and absurd misreadings. For example, the letters that Sam reads, first as "cir-" and then as a "c," an "i," and a "d," attempting to decipher his own writing, appear in Phiz's illustration in the sign that reads "CIDER" over the fireplace, only the first three letters of which are illuminated. If the letters on the page are already unstable and uncontainable, the illustration adds another layer of letters to generate another means of interpretation, or another means of "reading." And even as Dickens alludes to the concepts of consumption and consumerism in the images on the valentine's day card (in the cannibalism motif), so Phiz matches it in the pub adverts for cider and Guinness. Opposite the CIDER sign, which half conceals a picture of a clown, as if half revealing an underlying joke, is a picture of a boxer (above right) in a comical fighting stance challenging an unseen opponent. And in fact, Sam Weller (below left) has both of his hands in the air, like a dualist, mirroring the pictured fighter in counterpoise, flourishing his writer's pen and paper, while Tony Weller has one hand behind his back and flourishes his long quill-like pipe in the other, like another duelist, both exchanging gazes gamely, with the "Guinness Dublin Stout" sign just above the elder Mr. Weller's imposing head, slyly commenting on his ingenious application and (literally) stout defense of the "critical sentiments respecting literary criticism" he provides on Sam's letter. In short, the visual and verbal signifiers in this scene are as unruly and recalcitrant as its central characters.

Signifiers are in truth by nature unwieldy and recalcitrant, but in caricature, as we have seen, these material distortions and gaps can function to form new symbolic nodal points and meanings. Here in particular, the blotted-out word in dispute between being read either as "circumvented" or "circumscribed," which generates this interpretive play between text and illustration, marks a kind of splitting (as that between word and image) that reveals the signifier's inherent tension with itself (the two words having opposing connotations respecting borders and rules) and by doing so calls attention to its intrinsic surplus of sense (or as Sam asks, "But don't you think it means more?"). "Circumvented" has the significance, of course, of finding a way to elude or overcome laws or restrictions, or as the *Oxford English Dictionary* (OED) has it, "[t]o get the better of by craft or fraud; to overreach, outwit, cheat, 'get round,' 'take in.' Also, to evade or find a way around (a difficulty, obstacle, etc.)." It is, as Marcus points out, a linguistic crime that brings Pickwick to court in the trial scene that follows, and as Steig points out, it is his so-called love letters that ensnare Pickwick in unintended contracts and finally land him in the debtors' prison for breach of promise, all of which beg for a linguistic circumvention beyond the bourgeois Pickwick's means. Unlike Pickwick, however, Sam *is* able to circumvent the law linguistically, with his unpolished savvy, precisely *because of* his semi-literacy, or his uncanny ability to occupy or evade fixed linguistic positions: "Never sign a walentine with your own name," he says, and signs it "Your love-sick Pickwick" (543). In a parallel sense, Dickens and Phiz are, in the symbolic exchanges between words and images, similarly circumventing the laws and codes that govern mimetic representation, drawing on the gap or lack inherent to the signifier to generate a drive or excess of signification that gives their artform an uncanny excess or spectrality.

"Circumscribed," however, which the OED defines as "to draw a line round; to encompass with (or as with) a bounding line, to form the boundary of, to bound," seems to have something of the opposite meaning: to limit and to define, to "draw a circle around" something. Yet to encompass is also to bring into being, to define, to *de-limit*, as in the image of Tony's globular belly incorporating that which encompasses it. Writing and etching are brought to bear on one another even in this word "circumscribe," with its roots in the Latin prefix *circum*, to ring around, related to *circus*, the encircled (dis)play of the arena, and the verb *scribere*, "to write," "whose basic meaning," as Jensen says, "was 'to scratch, to score,' as indicated by its etymological connection with the Greek ... (*skariphaomai*) 'to scratch, to score' and Latvian *skripat* 'to score'" (31–2). As we have seen, Phiz's etchings, a literal form of writing/scoring, translates this play on the words "circumvented" and "circumscribed" in the configurations of frames and circles and the play with signs and pictures. And in the text, Dickens uses letters in ways that evade formal transcription, as in the Wellers' conflation of "Vs" and "Ws," as a boundless source of creativity and means to circumvent formal prose and clichés, for example in Tony Weller's critical sentiments about Sam's love letter: "'Wot I like in that 'ere style of writin,' said the elder Mr Weller, 'is, that there ain't no callin' names in it,—no Wenuses, nor nothin' o' that kind. Wot's the good o' callin' a young 'ooman a Wenus or a Angel, Sammy?'" (540). Letters and words here are distorted, switched about, substituted with marks, scarred, and there are nearly as many dashes, apostrophes and omissions as there are words. *Circum-scription*, in the sense of an exhibition of the writing itself, a material writing that slips between the text/image opposition, or a surface score/scar that distorts the sense of the mimetic sign, characterizes what is most radical about this "new art form" of Dickens and Phiz.

Steig makes important advances in the critical approach to Dickens's illustrated novels when he recognizes the ways in which illustrations can be "read" in dialogue with other scenes and illustrations that carry over various textual themes in various combinations, such as the illustration "the Valentine," which becomes more nuanced and expressive when "read" in conjunction with its subsequent illustration, "The Trial" (Figure 9): "in 'The Valentine' (ch. 32) and "The Trial" (ch. 33) these implicit parallels [that echo more implicitly throughout the novel] can be actively 'read.' The central link between chapters 32 and 33 is a love letter" (34). "Once this parallel is recognized," continues Steig, "the similar composition in the two etchings suddenly becomes visible," such as the "spatial relationship between a central, standing, admonitory figure and, on the left, the object of his exhortations" (34), these figures being Mr. Weller advising Sam while he is writing the love letter in the first illustration, and Serjeant Buzfuz flourishing the fabricated "love letter" at the sitting Pickwick in the second.

Once we acknowledge the benefits of this more fluid approach of "reading" across text and illustration, moreover, we can see that in fact the love letter is not the only theme to link these two chapters (33 and 34) and illustrations, but is part of a deeper network of symbolic connections. For one thing, it isn't just the letter itself that carries the parallel; it is the dramatization of the acts of reading and writing that is echoed between the episodes in text and image. In the first, Sam writes the letter and (mis)reads it aloud to his father who interprets, interjects, and critiques his style. In the second episode, Serjeant Buzfuz reads aloud and tendentiously misconstrues the innocent letters Pickwick wrote to his landlady, Mrs. Bardell, as love letters, critiquing and misreading figures of speech in literal terms. In the former case, the act of writing itself is given theatrical emphasis: Sam "pulled out the sheet of guilt-edged letter-paper, and the hard-nibbed pen. Then looking carefully at the pen to see that there were no hairs in it, and dusting down the table, so that there might be no crumbs of bread under the paper, Sam tucked up the cuffs of his coat, squared his elbows, and composed himself to write" (537). In "Tuck[ing] up his cuffs" and "squar[ing] his elbows" Sam makes a playful show of warming up, as if for sparring. Serjeant Buzfuz, too, makes a menacing show of the act of writing, but now with the consequential weight of the law behind his gestures: "'Now attend well, Mr Weller,' said Serjeant Buzfuz, dipping a large pen into the inkstand before him, for the purpose of frightening Sam with a show of taking down his answer" (573). That is, Sam Weller's letter-writing scene frames Pickwick's trial scene by anticipating the latter's more consequential motifs of writing, play, and power in a more playful and innocuous context, and the trope of names and naming becomes the focal point of this tension between the play and force of writing. The judge had already put Mr. Winkle

9 Phiz (Hablot K. Browne), "The Trial," etching for *The Pickwick Papers*, 1837.

Spectral mimesis

completely out of sorts by taking down his name in the court documents incorrectly and then attributing it to Winkle's own evasion, but when he attempts to repeat this strategy with the inimitable Sam Weller on the stand, he is, of course, uproariously circumvented:

> "What's your name, sir": inquired the judge.
> "Sam Weller, my lord," replied that gentleman.
> "Do you spell it with a 'V' or a 'W'"? inquired the judge.
> "That depends on the taste and fancy of the speller, my lord," replied Sam; "I never had occasion to spell it more than once or twice in my life, but I spells it with a 'V.'"
> Here a voice in the gallery exclaimed aloud, "Quite right too, Samivel, quite right. Put it down a we, my lord, put it down a we." (572)

Serjeant Buzfuz's legalistic trick of ensnaring Pickwick through theatrical misreadings is countered by the inimitable linguistic play and Disparity of the Wellers (it is, of course, the *other* Weller who "dares address the court" anonymously from the gallery). Putting Sam on the bench is not enough to circumscribe his words: try to pin him down to a single name and his echo or double, "a voice in the gallery," will appear with another competing reading. The dialogue between Sam and Tony Weller in the pub that centered on the creative misreading of letters, particularly "v" and "w," is here repeated in the court as a means to circumvent the circumscription of legal discourse. That is, it was by putting his name in writing (incorrectly) that the judge puts Nathaniel Winkle in an indefensible position: "How could I have got Daniel in my notes, unless you told me so, sir?" he asks, and the narrator tells us flatly that "this argument was, of course, unanswerable" (566–7). But just as Justice Stareleigh's notes are "unanswerable" and unchangeable because transcribed, codified as fixed positive signs in official documents, the language of the Wellers, which eludes circumscription literally to the letter, is recalcitrant to the judge's coercion because it resists being written down as such; it circumvents circumscription by (re)inscribing *the very elusiveness of difference itself* within written discourse: between a "v" and "w" "put it down a we."

Moreover, this irreducible difference or Disparity is inscribed in the proper name itself, not just that of Weller, but also implicitly in the name of the author's surrogate, "Samivel," which pivots on this differential play of phonemes, or the *surplus/lack of the letter* that (re)inscribes the play of *jouissance* within the proper name, the legally binding codification of identity. "Samivel" here, precisely by ventriloquizing this irreducible play of the letter, repeats the desubjectifying tendency of the signifier

Spectral character

to slip away from the speaker/writer/reader/critic put on comic display in the pub scene but now within the more consequential legal space of the courtroom; he enacts, that is, the signifier's obverse function not to bind but to unbind, its intrinsic death drive, in the very proper name, by opening the enunciation to the possibility of the *multiple*, as the invisible Weller in the courtroom reminds us when he tells the judge attempting to put down *one* Weller's name as a legal binding of an anonymous *you*—finding a line of flight between a "v" and a "w"—"put it down a we." As John Bowen puts it, the Wellers' "vaggery [*sic*] is marked by singular, plural letters which are no letters, and are neither part of speech nor writing, but the signs of an irreducible and collective plurality and play beyond both" (*Other Dickens* 70). What makes this "beyond" so radical, I would add, is that this play of *jouissance* that haunts signification always and by definition eludes being written down as such—it is the *ghostly and uncanny remainder/materiality of the signifier* that is repressed in discourses of realism but, in an age of the institutionalization of mimesis as a technology, *returns* as spectrality in Dickens and Phiz's uncanny forms, in, for instance, the form(s) of the Wellers.

Steven Marcus also notes this strangely *material* aspect of Dickens's writing as a play with (and "beyond") the opposition between grapheme and phoneme, suggesting "that Dickens's prolonged experience as a shorthand writer had a significant effect on what for a writer must be the most important of relations, the relation between speech and writing" ("Language into Structure" 141). Marcus draws upon the semi-autobiographic description from *David Copperfield* of David (like Dickens) learning shorthand in his youth, which Marcus sees as a potential origin of Dickens's ability to circumvent the semantically/culturally biding codification of speech in written signifiers:

> It was almost as if the nascent novelist had providentially been given or discovered another way of structurally relating himself to the language. Speech could now be rendered not only in the abstract forms of cursive or printed letters and units; it could be represented *graphically* as well—the other two forms of written transcription that [David] refers to are Egyptian hieroglyphics and Chinese ideograms (along with the written code of science, chemistry). What I am suggesting is that this experience of an alternative, quasi-graphic way of representing speech had among other things the effect upon Dickens of loosening up the rigid relations between speech and writing that prevail in our linguistic and cultural system. (141)

Ultimately Marcus sees this "loosening" of the structural relations of speech and writing as a loosening of the cultural logic or logos associated by Freud with the secondary (conscious) processes in favor of the less retrained and more prolific signifying mechanisms of the primary (unconscious) processes. I have been suggesting here another way of articulating this characteristic dimension of Dickens's style, not in terms of the primary process as a subjective phenomenon but in terms of this disparity between forms of signification, textual and graphic, being already *inscribed in the signifier itself*, as the "materiality" or ontological antagonisms already implicit in/as the *subject* as a *cut in the Real*. In any case it is worth noting the obvious here that not only did Dickens have his youthful encounter with stenography, but also his close artistic affinity with his illustrator Phiz, which sprang up providentially very early in the course of *The Pickwick Papers* and gave Dickens the opportunity to play, from the outset, with language's relation to its representational "outside" or "other," the visual image. All of these things may have given Dickens "another way of structurally relating himself to the language" that accounts for his uncanny tendency to tap into what Marcus refers to as the primary processes or what I'm calling the intrinsic spectrally of language. Another way of putting this is that the anamorphic play between word and image is already inscribed in Dickens's prose as such, since it is a play with an ontological lack or gap that is already intrinsic to the representation/reality split in the form of the Real.

To further illustrate this anamorphic play and splitting of perspective we can pursue the graphic/textual play between the pub scene and the trial scene, illustrated as "The Valentine" and "The Trial," a bit further. Again, the two scenes/illustrations are woven together in complex ways that reach across text and image and look forwards and backwards. For example, in his absurdly tendentious (mis)reading of Pickwick's writing in the trial scene, Buzfuz turns an offhanded reference in one of Pickwick's letters to taking a "slow coach" home into an encrypted allegory of Pickwick's transgressions with Mrs. Bardell: "And what does this allusion to the slow coach mean? For aught I know, it may be a reference to Pickwick himself, who has most unquestionably been a criminally slow coach during the whole of this transaction, but whose speed will now be very unexpectedly accelerated" (563). It seems likely that Phiz is making a graphic allusion to these images, but projected retrospectively into the pub scene, in the two paintings of coaches that appear on the mantelpiece in "The Valentine," one appearing quite speedy, with huge wheels and a sprinting dog, the other appearing larger, more stately and slow, making the two scenes and illustrations appear tightly compositionally interwoven. Of course, this connection is particularly playful, and in general the illustration "The Trial" seems essentially whimsical, perhaps even lacking in the gravity that is implicit in Dickens's critique of the British juridical system, which will intensify as Pickwick finds himself eventually arrested and taken to prison for evading fabricated monetary fines.

But if we look at these two illustrations not merely as thematically parallel, but almost literally as a kind of split representation, we can see in them, potentially, a kind of combined allusion to another, darker illustration by Daumier entitled, appropriately enough here, "Le Ventre Législatif" (The Legislative Belly) (Figure 10), which was part of Daumier's "attack on the National Assembly" (Vincent 48). One can see the compositional influences of "The Legislative Belly," an illustration reproduced to be sold on its own in January of 1834, on Phiz's "The Trial," with its direct perspective of rows in the gallery peopled by wigs and clerks, some snoozing, some chatting, some perusing papers, just as in Daumier's lithograph "[t]he statesmen are caught as by a candid camera" says Vincent, "in unposed activities, reading, sleeping, gossiping" (50).

10 Honoré Daumier, "Le Ventre Législatif" (The Legislative Belly), lithograph on wove paper, 1843.

Daumier's caricature uses the *visual* metaphor of *the belly* as a signifier to link the corpulent bourgeois politicians and judiciary of Louis-Philippe's *juste milieu* National Assembly to the state bureaucratic organism as a whole in its implicit function of consuming the revolutionary energy of the people as means of expanding its ponderous fiscal control—just as Pickwick's playful pecuniary innocence is for the first time in the novel subject to darker juridical forces of the bourgeois economic state, such as British equity courts and the debtors' prisons. Daumier's illustration also does something very dreamlike in transforming the image of the belly into a metaphor *by graphically displacing* it from the individual men onto the composition of the whole courtroom: "'The largeness of Daumier's humor,' David Rubens wrote, 'is not in the paunches of the individual men but in the curve of the benches which repeats the wrinkles of the tight vests and makes a huge 'belly' of the whole scene'" (Vincent 50). In Phiz's case, we can see a similar graphic displacement of the belly metaphor but echoed *between* the two illustrations: the metaphor/allusion is split between the giant belly of Tony Weller in "The Valentine," girded round by curved vertical and horizontal lines like Daumier's courtroom, and the tiered courtroom itself, in "The Trial," which, though lacking the curvature, repeats the tiered structure of the pub scene and its compositional drama. Of course, Mr. Weller Sr. (and his anamorphic belly) is absent from the "The Trial," since, as we have seen, even as Tony Weller's belly graphically echoes the whole courtroom in the first illustration, the courtroom *swallows up Mr. Weller's body/belly*, but not his voice, in the trial scene. The judge, after the anonymous interjection "put it down a we," attempted to apprehend the person who called out from the gallery "but as the usher didn't find the person, he didn't bring him; and, after a great commotion, all the people who had got up to look for the culprit, sat down again" (572). That is, the (visual) metaphor of Weller's belly from the pub scene is actually present in its absence in the courtroom, compositionally haunting the trial scene in the form of a more primal characteristic of Tony Weller's function in the text, his uncanny capacity for transgressing our strict sense of the inside/outside opposition of the body, in short, for swallowing things up. As Steven Marcus points out,

> Tony Weller generally appears as Mr Pickwick's complement, particularly in respect to the latter's benevolent disposition, for much of Tony's irresistible charm consists in his oyster like "power o' suction" his superb excess of receptivity. Whenever Tony comes on the scene, he is about to begin, has just concluded, or is in the process of ingesting immeasurable quantities of nourishment, making them disappear down his "capacious throat" (ch. 20),

not out of gluttony or animal appetite, but simply because of his pleasure in taking everything into himself, his infant-like urge to absorb. (*Dickens* 36)

Thus although "The Trial" by itself may appear relatively unsophisticated in its composition, it suggests a use of allusion and metaphor in visual expression that set Phiz apart as the particular illustrator that could engage Dickens in a creative interplay between text and image that would open up a whole new representational potential for his prose and for the novel form.

Seeing a ghostly trace of Daumier's art form in *The Pickwick Papers* allows us to see a totally new kind of representational influence, not on the level of content (an allusion to the pear image, say, or a character), but the influence of the dreamlike distortion and anamorphic play that made the very *form* of the French caricaturists' art form politically and ontologically forceful—that lent it its spectrality. Whereas Phiz's early illustrations seem on the surface exuberantly light and comic, seeing them in the context of Daumier's darker, more caustic and dreamlike visual satire on the bourgeois ruling class makes them appear more fitting for Dickens's early novels, which of course have the appeal of being humorous and even playful but are frequently more dark and subversive, and even in the trial scene Dickens gives us Daumieresque satirical "portraits" of the British judiciary in Serjeant Buzfuz, Serjeant Snubbin, Justice Stareleigh, and others.[3] But this particular pairing of the "The Trial" and "The Legislative Belly" has the added interest of linking Dickens and Phiz to the extensive and self-conscious ideological/ontological critique of mimetic representation we discussed earlier in the imagery of Daumier and Grandville, especially in terms of the antagonism between portraiture and caricature. Daumier's "The Legislative Belly" was part of a "campaign" directed at Louis-Philippe's whole *juste milieu* ideology, conceived by Philipon who had "invented a new line of attack on the *juste milieu* for [Daumier] to carry out" (Vincent 39) through a kind of mock portrait gallery of Louis-Philippe's politicians to appear in both *Caricature* and *Charivari*:

> This series stemmed from a witticism of Philipon's: since Louis-Philippe was having his portrait gallery at Versailles, Philipon would have his at the *Gallerie Vero-Dodat*; since Louis-Philippe had his court painter, Alaud, then Philipon would have his, Daumier; Philipon's portrait gallery would be a an ironic caricatural counterpart to the Pear's. (Vincent 40)

Philipon himself described the project as "a portrait series of the celebrities of the *juste milieu*—portraits which, realistically studied, should possess a satiric character, a burlesque element, known under the name of *charge"* (Vincent 41). The "Legislative Belly" was the artistic and dramatic culmination of this portrait series of individual statesmen, whose "likenesses" were taken (and transformed) by Daumier to appear in Philipon's illustrated journals as a counterpoise to the public gallery—a revolutionary struggle played out in the sphere of representation.

The idea of portraiture also makes a few appearances in *The Pickwick Papers* as well. In his valentine letter, in fact, Sam Weller references a kind of likeness reproduction device when he writes: "The first and only time I see you your likeness was took on my heart in much quicker time and brighter colours than ever a likeness was took by the profeel machine ... although it *does* finish a portrait and put the frame and glass on complete with a hook at the end to hang it up by and all in two minutes and a quarter" (542). Sam's playful comment in his letter comparing himself (favorably) to a portrait, or profile device, is well placed in a chapter that is particularly concerned with ekphrasis and the relation of text to illustration, but it also highlights the triumphant role of Sam's all-consuming perspective or gaze, which will become more explicit and significant in the courtroom and in the debtors' prison. When Sam is introduced into the courtroom, for instance, he "took a bird's-eye view of the bar, and a comprehensive survey of the bench with a remarkably cheerful and lively aspect" and further into his questioning, the judge, trying to intimidate him, "looked sternly at Sam for full two minutes, but Sam's features were so perfectly calm and serene that the judge said nothing, and motioned Serjeant Buzfuz to proceed" (573). Just as he circumvents the circumscription of the written word, Sam somehow seems to elude the gaze of the Other embodied by the surveillance of the judge and all the public display of the courtroom. Being the object of disciplinary observation does not faze Sam in his role as the one who gazes and who seems to occupy a position beyond the perspective of this scene, perhaps because he is not in that position to identify with the bourgeois state apparatus that Dickens is capturing in portrait caricature here.

Pickwick, however, *is* in that position to identify with the bourgeois gaze (being himself quasi-bourgeois, we might say, since he is a man, as Chesterton says, without a past), and this difference between Sam and Pickwick in relation to the gaze of the Other is at the center of an illustration of the scene depicting the trial's consequences—articulated, moreover, through the metaphor of portraiture. That is, as a result of the "Trial of Bardell Against Pickwick," and the pecuniary punishment that ensues, Pickwick is sentenced to confinement in the debtors' prison. When Pickwick is first admitted there, the turnkeys circle round him in a ritual they have adopted, to "take his likeness," as they call it (i.e., commit his face to memory), in order to brand him as a prisoner distinct from visitors who are free to come and go, hence the ironic title of the illustration, "Pickwick Sits For His Portrait" (Figure 11). As visualized in Phiz's illustration, Pickwick sitting for his "portrait" here means becoming a passive spectacle without agency, a kind of hapless object circumscribed by the specular desire of the gazer in a way that very nicely plays on the genre of bourgeois portraiture with its unspoken but awkward exhibition of selfhood or personhood. Dickens's repeated use of "likeness" in this scene makes it clear that he is playing with the representational and generic implications of the comic parallel, so that "taking a likeness" is here a literal and symbolic act of circumscription, whereby ones identity, captured in an image, becomes inscribed in a system or structure. The process of representation, or mimesis, is implicitly analogous to a mechanical locking-in of an apparatus: "We're capital hands at likenesses here," says one turnkey, "Take 'em in no time, and always exact" (662).

Pickwick's uneasy and rigid posture and nervous expression in the illustration, registering an uncharacteristic cognizance of a threat to his dignity, artfully combines characteristics of the bourgeois portrait sitter and the detained debtor. Sam, on the other hand, standing directly behind the portrait sitter, imperviously returns the gaze of the turnkeys, thereby (as is Dickens in this very act) taking *their* likeness. It might seem too facile to say that the gaze is inscribed into the picture itself in this illustration, if it were not for the fact that Sam himself unaccountably points out to Pickwick allegorical details in the room (and the illustration) suggestive of *mise en abyme*: "'There's a Dutch clock, sir ... And a bird-cage, sir,' says Sam. 'Veels within Veels, a prison in a prison. Ain't it, sir?'" (662). Why the reference to "wheels within wheels" in this satirical portrait scene on the threshold of Pickwick's imprisonment for misinterpreted acts resulting from his linguistic and economic innocence? Are these graphic metaphors merely referenced as random jokes? Or do they refer to the gaze within the gaze within the gaze of the illustration—our gazing at Sam (Dickens's surrogate) gazing at the turnkeys gazing at Pickwick—with all of its implications of the limits and transgressions of representation? From the viewer's perspective, it certainly feels like "veels within veels" to make a spectacle (an illustration) of Pickwick having become a spectacle (a "portrait") for his captors, but the illustration also shows that Sam in all his savvy, "reclined on the back of the chair," manages to stand above the fray, "reflecting" (as Dickens describes him) on the scene in a way

Spectral mimesis

11 Phiz (Hablot K. Browne), "Pickwick Sits for His Portrait," etching for *The Pickwick Papers*, 1837.

that transgresses its representational frame. Standing behind his counterpart Pickwick, beyond either being subjected to the likeness-taking gaze of the bourgeois portrait or the enclosure of the bourgeois state, Sam cuts a spectral figure in the illustration and in the scene; he conjures Dickens's gaze and haunts the narcissistic certainty of the bourgeois portrait with an *other* kind of vision, one that disrupts the institutionalized power of mimesis itself. Offering to obliquely shift our perspective not only of the scene but of the cultural forms of representation through which we see it, Sam is himself the anamorphic stain contained within the image.

Notes

1 Copyright © 2007 Johns Hopkins University Press. A previous version of this section on Rosa Dartle first appeared in *ELH*, vol. 74, no. 3, Fall 2007, 655–79. Other parts also appeared in *LFQ*, vol. 46, no. 1, Winter 2018.
2 In the *Book of Daniel*, in which Daniel has the gift of being able to read dreams and cryptic signs, the writing on the wall contains a warning against self-aggrandizement and fame.
3 For example, in a review in *Atlantic Monthly* in 1877, Edwin P. Wipple bemoaned that, "after his immense popularity was secured by the success of *The Pickwick Papers*, [Dickens] was smitten with the ambition to direct the public opinion of Great Britain by embodying, in exquisitely satirical caricatures, rash and hasty judgments on the whole government of Great Britain in all its departments, legislative, executive, and judicial" (Collins 318).

Part II

"Moor eeffocish things": effigy and the bourgeoisie

3

Where "the specular becomes the spectral" in *The Old Curiosity Shop* and *Dombey and Son*

That wild word, "Moor Eeffoc," is the motto of all effective realism; it is the masterpiece of the good realistic principle—the principle that the most fantastic thing of all is often the precise fact. And that elvish kind of realism Dickens adopted everywhere. His world was alive with inanimate objects. The date on the door danced over Mr Grewgious's, the knocker grinned at Mr Scrooge, the Roman on the ceiling pointed down at Mr Tulkinghorn, the elderly armchair leered at Tom Smart—these are all moor eeffocish things. A man sees them because he does not look at them. (Chesterton, *Charles Dickens* 65)

From image magic to effective realism

Two genres, two generations of movement, intersect with each other in [the commodity], and this is why it figures the apparition of a specter. It accumulates undecidably, in its uncanniness, their contradictory predicates: the inert thing appears suddenly *inspired*, it is all at once transfixed by a *pneuma* or a *psychē*. (Derrida, *Specters* 192)

"If the commodity was a fetish," said Walter Benjamin, "then Grandville was the tribal sorcerer" (*Arcades* 186). It may seem surprising that Benjamin would choose not just a *caricaturist*, but a particular caricaturist, J. J. Grandville, as the bearer of a supernatural power, a sorcery, in relation to the commodity. One typically thinks of the caricaturist in terms of a satirizing of people, not a spiritualizing of objects. But Benjamin, in the section of *The Arcades Project* on Grandville, is interested in the strange vitality material objects came to acquire in the nineteenth century, and the image of the sorcerer evokes a special relationship with objects that spoke to what fascinated Benjamin about Grandville: his uncanny art form awakens objects out of their inert materiality, uncovers the thing's hidden ambiguity, and destabilizes the normally rigid opposition between person and thing. Benjamin's observation obviously also extends Marx's well-known metaphor likening the commodity in modern capitalist society to the fetish in earlier "primitive" societies as examples of objects that have mysterious or unexplained power over humans, even over whole cultures. The implication of Benjamin's twist on Marx's claim is that if modern society repeats this "primitive" fantasy attributing mysterious power to objects, whereby the fantasy object casts a spell over society, as Marx suggests, there must be some modern art form, or other form of representation, that can conjure up that earlier, more primal fantasy formation that has been sublimated into the post-Enlightenment economic system of modern capitalism—and that art form is found in the lithographic images, or "caricatures" of Grandville. The question then becomes—why is it the *caricaturist* who holds this unique place, who conjures up images of the phantasms concealed in the commodity-form?

Benjamin's reflections on Grandville's art—part of his collection of fragments, reflections, and images embodying nineteenth-century industrialism, capitalism, and culture that make up his momentous *The Arcades Project*—point to certain rather arcane ideas about the origin of caricature itself, which I introduced briefly in the previous chapter. In comparing Grandville to a tribal sorcerer, that is, Benjamin could be drawing on the idea of a genealogy that traces caricature back to the ancient belief in "image magic," an idea articulated by Ernst Kris as explaining the uncanny force of caricature and its late appearance in history: "Of modern caricature it can be stated with certainty that one of its roots reaches back to the insulting and derisive representations on which punishments were carried out (in a real sense *in effigie*) when the culprit had put himself beyond their reach" (Kris 180). Kris traces the genealogy of caricature in three stages—conjuration, effigy, and modern caricature—in terms of the changing "mental attitudes toward image magic," all predicated on the belief that the *visual image* is more archaic than the linguistic sign and therefore more "deeply rooted" in the human psyche. According to Kris's genealogy, then, the first and most archaic stage, part of "witchcraft and sorcery," was characterized by a belief in *image magic*, which held that the "person and image are one" and actions carried out on an image were meant to have effects on a real person (a belief that sign and referent were somehow mysteriously interconnected, as in Einstein's famous "spooky action at a distance"). In the second stage, that of *effigy* proper, the image is treated as a *symbolic substitute* for the person and actions are carried out on it "*instead* of on the person." Note that there is a more distinct separation between the realms of representation and reality here, but that the effigy, as an image, functions as a means of transferring affect from the latter to the former (like a secret and quasi-magical passageway between the two). In the third and final stage, where effigy is transformed into *caricature*, the action (expressing an affect such as hostility for instance) is carried out on the representation *as such*, in the form of an "alteration of the person's 'likeness'" (Kris 203) and this further transition into the symbolic order (though Kris only hints at this) entails the transformation of the tendency involved from an aggressive one towards an individual into a pleasurable one towards a social group, that is, from hostility into laughter, but also, from an act *on* the signifier to an act *by* or *of* the signifier.

We don't have to accept Kris's distinctly psychoanalytic historical narrative of what we might call the historical/psychic sublation of image magic into caricature in order to find his analysis of the art form itself, and its relation to effigy, useful. In fact, the proliferation of caricature in the eighteenth and nineteenth centuries may have had more to do with, on the one hand, developing technologies, such as the lithograph, that allowed artists more room for tone, shading, and distortion (as opposed to steel etching, for instance), and on the other, expanding commodification and (as Benjamin suggests) advertising and the privatizing of the political sphere throughout the nineteenth century. In any case, what strikes me as interesting in Kris's interpretation of the form's history has more to do with the way in which "the definite, but not easily determined, measure of concern with the reproduction of reality" becomes a "prerequisite" of caricature in its last phase, so that as a form it draws on an antagonism between mimesis and distortion, being "the distorted reproduction of a recognizable likeness" (Kris 184). Thus, "caricature is a play with the magic power of the [visual] image"—and in particular of the effigy or visual signifier of the subject. Of course, the implication for Kris here is that the idea of magic is historically a pre-Enlightenment way of accounting for an unconscious—and thus illogical or unknown—influence something has over us. In a way, Kris sees *distortion* as a vehicle for the *return of the repressed* of this influence: "This kind of distortion gets its force from the primal connections with visual representation: under the surface of fun and play the old image magic is still at work." But simultaneously, the play between resemblance and distortion in modern caricature can have an effect in the Real, precisely by importing, as it were, into the present the inheritance of that repressed influence: "If the caricature fits, as Philipon's *Poire* obviously did, the victim really does become transformed in our eyes" (203).

There are three ideas I would like to take from Kris's theory of caricature (and effigy) to enhance to the concept of spectral characterization here. The first has to do with his point concerning the primacy of the visual image. It becomes difficult to discuss this idea from a historical point of view, but the idea that there is a certain force to the image itself, and particularly in its visual form, has a long and rich theoretical history, both within psychoanalysis and outside of it. I will not develop this here, but will just point, for one example, to Kristeva's concept of the "specular" image and its relation to the drive: "The specular," she says, "transforms the drive into desire, aggression into seduction" (72). In addition, I would recall the discussion from the last two chapters of the mirror image and Lacan's concept of the ego as specular image. And finally, Derrida points out that Marx works within the Platonic tradition that "associates in a strict fashion image with specter, and idol with phantasm, with the *phantasma* in its phantomatic or errant dimension as living-dead" (*Specters* 184).

The second insight that Kris offers relates to the form of effigy itself, and is something that has remained quite under-theorized about it, which is the question of how it differs from the mimetic sign. For Kris, in any case, the effigy presents not a mirror reflection of reality in the manner of mimesis, but a kind of short circuit between signifier and signified, a wormhole between the two sides, word and thing (to continue my quantum theory metaphors). This wormhole, or short circuit, however, is not predicated on some kind of occult force, but rather on the effect the signifier has on the Real, and this effect is itself predicated on the gap inherent to the signifier itself. As Žižek demonstrates in the signifier MOOR EEFFOC, from Dickens's childhood experience, the signifier can open up onto the Real of *jouissance* precisely when its purchase on meaning (or mimetic representation) *breaks down* and the trauma of subjectivity, or the fact that subjectivity is already inscribed in material reality, emerges in the image.

The third aspect incorporates the first two: it is that, to a certain extent, the force or "violence" of effigy is, in the case of caricature, directed not at an individual but at *mimesis* itself, and this violence, *which is now formal and so transformed into play*, is expressed precisely in distortion. Thus "likeness" that functions for Kris on the "secondary" level (both onto- and phylogenetically) is acted upon and *distorted* by something more "primary," which therefore "foils censorship" in order to convey something more, something beyond what the mimetic sign conveys (the "tendency," as Kris puts it) in and through this distortion. Kris points to the role of Freud's primary process here: "But by means of condensation, displacement and allusion, certain elements in the distortion point to the existence of other ideas, the distorting ones, we might say; these are the elements which betray the *tendency*" (Kris 184). But we know from Lacan that these primary processes are none other than the laws of the signifier: metaphor, metonymy, and the "sliding" of the signifier under the signified. What seems striking here is the way in which mimesis plays a role not as a reflection of reality but as a mask, a means by which both to conceal and signify something else, or reveal through concealment. As in the dream, a mimetic image is not a means of a communication as such, but material to be taken up as a signifier for some *other* signifying force or "tendency."[1]

Thus distortion is not merely a foil for mimesis; it is rather the very precondition of caricature, which functions by dislodging the seemingly natural and unassailable connection between signifier and signified in a given sign in order to expose something latent or masked by the meaning itself. This splitting up of the image in caricature that allows it to play with the relation between signifier and signified makes it similar in structure to dream images as well; as Lacan points out, this stems from the very structure of the linguistic sign (its split structure of signifier over signified, S/s) and is most observable in unconscious representations: "*Entstellung*, translated as 'distortion' or 'transposition,' is what Freud shows to be the general precondition for the functioning of the dream, and it is what I designated ... as the sliding of the signified under the signifier ... (its action, let us note, is unconscious)" (*Ecrits* 160). In other words, distortion is both inherent in and suppressed in the linguistic sign, but is brought into play in a more exposed and radical form in the 'sorcery' of effigial or spectral images such as those of Grandville and Dickens. Caricature as a form of representation is thus distinguished by its affinity with the structure of the unconscious sign, its internal duality and (thus) its tendency towards substitutions, as we see, for instance, in the frequent use caricature makes of *verbal* puns in the *visual* medium (as in Daumier's "The Pears" or Grandville's "The Dual Between High and Low Officers," which depicts the officers as elongated and dwarfed respectively) or its expression of abstract ideas in visual form. In other words, caricature can be characterized by its implicit *splitting of the visual image into a double sign*, a mimetic graphic sign and a spectral excess that haunts it with its own otherness or antagonism: "Caricature is a double thing: it is both drawing and idea—the drawing violent, the idea caustic and veiled," said Baudelaire ("On the Essence of Laughter" 136–7). It is this, we could say, that finally posits a possible answer to our earlier question about what makes Grandville a sorcerer of the commodity, insofar as it suggests that the caricaturist writes in the language of the unconscious. This language can be defined by a kind of image-writing, a writing with visual signifiers, what Freud calls *Bilderschrift* ("image script") in *The Interpretation of Dreams*, and which Derrida glosses as "not an inscribed image but a figurative script, an image inviting not a simple, conscious, present perception of the thing itself—assuming it exists—but a reading" (*Writing and Difference* 218).

Kris's reference to Daumier as an example of the latent potential of caricature is far from incidental. We could do no better to illustrate the split image of caricature than to return to Daumier's "Les Poires" (Figure 1), which captures what Lacan calls *glissement*, the sliding of the signified under the signifier that characterizes distortion, in its very process, held out before our eyes in its transformative power. This caricature, quickly sketched out on paper by Philipon and later perfected and executed as a lithograph by Daumier, visualizes the verbal pun on "*Poire*" (or a "fathead" in French) by demonstrating the metamorphosis of the image of King Louis-Philippe into a pear in uncannily precise visually articulated stages. The signifier "Louis-Philippe" could not have been transferred from a likeness of the king in the first sketch to the image of the pear in the last were it not for the internal splitting of the sign and the "sliding" effect (distortion) of the "bar" that divides it, allowing the transference of the signified, Louis-Philippe, by degrees, from a literal mimetic image (a resemblance) to a metaphoric mimetic image (a "likeness" exposing the underlying double or pun), to an alternate image (the pear) in which the spirit of the king still seems sadly trapped, like a specter. In the last image, that is, "identity" or personhood is no longer reflected in likeness, but captured in effigy. This caricature lays bare the very mechanism of caricature, since its distortion makes of the image not just an icon of the spirit of the king *but of the age*—it taps into a whole constellation of ghosts that haunt the era, conjuring associations between subjectivity, capitalism, commodification, and representation. The result is more than simply a slight to the king; it marks the discovery of a representational method of immensely subversive political and symbolic force, a breakthrough.

As a result of Daumier's "The Pears," the simple visual signifier of a pear turned out to be one of the most powerfully subversive images leveled at Louis-Philippe, the *Roi Bourgeois*. Once transformed by Philipon into a pear in the eyes of the world, the Bourgeois King, despite his attempts to punish and censor, was powerless to undo the spell, and the revolutionary artists of Philipon's circle not only used the image repeatedly, but also transformed the image itself, subjecting it to innumerable allusive variations and symbolic distortions. "The Pear continued in *Caricature* and *Charivari*," Philipon's two leading illustrated journals of the 1830s, the first of their kind, "becoming the chief symbol of the Citizen King" and was "the favorite caricatural device of the cartoonists Grandville and Traviés" (Vincent 23). In one Grandville print, for instance ("A Quelle Sauce les Voulez-vous?") "Grandville, Daumier, Traviés and Forest are all depicted stewing, roasting and boiling pears under Philipon's direction" (Kerr 48). Though the pear was used to symbolize the king far more frequently than any other image, other images became a short-hand of effigy as well until Philipon and his team of virtuosic caricaturists developed a veritable *language of effigy*, such that "each time an image or symbol appeared in a caricature its meaning was slightly modified. As a result, the symbols tended to become increasingly polysemic" (Kerr 45). Or, in other words, once identity or spirit (the head of Louis-Philippe and the age) is transferred from a mimetic likeness to an effigial image it becomes a signifier imbedded in a language more and more subject to symbolic play, to the laws of the signifier (surplus meaning/enjoyment) rather than those of the big Other. This language, that is, has a very dreamlike logic to it allowing for a complexity-in-simplicity found in condensations, displacements, and nodal points achieved through signifiers rather than the *logos*, a process that seems infectious and uncontainable:

> The pear was originally created as a symbol for the king's head and it continued to be used in that context, in Daumier's "Masques de 1831" for example. Very quickly, however, it came to symbolize the king's entire body and then his system of government. Using the pear in this wider sense, Philipon's artists could convey complicated ideas in simple visual language. (Kerr 85)

The image of the pear, as an effigy transforming the visual signifier of the king, has this double function of both quilting more and more associations into an image, but also of placing that image within a whole other form of language, not just a "visual language" but a spectral language.

The quilting point, what Lacan calls *the point de capiton*, between this spectral language and its epoch can be located in the symbolically overdetermined historical figure of Louis-Philippe, the signifier, the Bourgeois King of whom Benjamin said "[u]nder Louis Philippe, the private individual makes his entrance on the stage of history" (*Arcades*

8). Louis-Philippe represents transformation of the state into the private apparatus of the bourgeois ruling class, who in turn "promotes the reign of Louis Philippe as that of a private individual managing his affairs" (*Arcades* 8). The at first enigmatic section heading "Louis Philippe, or the Interior," containing Benjamin's reflections on the changing symbolic status of the individual and its relation to commodities in the nineteenth century, provides the interpretive key for this nodal point by leading in a seeming non sequitur from the bourgeois monarch to the bourgeois home: the individual's growing accumulation of private possessions put on display in the array of the *interior* reflects an increasing display of individual and psychological *innerness* in bourgeois art forms. This dialectical play between interiority and exteriority, centering on the image of Louis-Philippe's head, is perfectly captured in a caricature by Daumier, his famous "Masques de 1831" (Masks of 1831) (Figure 12). Vincent hints at this dialectic when he observes of this illustration that "these men are not to be seen as individuals; they are but masks which the pear himself puts on, through which he ventriloquially speaks. A mask, Daumier knew and drew, is a false face, a dead image, not a living face; it is a mode of

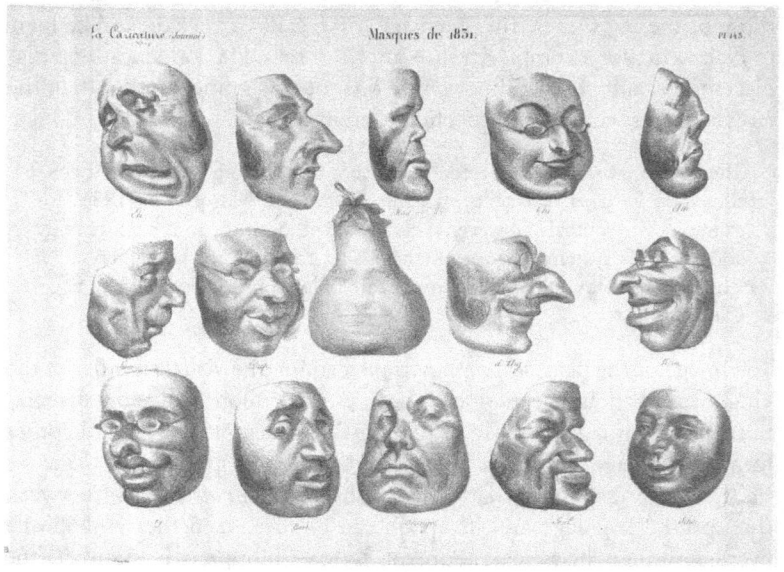

12 Honoré Daumier, "Masques de 1831" (Masks of 1831), lithograph published in *La Caricature*, March 8, 1832.

concealment and deception" (41). It is true that Daumier has very artistically depicted a gallery of "false faces" here, but what is more surprising is the fact that the "real" face "behind" the mask is not a living face either, *nor a mask*, but *an effigy*, a pear reduced to pure signifier with the ghostly traces of a face (not even Louis-Philippe's, but any face) washed over it. The king is placed in the same exhibit, in the same ontological set, as the "false face[s]" or "dead image[s]" that are supposed to conceal the true face behind them. In other words, if the monarch speaks ventriloquially through the masks, then something speaks ventriloquially through *him*; Louis-Philippe *is himself a signifier*, an effigy behind the masks that provides the illusion of innerness or spirit for the individual (hence: "Louis-Philippe, or the Interior"?).

This representational play of unmasking an effigy allegorizes the fact that the forces at work beyond the masks stem not from Louis-Philippe as such, seemingly the private individual "behind" the state politicians, but from the reified economic forces expressed as an interiority or ego *through the signifier* Louis-Philippe, the new emblem of the nineteenth-century economic individualism. As Kerr notes, for instance, "[b]y excluding the nation's intellectual elite in favor of a narrow-minded and rapacious bourgeoisie, the electoral law transformed the right to vote from a sacred duty into a lucrative monopoly. This was, in Philipon's eyes, part of Louis-Philippe's attempt to smother France's political passions under a blanket of collective egoism" (157). While unmasking the "bourgeois monarchy" as the mask of private capital, the "Masks of 1831" represents a decisive development in the logic of effigy and its use in spectral representation: like a mask, it draws on the distortion of mimetic representation of the individual as a means to expose or give expression to the implicit antagonisms of those forces reified in it, here the forces of capital. The point of the "Masks of 1831" would thus be to reveal the fact that the "bourgeois monarchy" merely masks a more elusive but no less oppressive form of power, the forces of capitalism that disguises and transforms collective revolutionary energy into rapacious "collective egoism." The dialectical tension between individuals (as masks) and objects (as autonomous) reflects the central contradiction of modern capitalism, termed commodity fetishism by Marx and articulated as "*automatic autonomy*, mechanical freedom, technical life" by Derrida (*Specters* 102). The dialectic or play between the two points to an uncanny Disparity structuring the opposition itself, or as Derrida puts it, in the commodity "autonomy is no more than the mask of automatism" (*Specters* 102), which is precisely why Daumier's "Masks of 1831" as a whole evokes a haunting sense of anamorphosis. Somewhere between the ghostly grin of the depleted effigy and the leering and twisted frozen masks that surround it, the *surplus jouissance* of a social system generated by commodities that represent the subject's "interiority" is traced in the image of the face. Here in Daumier's and Grandville's lithographs a radically new form of portrait is born: the distorted faces, at first called caricature, will later become the dreamlike grimaces of the modernist and postmodern portraiture, for example of Edvard Munch or Francis Bacon. This is why for Agamben caricature and fetish both share a unique relationship to the signifier: "Metaphor, caricature, emblem, and fetish point toward that 'barrier resistant to signification' in which is guarded the original enigma of every signifying act" (Agamben 149). If mimesis masks the gap of the Real of the subject, spectral representation grounds the subject in this Disparity through the dreamlike distortion of mimesis. It is thus that distortion plays such an important role in portrait caricature and modern art: it exploits this representational "bar" as the repressed possibility of signification itself, "the original enigma of every signifying act."

One could, then, in a kind of anamorphic split, see two different aspects of the effigy from two different perspectives. From one point of view, the effigy appears among other uncannily autonomous objects, such as the *fetish*, which gives it a certain privileged capacity to expose commodity fetishism. From another perspective, the effigy reflects a certain *kind* of signifier that embodies the extimacy, or inhuman core, of the subject: the unconscious image/signifier sometimes referred to as the *imago*. In the next two sections, I will explore the effigy from these two perspectives.

Mask—fetish—object

Marx famously locates the source of commodity fetishism in a kind of *ontological displacement* at the heart of capitalism, the *displacement of an intrinsic contradiction* onto a screen of "natural" value, so that the social relation between subjects (the forces of production) appears instead as the material relation between things (the commodity market)—or in Marx's words, "in the fact that the commodity reflects the social characteristics of men's own labor as objective characteristics of the products of labor themselves, as the socio-natural properties of these things" (164–5). Right away we can see, within the context of this discussion, that what is at stake in this thesis is precisely a *crisis of representation* (the problem of social Disparity, we could say, finding signification as such) and even more specifically of mimesis: something out of joint about *subjects* is disavowed and projected outward as a kind of *realist illusion* of a "natural" property of objects. The contradiction that we disavow at the level of subjects, that is, appears reflected in the sphere of objects as belonging "properly" to them, no longer appearing as a contradiction but as a natural surplus or material value. This contradiction, too—that social products appear as the "products of labor of private individuals who work independently of each other" (Marx 165)—is for Marx a kind of ontological fiction, a Disparity between private and social, particular and universal, which, not being expressed as such, must be treated as a (social) reality for capitalism to function. In order to fulfill this function of illusory reflection, however, the object, says Marx, must split and adopt two (mutually exclusive) personas, use-value and exchange-value, playing the parts of both objects and subjects in this theater of social reality.

In a sense, we could say, the subject has forfeited something ontological to the object as the price of this displacement, that being its will or autonomy, according to Marx, or in Lacanian terms, its *lack in the Other*, as a result, the *thing*, the commodity, must "manifest" the subject's autonomy in its place and mediate its presence (as non-lack) in the Symbolic Order translated into the language of exchangeability: "The labor of the private individual manifests itself as an element of the total labor of society only through the relations which the act of exchange establishes between the products, and, through their mediation, between the producers" (Marx 165). Producers thus seem to presence themselves in the social order only via "the act of exchange" between things. And since exchange-value is the expression of what has been displaced, in this social/ontological/representational sleight of hand (or play of mirrors, as Derrida puts it), from the subject onto the object, the commodity acquires an uncanny surplus effect, a "fantastic" and "supra-sensible" character haunting its materiality:

> The commodity-form, and the value-relation of the products of labor within which it appears, have absolutely no connection with the physical nature of the commodity and the material [*dinglich*] relations arising out of this. It is nothing but the definite social relations between men themselves which assumes here, for them, the fantastic form of a relation between things. (Marx 165)

This haunting is, of course, at the heart of the changing relationship with and perception of objects in the nineteenth century, since commodity fetishism is Marx's way of articulating the uncanny play between subject and object, inside and outside, as a result of which "the products of the human brain appear as autonomous figures endowed with a life of their own"

(Marx 165). Again, one can see how deeply bound up this sociohistorical change is with the question of representation: realism (as objectification or naturalization of the sign) reflects back the social fantasy, the "fantastic form" that appears as social reality, gives it its very status as reality.

It's worth pursuing a little further here this enigmatic idea of (what I am calling) ontological displacement and the questions it poses about what the subject forfeits, as well as the relationship this forfeiture has with the "fantastic form" of social reality/realism in which it results. If the subject forfeits a part of its being (essentially, its *lack*, which is what makes it a subject in Lacanian terms), it may also be said that this being is its form of desire—and Lacan's term *"jouissance"* precisely captures the correspondence in his system of these two terms, being and desire. The capitalist subject, then, forfeits its *jouissance* over to the object (the commodity) in the Gaze of the Other. Derrida, however, in particular explores the commodity-form's uncanny ontology that plays out in Marx's analysis through images of mimesis and mirrors. The uncanniness of the commodity results, as Derrida says, from "an abnormal play of mirrors," whereby "those who are looking for themselves can no longer find themselves in" the mirror reflection (*Specters* 195) of the commodity-form: "Men no longer recognize in [this mirror] the *social* character of their *own* labor. It is as if they were becoming ghosts in their turn. The 'proper' feature of specters, like vampires, is that they are deprived of a specular image, of the true, right specular image (but who is not so deprived?)" (195). The ontology of capitalist culture, capitalist ontology, seems to initiate a strange play of perspectives, of reflections and refractions in which the "ghosts that are commodities transform human producers into ghosts" (Derrida 195). This can only happen through the vanishing mediation of mimesis—the fantasy structure of reality must be first of all naturalized, naturally naturalized, as it were, if it is to carry the weight of social objectivity: "If, then, it phantomalizes, that is first of all because it naturalizes. The 'mysteriousness' of the commodity-form as presumed reflection of the social form is the incredible manner in which this mirror sends back the image ... when one thinks it is reflecting for men the image of the 'social characteristics of men's own labor': such an image objectivizes by naturalizing" (Derrida 195). It is in the very act of reflection, in the image of the mirror precisely as a function of identification—seeing oneself *within* reality or the *subjectivization* of the real—that this objectification of the subject is carried out: "The returned (deformed, objectified, naturalized) image becomes that of a social relation among commodities, among these inspired, autonomous, and automatic 'objects' that are séance tables" (Derrida 196). Derrida gives a very precise formula for this mimetic/ontological process: "The specular becomes the spectral at the threshold of this objectifying naturalization" (196).

Interestingly Derrida does not pursue the specific role of the money-form in this play of mirrors, whereas, in fact, money is the very key, the piece that is needed to fill in the gap of representation (that exchange-value is not "naturally" universal), sending back an image of reality appearing complete and whole. If the commodity-form is able to successfully distort the image of the individual's social character it is only because it can properly efface this distortion in a *naturalizing* movement towards a complete and universalizing reflection of objective (that is, projected out of/detached and excluded from subjective) reality. The money-form is the "threshold" on which this transpires, which is also a strange pivoting of perspective. As Marx observes,

> If I state that coats or boots stand in relation to linen because the latter is the universal incarnation of abstract human labor, the absurdity of the statement is self-evident. Nevertheless, when the producers of coats and boots bring these commodities into relation with linen, or with gold or silver (and this makes no difference here), as the universal equivalent, the relation between their own private labor and the collective labor of society appears to them in exactly this absurd form. (169)

It is thus the money-form that structures the subject's perspective so that social reality's intrinsic contradiction—that the universality of exchange-ability is a necessary absurdity needed to conceal the "social character of private labor" (Marx 168)—appears as an unquestionable, objective, and "socio-natural" form of reality: "What appears to happen is not that a particular commodity [for example gold] becomes money because all other commodities express their value in it, but, on the contrary, that all other commodities universally express their values in a particular commodity because it is money" (Marx 187). In other words, the *money-form is a kind of reverse-anamorphosis* that puts a *gap* in the social/ontological structure into (illusory) perspective that appears rational, naturalized, self-evident, and complete. And we could say that *this* is Marx's great insight or gesture: he demonstrates that social critique is ontological insofar as it can push us outside of our own subjectivizing perspective, allow us to see from that eccentric position beyond the Gaze of the Other that subjectivizes us into the fantasy formation of social reality. The naturalizing of this fantasy formation, on the other hand, is bound up with and overdetermines all the forms of bourgeois realism of the nineteenth

"Moor eeffocish things"

century, from the novel to the portrait to rationalism in political economy and the sciences, etc.

Adorno takes up this concept of realism as a form grounded in bourgeois ideology/fantasy in his essay on Dickens's *The Old Curiosity Shop* and he notes that while Dickens may be compared to the nineteenth-century Realist novelists in terms of *content* (focusing on "poverty, despair, and death" that have "already been recognized as the fruits of a bourgeois world"), he should be contrasted with them in terms of *form*, since there one finds "the outlines of a completely different sort of view of the world," a view Adorno sees as more "prebourgeois" than bourgeois (*Notes to Literature* 171). What is at stake in this distinction between a prebourgeois vision of the world as depicted by Dickens and the bourgeois vision of the world as depicted in the realist novel is nothing less than the concept of the individual, of subjectivity:

> In [Dickens's prebourgeois world] the individual has not yet reached full autonomy, nor, therefore, complete isolation, but instead is presented as a bearer of objective factors, of a dark, obscure fate and a starlike consolation that overtake the individual and permeate his life but never follow from the law of the individual, as do, for instance, the fates of the characters in Flaubert's novels. (Adorno, *Notes to Literature* 171)

Adorno, in other words, also begins from this assumption that the bourgeois position is marked by its inability to see itself, or its position, "properly," to see its "right specular image" from within its own perspective, since this very perspective is what subjectivizes its view of reality; it is its point of identification. This is why Adorno emphasizes *form itself* as a potential means of critiquing bourgeois ideology of the individual. Dickens's novels, claims Adorno, work in a different *form* from that of the nineteenth-century realist novel, in part by evoking allegory as a prebourgeois form, but also in the adoption of illustration to effect a different *formal relationship* to its object:

> For the novel form in Dickens, that means, more specifically, that there is no psychology in it, or rather, that it absorbs psychological approaches into the objective meanings the novels depict. There are good reasons why these novels were published with illustrations; they are themselves illustrations of objective meanings by means of human figures rather than free representations of human beings. (172)

Adorno nicely articulates the shift of perspective, in Dickens's form, regarding the representation of the "individual": the position of the individual in Dickens's novels is not the end or object of representation, but

Where "the specular becomes the spectral"

a *means of*, or method of representation. Subjects are representational *material* (like facial features in caricature), a form of "illustration" that places the reader in a different, and I would say desubjectivizing, position to see the "psychology" of the individual—not as a thing, but as an approach to depicting an "objective meaning." In this sense, Dickens's novels not only look idiosyncratically back to allegory (particularly in *The Old Curiosity Shop*), but astride to caricature and ahead to surrealism and modernism. Adorno, I would even say, seems to have intuited what I'm calling Dickens's spectral form of representation in his insight that "[the novels] are themselves illustrations" and even more in his striking claim that, along with Dickens, "only Daumier has depicted the bourgeois spirit world as incisively as this, and reference to the 'humor' with which such figures are drawn could serve only to rob knowledge of them of its seriousness" (174). Dickens and Daumier, it seems, were able to see and depict spirits, the bourgeoisie's ghosts, in a way that Realism, with its focus on the individual, was not, insofar as they shared a form of art that went "beyond the bourgeois practice of art" by "rejecting" "the highest norm of bourgeois art, the individual and his psychology" (Adorno, *Notes to Literature* 173).

By the mid-nineteenth century, despite his popularity (or perhaps in part because of it), Dickens was in fact already under steady criticism for his idiosyncratic means of characterization, a criticism implicitly situated from within the (ideological) perspective of the realist form and filtered through its lens of the individual's psychology. George Eliot famously claims, for instance, that Dickens "scarcely ever passes from the humorous and external to the emotional and tragic, without becoming as transcendent in his unreality as he was a moment before in his artistic truthfulness,"[2] as if the very limit-point of Dickens's characterization were precisely the *sine qua non* of "artistic truthfulness" in the bourgeois art form, psychological innerness. Eliot's critique is formulated in very interesting terms. One almost feels this formula could be measured on a meter: the more "external" Dickens's representation of a character is, the more "autistic truth" it registers, the more internal or emotion, however, the less ... until it becomes transcendentally unreal. In other words, as Dickens approaches the core characteristic of the bourgeois art form, interiority, his novels to that very degree become *excluded from the genre or form* itself. That Dickens was conscious not only of the predispositions about representational form in this kind of criticism but also of its ideological implications is apparent in his career-long persistence in decidedly avoiding the interiority of character the realist novel form increasingly demanded (or rather, as Chesterton says, he created his own kind of "eerie realism") and even in the many self-conscious allusions to his own characterization in his novels. In *The Old Curiosity Shop*, for instance, Dickens embeds his characters in a "spirit world" teeming with inanimate objects that resemble humans and with humans that resemble inanimate objects or nonhumans: Jarley's Waxworks, Punch and the marionette theater, Quilp the demonic dwarf, a factory worker "nursed" by a factory furnace, etc. Mrs. Jarley of the waxworks draws a very self-conscious contrast between her wax figures and the marionettes from the Punch theater that could almost be heard as Dickens's satirical response to the kind of criticism later articulated by Eliot:

> "[The waxworks] isn't funny at all," repeated Mrs Jarley, "It's calm and—what's the word again—critical?—no—classical, that's it—it's calm and classical. No low beatings and knockings about, no jokings and squeakings like your precious Punches, but always the same, with a constantly unchanging air of coldness and gentility; and so like life, that if wax-work only spoke and walked about, you'd hardly know the difference." (209)

Dickens clearly sees his means of characterization as closer to the gestural and wild theatricality of Punch's marionette's than to the static and controlled lifelikeness of Jarley's waxworks. Adorno points out that in their "constantly unchanging" nature Jarley's waxworks, symbols not of lifelikeness but of "death" at the heart of the bourgeois "spirit world," are appropriate elements of the "Hell space" that is bourgeois industrial society (*Notes to Literature* 176). Mrs. Jarley's revealing descriptions in praise of the waxworks, including their "calm and classical" (with her Freudian slip on "critical") quality and their "unchanging air of coldness and gentility" give us a glimpse into Dickens's skepticism about realism's "artistic truthfulness"—so devoted to reflecting "lifelike" subjects, self-contained and preserved, that it reflects nothing so much as deathly frozen objects or types.

It is no coincidence, then, that in the novel in which Dickens first makes explicit targets of both the bourgeois milieu (debt and alienation, for instance, as opposed to specific institutions or abuses) and mimetic realism (turning to allegory), effigy becomes such an explicit aspect of his representation of character. The illustration of Nell sleeping while surrounded by grotesque masks, gargoyles, grimacing carvings, like a doll among an array of idols, sufficiently depicts the ambiguous relation between humans and objects that the novel takes as one of its motifs. But we could find no better illustration of the significance of effigy in this novel than in the dreamlike scene staging a strange ritualistic interaction between an effigy and a dwarf; the one in which Quilp takes revenge on another character *in effigie* by jabbing a hot poker into the detached figurehead of a ship. Late one evening when Sampson Brass, Quilp's lawyer in his claim on the property of Nell and her grandfather, pays Quilp a visit in his countinghouse on the wharf, he finds the dwarf directing his boiling rage, in lieu of Kit Nubbles (as defender of Nell), at a "great, goggle-eyed, blunt-nosed figure-head of some old ship, which was reared up against the wall in a corner near the stove, looking like a goblin or hideous idol whom the dwarf worshipped" that had originally been "intended for the effigy of some famous admiral" (474) (Figure 13). The fact that Dickens refers to this surreal effigy as a "substantial phantom" (474)—like the commodity, at once material and phantasmal—and the primal and dreamlike energy engendered by the effigial object in this scene, invoking both ritualism and violence, suggests something darker and more far-reaching than just a dramatic flourish. Moreover Quilp's questions are almost uncannily self-reflexive of the effigy's representational status: "Is it like Kit—is it his picture, his image, his very self?" he demands of Samson. In Quilp's series of questions qualifying the mimetic term "like"

13 Phiz (Hablot K. Browne), "Revenge Is Sweet," engraving for *The Old Curiosity Shop*, 1840.

regarding the effigy—from "picture" to "image" to "self"—it is almost as if Dickens evokes the reversal of the three representational stages described by Kris from magic exchangeability to mimetic likeness.

On the surface, then, the effigy in Quilp's countinghouse represents Kit and is used by Quilp to inflict punishment on him *in absentia*, but the roots of this effigy reach much deeper into the novel than this. For one thing, the "likeness" of the effigy is not limited to Kit, but, curiously enough, extends to Quilp himself, as Sampson was "uncertain whether Mr Quilp considered it like himself, and had therefore bought it for a family portrait" (474). The effigy is therefore also a *material double of Quilp*: just as Quilp is a "stunted figure" (224) the effigy is "sawn short off at the waist" to fit into the room, the two are diametrically opposed in size, and they both shared an "excessively wide-awake" look and a menacing grin. The effigy is thus not only a nodal point between various characters in the novel linking Kit, a good character from Nell's circle, to the evil Quilp, establishing a strange chain of associations; it also reveals a strange anamorphic aspect of Quilp's character, which is already apparently quasi-human/quasi-animal—the fact that Quilp is, from a certain point of view, *himself an effigy*. When Little Nell travels with the waxworks and sleeps among the wax figures, for instance, this "resemblance" between Quilp and an effigy appears to Nell in her fantasy when she "tortured herself—she could not help it—with imagining a resemblance, in some one or other of their death-like faces, to the dwarf, and this fancy would sometimes so gain upon her that she would almost believe he had removed the figure and stood within the clothes" (224). The dream image of a mimetic "calm and classical" waxwork figure concealing an effigial animal-like dwarf within it could easily be imagined as one of Grandville's dreamlike representational allegories (along with the monkey portrait painter or the Raphael ape). Thus the function of Quilp as an effigy plays a representational role in the novel by establishing non-mimetic links between various characters that blur the lines of separate identities between them, and even between persons and objects, as we see illustrated in another of Nell's dreams in which Quilp "was somehow connected with the wax-work, or was wax-work himself, or was Mrs Jarley and wax-work too, or was himself, Mrs Jarley, wax-work, and a barrel organ all in one, and yet not exactly any of them either" (215). Quilp has that same elusive ontological *surplus* of the commodity that ignites its infectious and spectral exchange-value, its universal exchangeability.

Considering Quilp himself as effigial, then, the scene depicting him conjuring up an effigy in his countinghouse could be compared to Daumier's "Masks of 1831," which reveals beneath the masks of the national assembly not the king himself, but a signifier, an effigy-beyond-the-effigy of certain antagonistic social forces, such as bourgeois capital or the surplus *jouissance* beyond the mask of private individualism. The doubling between Quilp and the figurehead effigy similarly reveals Quilp as a material signifier or "bearer of objective factors" (Adorno, *Notes to Literature* 171), as an anamorphic effigy-beyond-the-effigy, and the point of condensation between them, the nodal point that ignites their doubling, is the key to unraveling the signifier's meaning. Their point of condensation is indicated by the fact that in the illustration the effigy stands against a stove and Quilp, coiled up like a spring, strikes it with a hot poker and "mean[s] to burn him at last," as though he were stoking and consuming some kind of energy from it by means of (or as) heat or fire, and by striking it, moreover, Quilp makes "himself more fiery and furious … heating his malice and mischievousness till they boil" (473) as if he were somehow himself a part of, or an extension of, this "substantial" energy/enjoyment, an object of the same fiery surplus *jouissance*.

The image of fire, that is, functions throughout the novel as a signifier for some prebourgeois and repressed drive that structures the bourgeois social fantasy of progress from deep within its dark underbelly, caged up like a beast in the heart of the factory.[3] The symbolic force of this visual signifier can be traced to the extremely dreamlike scene in which Little Nell and her grandfather are driven in despair to spend the night in a factory where they find laborers working like slaves as if in the bondage of demonic spirits in the form of fire:

> In this gloomy place, moving like demons among the flame and smoke, dimly and fitfully seen, flushed and tormented by the burning fires, and wielding great weapons, a faulty blow from any one of which must have crushed some workman's skull, a number of men laboured like giants … Others, again, opening the white-hot furnace-doors, cast fuel on the flames, which came rushing and roasting forth to meet it, and lick it up like oil. Others drew forth, with clashing noise, upon the ground, great sheets of glowing steel, emitting an insupportable heat, and a dull deep light like that which reddens in the eyes of savage beasts. (341)

As a visual signifier (or dialectical image), fire embodies this suppressed contradiction at the heart of the bourgeois "spirit world"—on the one hand, as in Quilp's ecstatic malice, reflecting the voracious enjoyment of sheer consumption literally transforming landscapes on a national scale, on the other hand, reflecting the demonic enslavement to that same primal substance (pre-industrial nature) that fuels this need for consumption as new world order. *The Old Curiosity Shop* captures, with illustrative simplicity, this complex antagonism in the image of the factory furnace, which appears to transform raw substance into surplus value with an almost alchemical sorcery, but that simultaneously yields a glimpse of the savage violence lurking within the private commodity like the dull glow that "reddens in the eyes of savage beasts." The dialectical image of fire is thus particularly suited to give expression to the contradiction at the heart of the capitalist industrial society whose technological progress both represses and repeats something primal (even "savage"), just as the rationalized economic commodity represses and repeats the irrational worship of the tribal fetish.

If the image of fire links Quilp to the industrial factory through the effigy that is both a "hideous idol whom the dwarf worshipped" and a "substantial phantom" he derives pleasure from defacing, it is in order to materialize a lack that seems to flicker beyond all the fantasy formations of the bourgeois social reality it underlies, inasmuch as what Quilp puts on display more than anything is the insatiable desire of consumption—not the desire *to* consume (for he seems unaffected by what he consumes), but *consuming desire*, the surplus *jouissance* of consumption. As such, Quilp consumes fiery substances with inexhaustible relish: throughout sleepless nights he "kept his cigar alight, and kindled every fresh one from the ashes of that which was nearly consumed, without requiring the assistance of a candle" (40), he "drank boiling tea without winking" (41), and gulped down, straight from the "hot saucepan," "burning hot" spirits that "had been but a moment before, when he took it off the fire, bubbling and hissing fiercely" (477). Accordingly, the dull red glare of molten factory steel that reflects the hunger in the "eyes of savage beasts" reappears in Quilp's countinghouse, which gives off "a faint light, twinkling from the window ... looking inflamed and red through the night-fog, as though it suffered from it like an eye" (472), and in Quilp himself when, as he ravenously mutilates the Kit effigy, his "cunning eyes ... were turned toward the fire and reflected its light" (476).

Fire is not merely a symbol associated with Quilp; the dwarf and fire seem to be different *forms* of the same spectral or uncanny, but material, *effigial substance*. Thus when Quilp does finally burn the effigy of Kit (which he eventually does by accidentally knocking over the furnace and burning down his countinghouse in his attempted escape) it marks his own death, which is surrounded by images of wildly burning fires that seem to consume the entire milieu, as his cries "seemed to make the hundred fires that danced before his eyes tremble and flicker, as if a gust of wind had stirred them" and "the sky was red with flame" (525). And just as the effigy that Quilp left to burn in his wharf house, its face "horribly seared by the frequent application of the red-hot poker," seemed only to "provoke its tormentor" with its material invulnerability, Quilp's corpse, with "something of the glare upon its face" from the fire, is left lying like an effigy itself, its hair "[playing] in a kind of mockery of death ... about its head" (518, 526). Quilp dies bodily but not symbolically because effigy is beyond or outside of the life/death opposition of the human. As I will discuss further in regards to *Dombey and Son*, this aspect of effigy completely reframes much of the supposed inconsistency that has been attributed to Dickens's critiques of social systems—that it devolves social critiques onto evil individuals. But here we see that the *effigy* cannot be killed precisely because it is *not an individual*—it is a nodal point of socio-symbolic forces, a material lack/surplus, a signifier in the Real of the social forces it reflects.

Thus when Adorno says that Little Nell and her grandfather are "formed of the same material" (or that "neither could exist as an autonomous human being," 173) we might go so far as to take it literally, and when Quilp's lawyer Brass asks Quilp for water, and Quilp threatens to give him "melted lead and brimstone ... nice hot blistering pitch and tar" (477), or when Brass warns Quilp of the danger of a secret "combining together, of friends," and Quilp lashes out as if exposed, "Why do you talk to me of combining together, Do *I* combine?" we come to recognize that the fire of the factory furnace in *The Old Curiosity Shop* symbolically reaches back in some way to some elemental substratum of materiality that dissolves subject and object alike into primal substance, perhaps something like the strange ontological factory furnace of the individual in Blake's mythic industrial and infernal city, Golgonooza. Quilp embodies the all consuming energy of this primordial signifier, fire, and it is for this reason that what he reflects is, by nature, debt/voracious greed, or lack/surplus itself: Quilp's enfeebled yet indefatigable little body seems to present us nakedly with something like a *jouissance* of the death drive itself. Chesterton seems to have intuited this when he says of Quilp that "[h]e is energy, and energy by itself is always suicidal; he is that primordial energy which tears and which destroys itself" (281).

This idea of the effigy as a nodal point connecting various characters and images (as well as objects) in the novel to an overdetermined metaphor bearing their "objective factors" finds more subtle development in the later novels, such as *Dombey and Son*, which abounds in effigies, both literal and figurative (it is here, for instance, that we first see the hanging doll in the illustrations that will later appear repeatedly in *Bleak House*). Quilp battering the effigy of Kit finds more sublimated repetition, for instance, in Major Bagstock, himself almost an automaton, jabbing at objects and images in dumb shows of his unspoken motives, for example:

> "Granger, Sir," said the Major, tapping the last ideal portrait [an image he drew in the dirt with his cane], and rolling his head emphatically, "was the Colonel of ours; a de-vilish handsome fellow, Sir, of forty-one. He died, Sir, in the second year of his marriage." The Major ran the representative of the deceased Granger through and through the body with his walking stick. (282)

There is also an abundance of effigy-like characters. There is Cleopatra (Mrs. Skewton), who is turned into a grotesque doll after her stroke. There is Bunsby, another man of wood, who is like a human bulkhead: "immediately there appeared coming slowly up above the bulk-head of the cabin, another bulk-head—human, and very large—with one stationary eye in the mahogany face, and one revolving one, on the principle of some lighthouses" (323). But at the center of all of these effigie-like characters is the actual effigy of the Wooden Midshipman, an inanimate yet central object in the novel, which is present from beginning to end, appears in chapter headings, and often serves to establish transitions and association between scenes and characters.

In order to understand the function of the Wooden Midshipman in *Dombey and Son*, therefore, one has to look for the nodal metaphor of this novel. It is a staple of Dickens criticism to note that after *Dombey and Son* most of Dickens's longer novels have the unique trait of being uniformly structured around a central metaphoric image, such as fog in *Bleak House*, prisons in *Little Dorrit*, and dust heaps in *Our Mutual Friend*. It is usually assumed that *Dombey and Son*, on the other hand, while it was clearly the first of the more coherently structured of Dickens's long novels, was formally centered on a psychological motif, such as pride, rather than a metaphoric image like the prison. In fact, though not as pervasively as the other novels, *Dombey and Son* is, I would argue, structured by a particular metaphoric image, that of *mirror reflections*, which functions as a concrete expression of the reproducibility and exchangeability the commodity-form introduces at the heart of bourgeois culture. Thus, in the chapter introducing Mr. Brogley, pawnbroker, into the novel, at the end of a long passage describing the stock of personal goods scattered about Brogley's pawnshop, Dickens's narrator introduces the following visual image as a metaphor to ontologically intertwine commodities with people that eventually becomes the central symbolic image of the novel, mediating relations between characters, motifs, and things:

> Of motionless clocks that never stirred a finger, and seemed as incapable of being successfully wound up, as the pecuniary affairs of their former owners, there was always great choice in Mr Brogley's shop; and various looking-glasses, accidentally placed at compound interest of reflection and refraction, presented to the eye an eternal perspective of bankruptcy and ruin. (114)

The melancholic *mise en scène* of Brogley's desolate pawnshop, which strangely appears as a kind of filmic cutaway preceding and preparing for Brogley's sudden appearance in Captain Cuttle's nautical trade shop in possession of a "bond debt," is teaming with ghostly commodities—such as a "cabinet piano, wasting away, a string a day, and faithfully resounding to the noises of the street in its jangling and distracted brain"—and thus opens the symbolic space for self-consciously reflecting on representational forms within the novel itself. For instance, the optical terms "reflection and refraction," the successive placement of the looking glasses in the shop, which both reproduce images through light rays ("reflection") and bend or break images or light rays into component parts ("refraction"), and the phrase "presented to the eye," all evoke the motif of perspective devices, an important facet of this structuring specular metaphor of mirror reflection, as I will develop further shortly. This spectacle of endless reflections/refractions "present[s] to the eye," moreover, another spectral perspective shift—distorting or turning a mimetic into an effigial image—causing the inanimate objects in an unpeopled pawnshop to suddenly reveal a vertiginous vista of ghostly subjects, embodied in those very objects, suspended in a spatiotemporal *mise en abyme* of debt ("an eternal perspective of bankruptcy and ruin").

Not surprisingly, perhaps, Dickens forges new symbolic connections through techniques of comedy and linguistic play, specifically through the potential the joke structure offers to make illogical but overdetermined connections between disparate entities, but also through the play between visual and verbal images. The pun on the phase "wound up," that is, forges a linguistic connection between clocks and monetary affairs that evokes a certain substitutability or exchangeability between objects and persons established by the regime of capital and debt; but the introduction of mirror *reflections* into the scene takes the next step in transforming both the objects and their former owners into signs or images—that is, into a state of visual spectrality or virtuality in which the potential

"Moor eeffocish things"

equivalence is externalized and actualized (just as in the pawnshop the object becomes pure potential exchange-value, its presence only a placeholder for money). The economic metaphor of *compound interest*, applied rather sublimely to the optical effect of the "accidentally placed" looking glasses, synthesizes the whole trope into a visual metaphor of the existential deadlock of the capitalist subject, its unchanging "eternal perspective": the profit–debt deadlock captured in the reflections and refractions, each of which can generate further reflections and reflections, also reflects the logic of capital, the mysterious proliferation of surplus value in the circulation chains of commodities that drives capitalist expansion and that Marx formalizes in the movement from C–M–C (Commodities–Money–Commodities) to its mirror inversion M–C–M (surplus value in the money-form), the underbelly of which process is manifested in the pawnshop as "bankruptcy and ruin." With this subtle perspective/representational motif, it is as if in Brogley's pawnshop we have gone through the looking glass of speculative capitalism.

The nodal pun on "wound up" has a particularly overdetermined significance in this milieu of the pawnshop since it locks the two signified, clocks and debtors, into a reciprocal relationship between being in debt and being unable to progress, to register time as an actively unfolding present: the pawnshop is the place where personal and useful possessions are taken out of circulation (neither used nor sold) for an interest fee in order to "buy time" on money owed or past bills unpaid, that is, where *time* is liquidated through objects by effectively making their use-value and exchange-value virtual, indefinitely deferred. Stopped clocks recur as a motif throughout novel,[4] and the graveyard of reflections of motionless clocks as substitutes for the ruined debtors reflects the reification of time that, as Lukács points out, structurally follows the fetishization of the commodity: "Thus time sheds its qualitative, variable, flowing nature; it freezes into an exactly delimited, quantifiable continuum filled with quantifiable 'things' (the reified, mechanically objectified 'performance' of the worker, wholly separated from total human personality): in short, it becomes space" (90).

Though Phiz never illustrates Brogley's pawnshop, he does illustrate Mr. Brogley's visit to Captain Cuttle's stock and trade shop (also packed to the brim with miscellaneous objects) to assess the property for repossession if Cuttle can't pay off the bond that came into Brogley's possession (Figure 14). The illustration is rich (overflowing, like Dickens's description of Brogley's shop) in iconic details, but what interests us here is what Phiz does *graphically* with the mirror reflection metaphor as a

Where "the specular becomes the spectral"

14 Phiz (Hablot K. Browne), "Captain Cuttle Consoles His Friend," etching for *Dombey and Son*, 1846.

means to express something about the human/commodity relationship. Phiz depicts Mr. Brogley in a gesture chosen from a number of gestures described by Dickens: while Cuttle is being consoled by his friends and family as he contemplates his immanent financial ruin, Brogley is "catching up keys with loadstones, looking through telescopes, endeavoring to make himself acquainted with the use of the globes, setting parallel rulers astride on to his nose, and amusing himself with other philosophical transactions" (121). That, of all of these "philosophical transactions," Phiz illustrates Brogley "setting parallel rulers astride on to his nose," is not

"Moor eeffocish things"

merely chance, since in a later illustration, "The Wooden Midshipman on the Lookout" (Figure 15), Phiz repeats *this exact gesture* of Brogley's unfeeling mockery of Cuttle's financial ruin but now *displaced onto the figure of the Wooden Midshipman*, who is perched defiantly outside the doorway of Captain Cuttle's shop with his quadrant (shaped like the parallel rulers of the earlier plate) astride on his nose. Phiz makes this mirror

15   Phiz (Hablot K. Browne), "The Wooden Midshipman on the Lookout," etching for *Dombey and Son*, 1847.

reflection (across plates) between the man and the effigy unmistakable in the repeated shape of the objects they hold (quadrant and ruler), and in the repeated gesture and pose they assume, thereby adding a graphic dimension to the symbolic identification between the two figures that is central to the text and to any understanding of the Midshipman's function in it.

The Wooden Midshipman, as the central effigy of the novel, generates an almost irrepressible proliferation of animating metaphors, mostly working to establish his superiority (however comically) over the humans around him due to his superhuman detachment from mortal concerns— life, death, financial affairs, emotional attachment, etc.—which he enjoys precisely because of his inanimate effigial status, as seen in his unwaveringly "wide-awake" gaze, a quality he shares with other Dickens effigies, such as Quilp and the Kit effigy. The Midshipman, then, said to be "intent on his own discoveries, and caring as little of what went on about him, terrestrially, as Archimedes at the taking of Syracuse" (251) is a kind of nodal effigy, as it were, combining the figures of a "scientific" observer (whose gaze is augmented by optical devises), a commodity, and a vampiric profiteer (with colonialist implication). This effigy thus mirrors an aspect of the pawnbroker Brogley, who profits by calculating on the inevitable debt and financial decline of certain members of capitalist society, in that they both embody a certain *value* attached to the ability to take a "philosophic," "scientific" or objective perspective of this structural inequity and human loss that surrounds them; or, as Dickens's narrator puts it: "with his quadrant at his round black knob of an eye, and his finger in its old attitude of indomitable alacrity, the midshipman ... absorbed in scientific pursuits, had no sympathy with worldly concerns" (251). The emphasis on the Midshipman's "scientific" detachment as essential to his effigial character (his *thingly* loftiness), in other words, reflects a particular characteristic of Brogley's social role, since the pawnbroker by nature exploits a certain emotional attachment between debtors and their pawned objects, which keeps them from selling their possessions outright; but they also both reflect the structure of mirror inversion implicit in speculative capitalism between profit, imperial and entrepreneurial pursuits, and technological progress, on the one hand, and debt and financial "ruin" on the other, as the mirrors in Brogley's shop quite literally illustrate. Thus Phiz's graphic parallel between the two figures, man and effigy, reflects the way in which the two characters are both facets of the same spectral force that haunts the novel and the world it depicts; in fact, although Brogley's character disappears from the text, the Midshipman represents him *in* effigy as if in the illustration depicting the Midshipman with his quadrant to his eye, Brogley the pawnbroker *were metamorphosed into a fetish*, into the novel's most irrepressibly animated fetish object.

Just as Quilp, insofar as he is effigial, taps into the primordial force of the factory furnace at the heart of industrialism, the Midshipman as effigy taps into the primordial image of the fetish object at the heart of commodity culture, as we see when Dickens compares the Midshipman's supernatural indifference to that of a "fierce idol" to its "votaries": though characters show sentimental attachment to the Midshipman, "no fierce idol with a mouth from ear to ear, and a murderous visage made of parrot's feathers, was ever more indifferent to the appeal of its savage votaries, than was the Midshipman to these marks of attachment" (251). It is important to consider this uncanny play between savagery and indifference in the imagery of the Midshipman and the motifs that link it to Brogley. Just as Quilp functioned as the mask of the *jouissance* of surplus value, The Midshipman functions as the mask of the *fetishistic disavowal* of the capitalist subject: the bourgeois Rationalist spirit, or the drive to calculate and abstract (the Midshipman's quadrant, for instance, is a tool to calculate the stars as means of navigation) that guards its opposite, a repressed fear of lack that drives a primal desire for mastery through violent exploitation and social inequity.

Fetishism in its various dimensions, accordingly, is at the heart of the illustration dedicated to the Midshipman, "The Wooden Midshipman on the Lookout" (Figure 15), which depicts the scene in which Florence Dombey and Susan Nipper visit Walter and Captain Cuttle before Walter is shipped off to sea by Dombey's firm as a result of the financial upheaval Brogley's bond caused their home. The scene illustrated centers on a curious exchange across the shop's threshold, under the Midshipman's gaze, of Florence's shoes (which Walter had saved from his first encounter with her when she had run off without them) for Florence herself:

> But that ancient mariner [the midshipman] might have been excused his insensibility to the treasure [the shoes in the trunk] as it rolled away. For, under his eye at the same moment, acutely within his range of observation, coming full into the sphere of his startled and intensely wide-awake lookout, were Florence and Susan Nipper: Florence looking half into his face half timidly, and receiving the full shock of his wooden ogling! (253)

The motifs of mirroring and doubling (or reflection and refraction) in this illustration proliferate throughout: working from the front of the procession of figures coming down the street, Phiz depicts the two

Where "the specular becomes the spectral"

central women, then two identical gentleman in top hats facing each other, two horses (their heads at mirror angles), and finally, leading up and around the corner, the backs of two gentlemen, one in black one in white, with identical hats. And even circles and triangles (shapes that make up the quadrant's quartered circle) echo throughout the illustration. The more fundamental mirroring, however, is that the narrative depicts the exchange of a (typically fetishistic) object for its owner (Florence's shoes for Florence) while its illustration marks the substitution of a *person*, and one who exploits the human attachment to objects, for a personified *object* (Brogley for the Midshipman, who as we have seen echoes or doubles him here and replaces him). Between text and image, in other words, there is an inverted reflection of an exchange of fetish for flesh and flesh for fetish. Taking place on a threshold, the illustration/narrative of these transactions reflects the threshold both between text and image and between subject and object. At both limit and center of this threshold illustration is the Wooden Midshipman, himself a liminal figure that guards a doorway with his "intensely wide-awake look-out," like an arcane talisman overseeing an ontologically liminal dimension; similarly, Smallweed, the effigy-like villain from *Bleak House*, sits before the fire (and then before a well of wills and legal documents) like a "sentinel ... long forgotten on [his] post by the Black Serjeant, Death" (259).

The motifs of threshold and exchange enter into the *perspective* as well. In "Captain Cuttle Consoles His Friend" (Figure 14), the perspective is *telescoped* as we look through one room in which humans gaze at each other sympathetically into another room in which the inhumanly indifferent pawnbroker is gazing though an object among other objects, including a wide-eyed doll hanging from the ceiling. "The Wooden Midshipman on the Lookout" (Figure 15) is more temporally linear in perspective, tracking the perspective of the two women walking into a shop from the street and culminating in an a startling exchange of gazes between human and object, "Florence looking half into [the Midshipman's] face half timidly, and receiving the full shock of his wooden ogling!" As she walks past this threshold effigy to enter the shop, Florence suddenly finds herself in a position to see that an object (the Midshipman) *sees her*, as if she unexpectedly occupies the eccentric position (only "half" looking) from which the anamorphic object springs to life and gazes back: the very definition, as we will discuss presently, of the moor eeffocish thing.

We have thus seen how the novel's structuring metaphor of mirror reflection, established in Brogley's shop as a perspective play between the commodity-fetish object and the entranced human subject under the objectifying spell of Capital, reflects and refracts throughout the novel and all of its various milieus; but it is Carker, Dombey's manager and the novel's antagonist, who embodies it in its most insidious and animate form:

> Undertakings have been entered on, to swell the reputation of the house for vast resources, and to exhibit in magnificent contrast to other merchants' houses, of which it requires a steady head to contemplate the possibly—a few disastrous changes of affairs might render them the probably—ruinous consequences. In the midst of the many transactions of the House, in most parts of the world: a great labyrinth of which only he has held the clue. (719–20)

Like the Wooden Midshipman, who cares "little of what went on about him, terrestrially, as Archimedes at the taking of Syracuse," Carker, even more than Brogley, has the "steady head" to "contemplate" the financial "transactions" that will lead not only to Dombey's bankruptcy and ruin, but to a "great labyrinth" of "ruinous" reverberations throughout the world. But while Brogley is subjected to the logic of the commodity-form and its fetishistic disavowal, in that he is absorbed into the ostensibly benign figure of the Wooden Midshipman, Carker possesses an uncanny power over the forces of the commodity-fetish; he holds the secret ("only he has held the clue") to the dizzying "labyrinth" he has spun, like a sorcerer, out of capital. The spectral forces of reflection and refraction that underlie the novel's symbolic world, in other words, seem to find spectral expression in the figure of Carker, which is what gives his character a sense of being overcharged, overdetermined, effigial. Brogley's Grandvillesque metamorphosis into a wooden effigy, then, is not the end of his symbolic permutations: later he is reflected and refracted in the many "shabby vampires" (the nameless brokers) who "over-run [Dombey's] house" in order to auction off his property after his financial ruin, all of them acting like so many replications of Brogley, "sounding the plate-glass mirrors with their knuckles, striking discordant octaves on the Grand Piano, drawing wet forefingers over the pictures ... opening and shutting all the drawers, balancing the silver spoons and forks," etc. Accordingly, once his possessions have been changed back into commodities on the market, Dombey's house is transformed into a large-scale replication of Brogley's pawnshop in which "chaotic combinations of furniture also take place. Mattresses and bedding appear in the dining room; the glass and china get into the conservatory," etc. (798). That is to say, once Dombey has lost his claim to capital, and thus the claim to possession over his things, these things temporarily lose their (human) use-value so that their exchange-value is liberated from human attachment; they thus become, like the objects in Brogley's shop, uncannily alive, *moor eeffocish*.

In fact, *Dombey and Son* is teeming with *moor eeffocish things*, with objects that seem to flicker between the animate and inanimate, that possess an eerie sentience despite their muteness. Chesterton derives the term "moor eeffocish things" from Dickens's autobiographical fragments and uses it to explain the unsettling intensity of objects that, having been perceived only "dreamily" in the past, somehow acquire a surplus symbolic valence in the present, an elusiveness *realness* beyond the observer's grasp. Thus Chesterton associates this ontological surplus in objects with an uncanny kind of *realism* characteristic of Dickens, the "unbearable realism of a dream" as he calls it, which stems from originally experiencing places in a semi-conscious state: "This kind of realism can only be gained by walking dreamily in a place," he explains, and "the scenes we see are the scenes at which we did not look at all—the scenes in which we walked when we were thinking about something else" (*Charles Dickens* 65). The root-phrase "Moor Eeffoc" originates in Dickens's description, preserved by Forster and quoted by Chesterton, of the nearby coffee shops Dickens haunted during his time working for the blacking factory as a child, the recollection of one of which in later life triggers an uncanny experience, a kind of return of the repressed encountered in an everyday scene. The passage appears first in Forster's *The Life of Charles Dickens* as follows:

> The coffee-shops to which I most reverted were: one in maiden Lane; one in a court (non-existent now) close to Hungerford Market; and one in St. Martin's Lane, of which I only recollect that it stood near the church, and that in the door there was an oval glass plate with COFFEE-ROOM painted on it, addressed towards the street. If I ever find myself in a very different sort of coffee-room now, but where there is such an inscription on the glass, and read it backwards on the wrong side, MOOR EEFFOC (as I used to do then, in a dismal reverie), a shock goes through my blood. (26–7)

Since Chesterton transforms this strange inverted signifier into an adjective to describe those objects which Dickens "endows with demoniac life" (*Charles Dickens* 65), he must have been fascinated by the phrase itself, "MOOR EEFFOC," and so must have Benjamin, who in the *Arcades Project* quotes the same passage from Chesterton quoting Forster quoting Dickens. And it has since captured the imagination of modern critics and theorists from John Bowen to Slavoj Žižek. This "wild word," as Chesterton calls it—as though it were somehow dangerously undomesticated, un*homely*—with all its double letters, its internal typographical mirroring, has a kind of eerily spectral echo to it, as though it could conceal or evoke a presence ... we could even imagine it as the incantation spoken by the "tribal sorcerer" of the commodity-fetish, of which Benjamin speaks when describing Grandville.

In any case, an interesting play of perspective centers on the signifier itself in Dickens's autobiographical fragment, since to read the inverted words "MOOR EEFFOC," inscribed on a glass door, one has to *look at* something that was meant to be *seen through*, overlooked, or imagined only from another viewpoint. One presumably passes the inscription every day without ever seeing it "backwards on the wrong side," so that inscribed in the most comfortable of bourgeois public spaces, the coffee room, is something hauntingly absurd, just out of view, an uncanny mirror effect. Moor Eeffoc is thus analogous, in the linguistic medium, to the anamorphic image in which something unexpected leaps out at the viewer only when seen from an oblique perspective; one sees moor eeffocish things, says Chesterton, "because he does not look at them" (*Charles Dickens* 65), as a result of which the subject experiences a kind of ontological displacement in relation to the object (as the older Dickens haunted by the young Dickens reading the words "backwards on the wrong side"). The "shock" that runs through Dickens's blood here is mirrored in the "full shock" Florence experiences from the Midshipman's "wooden ogling": both are the effect of receiving the *gaze of an object*, exactly Žižek's definition of anamorphosis, of the shock "that reality already involves our gaze, that this gaze is included in the scene we are observing, that this scene already 'regards us'" (*Ticklish Subject* 78). The detail of the door or threshold in this story is important here, because MOOR EEFFOC, seen only "backwards on the wrong side," implies a perspective that is never quite inside, or never at home on the "right side," but somehow split between both inside and outside, familiar and foreign. As a result of this play between inside and outside, the signifier *Coffee Room* has the power, once inverted, to return Dickens to a traumatic childhood scene, to take him out of himself; but in a remarkable example of what Freud called *Nachträglichkeit*, the *gaze of each scene already haunts the other*—the gaze of the adult Dickens seeing the signifier COFFEE ROOM can always return the child's gaze reading MOOR EEFFOC on the other side, but also the *original scene was already regarded by the future adult's look*, MOOR EEFFOC always already contained the empty place of the gaze the adult Dickens would later occupy.

Where "the specular becomes the spectral"

MOOR EEFFOC is thus an anamorphosis of the signifier, a traumatic return of the uncanny *materiality of the signifier* that decenters the self-presence of the subject in an encounter with the Real. It exposes, that is, the nature of the signifier in the Real to be that of a *spectral materiality*. This is why Žižek uses Dickens's autobiographical fragment, and Chesterton's adoption of it to typify Dickens's "eerie realism," as an illustration of the relation between ontology, reality, and trauma according to psychoanalysis. In his chapter from *Disparities* titled "MOOR EEFFOC," Žižek recasts Freud's notion of "primordial repression" in ontological (or we could say here *hauntological*) terms by showing how it is inaugurated in the very trauma, or "catastrophe" that is the "emergence of subjectivity, of the human mind, out of nature" (185). "The exclusion of the Real from *this* 'catastrophe' ... is what introduces the gap that separates the Real from reality—it is on account of this gap that what we experience as external reality always has to rely on a fantasy, and that when the raw Real is forced upon us, it causes the experience of the loss of reality" (185). Chesterton's description of Dickens's "unbearable realism," which postulates that (in Chesterton's words) "the most fantastic thing of all is often the precise fact" (*Charles Dickens* 65), thus acquires its full ontological significance when Žižek adds that in Dickens's realism "a detail of reality itself gets spectralized" (*Disparities* 187). The autobiographical fragment's remarkable illustration of the *Nachträglichkeit* (a dialectical or delayed-activation effect) sparked between an adult's ordinary encounter with an unremarkable inscription, COFFEE ROOM, and a childhood encounter with a meaningless signifier, MOOR EEFFOC, captures precisely why *realism* cannot be conceived in terms of a representation of "objective reality" independent of the subject: the "objective reality" is itself always already a world of meaning bound up with and indissociable from signifiers, signifiers that (primordially) repress a traumatic Real of *jouissance* that underlies this objectivity. But in certain uncanny moments the signifier within that reality can in fact capture the "mysterious points within the universe of meaning where meaning breaks down and is overshadowed by a nameless abyss of *jouissance*, and this is why when I stumble upon the meaningless signifier MOOR EEFFOC, 'a shock goes through my blood'" (Žižek, *Disparities* 186). Thus in the "spectralized detail" of reality, the signifier that gives it its meaning within the symbolic network is also haunted by its own meaningless excess, its own traumatic tear in that same fabric, the *tear or scar of the subject*.

What I would highlight here is that the *moor eeffocish thing* is precisely an *objet petit a* that contains a little piece of the Real that, as Žižek points out in accordance with Chesterton, distorts reality when directly gazed at but also *constitutes* it when overlooked. It is the uncanny object that introduces a strange *out-of-jointness*, an *extimacy*, in the opposition between subject and object that structures "objective reality" and neatly sections off the "interiority" upon which "depth" of character often depends: "'a shock goes through my blood' when I stumble upon a small material detail which stirs up something in my 'inner life'—not some 'deeper meaning' but something traumatic, nonsymbolizable, extimate (external in the very core of my being)" (Žižek, *Disparities* 189). This is also the function of effigy in *Dombey and Son*.

The effigy, then, is the ultimate moor eeffocish thing and as a *form* of characterization is, in a structural sense, anamorphic, as we have seen in the ontological inversions between humans and objects it effects in Dickens's characters. The remarkable thing, then, is that by the logic of effigy *characters as well can be moor eeffocish things*. Jonathan Crary points out that Dombey himself is a kind of effigy: "[His] rigidity attracts much notice: he looks 'like a man of wood, without a hinge or joint in him,' and turns his head in his neckcloth 'as if it were a socket.' Critics have taken this as a sign that he lacks human affection. Of course, he does. But the more pressing reason for his woodenness is that Dickens likes wooden men" (88). Both of these explanations of Dombey's "woodenness" are ultimately unsatisfying: the idea that it indicates a lack of human emotion (the psychological approach) fails to account for the cumulative effect of the pervasive images of woodenness and effigy throughout the novel (and Dickens's work more generally), while the idea that it is only because Dickens "likes wooden men" simply posits the fact without offering any explanation for it. Moreover, either response would seem to lead us to the same conclusion: Dombey's character, the central character in the novel, is "flat," a psychological sketch without any psychological complexity (demonstrating only a lack of qualities), in the same way that George Eliot suggested Dickens failed to represent innerness. And by extension, *many* of the characters in *Dombey and Son* would have to be considered flat. Obviously this is the wrong way to pose the question of Dombey's woodenness as an essential part of his characterization. If we start rather from Adorno's premise that Dickens's approach intentionally breaks from the form of bourgeois Realism precisely "by not taking as its own criterion the highest norm of bourgeois art, the individual and his psychology" (173), we will be in a better position to reformulate the question of characterization here without resorting to the "flat" and "round" metaphors according to which the "psychological" approach is grounded

Where "the specular becomes the spectral"

in mimesis. Dickens's insistence on wooden and object-like characters in *Dombey and Son* (The Midshipman, Brogley, Bunsby, Dombey, Carker, Cleopatra, etc.) is not simply indicative of his predilection for wooden figures, or even a result of his own attraction to their uncanny effect (as Crary goes on to suggest), but a *formal* means of subverting the bourgeois image of the subject by unmasking and distorting the primacy of innerness implied in mimetic realism—as in caricature, Dickens's representation of human figures takes mimesis itself as the target of its subversion. Dombey, therefore, is not simply "wooden," but is *moor eeffocish* in a way that haunts mimesis: underlying his human likeness is a kind of irrational, unassimilable material substrate, a lifeless wooden form, just as his name can be split into the two words *me* and *body*. This gives his character an underlying anamorphic effect: from a certain perspective, Dombey is a wooden effigy of a man, a material double of himself subject to symbolic inversions, like the inscription on the coffee room window.

We can see Dombey, then, as part of an ideologically subversive representational method that Dickens brings to full fruition in *Dombey and Son* and continues to develop until the end of his career. Dombey's ontological anamorphosis is illustrated best in a rather brilliant inversion of a fundamental motif of bourgeois Realism—the portrayal of internal "depth" that gives character its "roundness"—whereby instead of "getting inside" Dombey's character to create an illusion of innerness, the narrator externalizes Dombey's consciousness in the form of reflections in a piece of wooden furniture, using the motif of mirror reflections and the metaphor of the sea as a means to effect a *visual* and *material* composite of psychological "innerness" (remembered images, projected future, and affects), a projected sense of depth, and an inanimate object. In preparation for this projection of his consciousness, the narrator surrounds Dombey with moor eeffocish things in a moor eeffocish dining room that is

> in colour a dark brown, with black hatchments of pictures blotching the walls, and twenty four black chairs, with almost as many nails in them as so many coffins, waiting like mutes, upon the threshold of the Turkey carpet; and two exhausted negroes holding up two withered branches of candelabra on the sideboard, and a musty smell prevailing as if the ashes of ten thousand different dinners were entombed in the sarcophagus below it. The owner of the house lived much abroad ... and the room had gradually put itself into deeper and still deeper mourning for him, until it was become so funereal as to want nothing but a body in it to be quite complete. (469)

"Moor eeffocish things"

This room, in which objects are alive with symbolic surplus and mourn the loss of a human presence, manifested as a perceived absence of a corpse, itself marks a certain externalized liminality, as if the very threshold of consciousness belonged to the world of things or to a space neither inside nor outside the subject, to a room. Baudelaire describes his experience of "entering" Grandville's works in terms that could easily apply to the disturbing recalcitrance of household objects in *Dombey and Son*:

> There are some superficial spirits who are amused by Grandville; for my part, I find him terrifying ... When I open the door of Grandville's work, I feel a certain uneasiness, as though I were entering an apartment where disorder was systematically organized—where preposterous cornices were propped up against the floor, where the pictures showed their faces through an opticians distorting glass, where all the objects elbowed each other about obliquely, the furniture stood with its feet in the air, and the drawers slid inwards instead of out. ("Some French Caricaturists" 172)

What Baudelaire finds in Grandville's work is a completely moor eeffocish world, a world in which each object, every trinket, possesses a dreamlike vitality in a kind of mockingly impervious mirror reflection of subjective "depth." The Grangers' moor eeffocish dining room in *Dombey and Son*, the narrator tells us, thus lacks only one thing, a human "body," and Dombey, the central effigial character of the novel, is introduced into the scene as a "representation" of the missing corpse: "No bad representation of the body, for the nonce, in his unbending form, if not in his attitude, Mr Dombey looked down into the cold depths of the dead sea of mahogany on which the fruit dishes and decanters lay at anchor: as if the subject of his thoughts were rising towards the surface one by one, and plunging down again" (414–15). A long passage follows in which images of characters and scenes from Dombey's past and future rise and fall as projections reflected/refracted in the mahogany tabletop before him. Placed in the moor eeffocish room, Dombey's wooden "unbending form" here, itself the "representation" of an absent dead "body," has the effect of being a spectralized effigy of himself gazing at its own displaced interiority in mahogany reflections and refractions, much like the debtors' ruined lives seen only through objects in the looking glasses in Brogley's pawnshop. In this uncanny projection, Dombey has anamorphically become *me-body*. The resistance to the ideology of innerness in this passage is palpable: not only is Dombey a wooden man, his very *consciousness* is objectified in wood as something alienable from and external to his "unbending form," his subjectivity a flickering perspective play between a wooden form or "representation of the [dead] body" and "the dead sea of mahogany." This passage turns Eliot's criticism that Dickens never passes from the "external" to the emotional and psychological interior of the individual without becoming "transcendent in his unreality" on its head; in fact, Dickens transforms the internal *into the external* here, transcending the opposition itself and thus bringing the traumatic Real of subjectivity to bear on the psychological realism that posits "reality" on expelling this spectral or moor eeffocish "unreality." This is precisely why Dickens's realism is for Chesterton the "unbearable realism of a dream" (*Charles Dickens* 65). This particular form of dialectical play with psychological interiority finds full expression in the character of Twemlow from *Our Mutual Friend*, who, as a formal progression beyond the wooden Dombey, and extending this scene in which his consciousness is embodied in a mahogany tabletop, *literally becomes indistinguishable from a dining room table*, a perfect dream-composite of psychological innerness and bourgeois interior.

This scene in which Dombey's consciousness is reflected in the mahogany table, moreover, provides us the key to another dimension of the symbolic importance of the reflected image in *Dombey and Son*. Analogously to the function of the element of fire in *The Old Curiosity Shop*, the reflection, or mirror image, in *Dombey and Son* serves as a nodal point between subject and object, subverting the traditional distinction between the two: as in Brogley's shop, reflected images of subject and object are ontologically equivalent, and as such, exchangeable. But subjects are not only *exchangeable* with objects, they are also ontologically indebted to them. Thus when Dombey is finally financially ruined by Carker and sits in his room watching his clock, as the ruined debtors must have done before their broken clocks ended up in Brogley's shop, he contemplates the separation of his spirit from his body as the logical extension of the separation of the "other link" between his proprietorship and his possessions: "He might yet give up what his creditors had spared him ... and only sever the tie between him and the ruined house, by severing that other link" (807). At precisely this moment Dombey catches a glimpse of himself in the mirror and sees that "a spectral, haggard, wasted likeness of himself, brooded and brooded over the empty fireplace" (807). For the next few paragraphs the narrative relates not what *Dombey* did and thought, but what "it" did, referring to his reflection, Dombey again in his despair becoming a "spectral" image, or, as the narrator says, a "likeness of himself." And as in the previous scene, it is again the reflection, the likeness, to which his thoughts are attached, but at this point Dombey seems completely in the position of spectator, not even allowed access to the thoughts of this representational double of himself:

> It was thinking that if blood were to trickle that way, and to leak out into the hall, it must be a long time going so far ... When it had thought of this a long while, it got up again and walked to and fro with its hand in its breast. He glanced at it occasionally, very curious to watch its motions ... Now it was thinking again! what was it thinking? ... It sat down again, with its eyes upon the empty fireplace. (808)

Only when Florence enters the room does "its" alienated and displaced perspective seem to shift from the likeness back to Dombey as he reclaims possession of his own subjectivity and "only saw *his own* reflection in the glass, and at his knees, his daughter" (808, emphasis added).

Two other excellent examples from *Dombey and Son* of this tendency to push the bourgeois representation of subjectivity past its limit are Cleopatra (Mrs. Skewton) and Major Bagstock. Mrs. Skewton is dismantled every evening like a marionette or an automaton: "The painted object shriveled underneath [her maid's] hand; the form collapsed, the hair dropped off, the arched dark eyebrows changed to scanty tufts of grey; the pale lips shrunk, the skin became cadaverous and loose; an old, worn, yellow, nodding woman, with red eyes, alone remained in Cleopatra's place huddled up, like a slovenly bundle, in a greasy flannel gown" (380). And after her stroke she is transformed into a mere puppet. Reduced to a "bundle," Cleopatra is a precursor of characters like the Smallweeds, but in the Smallweeds Dickens pushes the absurdity even further and removes even the pretenses of logic (such as her physical affliction) behind these dreamlike symbolic condensations. Bagstock's character is pushed in the other direction, towards expansion and the explosive: an "overfed Mephistopheles," he falls into fits of silent reverie in which, for instance, "his whole form, but especially his face and head, dilated beyond all former experience; and presented to the dark man's view, nothing but a heavy mass of indigo. At length he burst into a violent fit of coughing, and when that was a little better burst into such ejaculations as the following" (127). Bagstock is a self-aggrandizing, self-consumed, self-satisfied sycophant with an insatiable appetite, but he also seems to *become* these characteristics ontologically—his body and "physical" presence as a character become a *material* means of expression or representation almost to the point of bursting apart, much like another Joshua, Josh Bounderby from *Hard Times*. This symbolic pressure on the boundaries of the individual is, of course, pushed all the way to the extreme in the spontaneous combustion of Krook. Bagstock is also associated with the Wooden Midshipman effigy, as well as with Quilp's figurehead effigy (and Quilp), in his "wide awake look," his unsleeping and uncanny gaze: "'Wide awake is old Joe—broad awake, and staring, Sir!' There was no doubt of this last assertion being true, and to a very fearful extent; as it continued to be during the greater part of that night" (127). Effigies don't sleep because they are always a kind of revenant of the unconscious Gaze, the Gaze projected externally into the objective scene of reality.

But the character who stands in the midst of all of these watching effigies, and who is perhaps the most revealing example of this effigial means of representation in the novel, is Carker. Many critics have attempted to account for the uncannily eerie power of Carker's face and menacing smile; most notable perhaps is Lukacher's analysis of Carker's teeth as an indication of his role as a "predatory capitalist." "It is through the figure of Carker's mouth and teeth," says Lukacher, "that the menacing anxieties of the age come most sharply into focus. They are figures for the hypnotic and destructive power of capital over individuals and over society at large." Thus for Lukacher too, Carker's teeth and mouth have an emblematic, if not effigial, force. They are "the fetish object par excellence. They embody the secret mystery of both his sexual and economic power" (299). Lukacher's analysis, however, illustrates well the differences in psychoanalytic approaches to character, for in pursuing the sources of these overdetermined social symbols, Lukacher turns to a wholly psychological explanation by linking the etymology of Carker's name ("to cark" means to care or worry) to Dickens's own anxiety over modern capitalism and his "experience of the streets," which leads him back to the "primal scene" of Dickens's childhood victimization in the factory. This approach winds up ultimately trading the social force of Dickens's characterization for the (individualized) sexual symbolism of Dickens himself, as the idea of a psychoanalytical fetish (as opposed to the commodity-fetish) leads Lukacher to stress the "'milk white' bosom" of Edith as the "primordial object" of Carker's oral eroticism. Lukacher's psychoanalytic reading of Carker is very powerful; but if we consider it in the context of our discussion of representation and characterization, we can see how, precisely when he attempts to explain the uncanny force of Carker's character traits, Lukacher assumes a mimetic form of psychological innerness that may not do justice to Dickens's art form, thus leading him, like other critics before and since, to question whether Dickens's characters weren't actually somehow self-contradictory, or even self-defeating. This becomes most apparent when, since Carker's character is ultimately explained through perversion or deviance, Lukacher must ask, in response to Carker's "predatory capitalism," "whether it is the economic system that must be changed or merely the villains into whose hands the system has unfortunately fallen" (300). Again we can see a kind of critical dilemma here: if we are trapped in the implicit assumption that Carker is a mimetic representation, then the force of that earlier insight about the darker objective forces he emblematizes, the "hypnotic and destructive power of capital ... over society" must ultimately be resolved in terms of the individual and its psychology, so that much of the critical force of Lukacher's critique is finally cancelled out in self-contradiction, at least from a social perspective, when he concludes that "in *Dombey and Son*, Dickens managed both to rail against social injustice and to defend the status quo" (300).[5]

Is there a way, then, of explaining the uncanny effect of Carker's character traits, his mouth and his teeth, which are again more distorted then mimetic, like Rosa's scar and irony, without ultimately psychologizing his character, which would only lead us again to attribute a self-contradiction to Dickens (that he is attacking and defending the same system)? To do so, of course, we will have to turn from the mimetic approach, and consider the possibility of seeing his character in terms of other, spectral forms of representation, such as effigy, anamorphosis, and dream-distortion.

I suggested above that Carker is part of a constellation of effigy-like characters that include Brogley, the Wooden Midshipman, and the nameless brokers, all of which revolve around the reflection/refraction metaphor as the expression of the subject/object antagonism embodied in the commodity-form. More specifically, if the Wooden Midshipman is the anamorphic expression of the social forces (the "hypnotic and destructive power of capital") contained within the seductively private commodity-form, the fetishized object as the *moor eeffocish thing* mirroring the capitalist subject's own objectification, then Carker's mouth and teeth expose the surplus *jouissance* of that force itself, the force of capital as lack/surplus, or *as that same* primal sexual desire with which Lukacher wanted to exchange. This is why Carker is repeatedly compared to leering masks and semi-human effigies in a state of unreadable or inhuman enjoyment: "Mr Carker bowed his head, and rising from the table, and standing thoughtfully before the fire, with his hand to his smooth chin, looked down at Mr Dombey with the evil slyness of some monkish carving, half human and half brute" (576). Carker is thus not a psychologically depicted character who abuses the capitalist system, but an *effigy*, a spectral embodiment of the *jouissance* of capital itself, like the grinning and leering faces of Daumier's "Masks of 1831" that provide the masks for an effigial signifier in order to give abstract economic forces an uncannily human form of *jouissance*.

Carker's mouth conceals his savage white teeth, but flashing them through his *smile* is a source of inhuman power over humans: "Stretching his mouth wider" at every pause in his conversation with Captain Cuttle, we are told, a "cat, or monkey, or a hyena, or a death's-head, could not have shown the Captain more teeth at one time, than Mr Carker showed him at this period of their interview" (229). Even the anamorphic sliding of signifiers here—cat, monkey, hyena, death's head—conjures a Grandville-type metamorphosis. Thus, just as the seemingly endearing "philosophic" indifference of the Wooden Midshipman's aspect masks the savage inhumanness of a "fierce idol *with a mouth from ear to ear*, and a murderous visage" (emphasis added), the smooth and urbane mask of the accountant conceals the savage toothy grin of "Mr Carker, with *his mouth from ear to ear*" (230, emphasis added). And Mr. Carker too, like the Midshipman-as-idol, displays the power to transform those around him to "savage votaries" of capital. Carker's teeth and grin are so uncanny and spectral because they are effigial and anamorphic; they flicker between human and nonhuman in a way that evokes an inhuman gaze within the human look and vice versa. As effigies, in other words, Carker and the Midshipman gaze at us at once from within and from beyond the logos. Carker's smile, then, is the key to his anamorphic form, inasmuch as it marks the perspective shift that reveals him as an effigy, a "fierce idol with mouth from ear to ear" lurking behind the mask of the realistic character.

Thus, as Quilp is to the furnace fire—a dreamlike *revenant* of oppressed labor force lurking beneath the production of bourgeois industry—Carker is to the commodity's mirror reflections in the pawnshop—a *revenant* of the fetishistic logic lurking within imperial and speculative entrepreneurism. And just as Quilp is associated with fire and dies by water, Carker is associated with the savage idol/fetish and *shattered* by the fiercely demoniac railroad train "that spun him round and round, and struck him limb from limb, and licked his stream of life up with its fiery heat, and cast his mutilated fragments in the air" (749). But as an effigy identified with a commodity-fetish, the Midshipman, Carker is not ultimately to be destroyed in *Geist*, or spirit: the very next words in the novel following Carker's gruesome dismemberment, the first words of the following chapter, are "The Midshipman was all alive" (749), as if to affirm with uncanny alacrity the unscathed vitality of the system of which Carker is only an effigy, despite his personal destruction.

In fact, characters that represents objective social forces in effigy can be found in many of Dickens's novels, and understanding their status as effigy is a powerful critical way of avoiding attributing that fallacy to Dickens that Lukacher (and many others) does, accusing Dickens of "rail[ing] against social injustice and [defending] the status quo." Smallweed, for instance, is an excellent example of this in *Bleak House*. Smallweed, like Carker, is not meant to be a *mimetic* representation of a greedy, covetous capitalist; he is an effigy, a giving-body to the desubjectifying forces of lack at work *in surplus-generating capital*. Thus Smallweed is of the category of characters like Quilp, Fagin, and Uriah, physically dwarfed, crippled, or enfeebled villains whose special power lies in the manipulation of debt, who seem born to enact the crippling power of debt of all types. Smallweed is explicitly compared with an effigy repeatedly throughout the novel, specifically as a "guy" (329, 665), which the footnote in the Norton Critical Edition glosses as "Grotesque scarecrow-like effigies (guys) [that] are carried through the streets by children" to celebrate the capture of Guy Fawkes for conspiring to blow up Parliament. Smallweed too is carried through the streets with an air of ancient ritual: the Smallweed family, as it approaches George's shooting gallery, "consists of a limp and ugly figure carried in a chair by two bearers, and attended by a lean female with a face like a pinched mask, who might be expected immediately to recite the popular verse, commemorative of the time when they did contrive to blow Old England up alive, but of her keeping her lips tightly and defiantly closed as the chair is put down" (329). Drawing on aspects of other effigies and effigy-like characters, Smallweed is vindictive and grotesque, like Quilp, with a bottomless capacity for creative insults; like Carker, he draws power by calculating and manipulating debt and documents; and like the Midshipman and Dombey, he is a spectralized material likeness of a human form, compared to a "guy," a "broken puppet," a "doll," a "clothes-bag," a "shapeless bundle," among other objects resembling (or failing to resemble) a human being. Accordingly, Smallweed seems to flicker on the threshold between the animate and inanimate, as he continually collapses into a shapeless form and must be reanimated by Judy after the exertion of throwing his cushion at Mrs. Smallweed: "The excellent old gentleman being, at these times, a mere clothes-bag with a skull-cap on the top of it, does not present a very animated appearance, until he has undergone the two operations at the hands of his grand-daughter, of being shaken like a great bottle, and poked and punched like a great bolster" (259).

Like a fetish object or commodity-form, Smallweed is the material form for something else, a "clothes-bag," a "bolster," or prop for a certain *Geist* of Victorian society; his character functions as the *representation material* of the spirit-form of property and money. He thus *repeats* and illustrates the repressed violence and greed and insidiousness of the novel's world in a way that must be distinguished from a "realistic" representation of a character depicted as *himself* violent and greedy. As a spectralized object of the social fantasy, he materializes disavowed forces of capital in a form at once realistic and allegorical, concrete and phantasmal. He is like a dream image in a representational sense. In accounting for the fact that in dreams thoughts are acted out ("represented as a scene") Freud says that there are two features that "stand out as characteristic of the form taken by dreams. One is the fact that the thought is represented as an immediate situation with the 'perhaps' omitted, and the other is the fact that the thought is transformed into visual images and speech" (*Dreams* 573). Smallweed seems more like a transformation into "visual images and speech" of the social unconscious of Victorian society than a human figure who acts consciously and autonomously on behalf of himself. And the proper name hooks Smallweed into latent forces of the novel through a concrete metaphor: Smallweed is weed-like in that he clings and corrodes, he is small and weak but patient and insidious, and he fastens on to healthy entities (George) or dead matter (Krook) and sucks the life or energy from them. The character of Smallweed himself is like a dreamlike dumb show of this metaphor: "'When you go winding round and round me,' says [George] ... , 'damme, if I don't feel as if I was being smothered'" (*Bleak House* 428), and in a literal sense, "some degree of force is necessary on the trooper's part to effect a separation" from George's body, when Smallweed attaches and clings on to him (438).

The signifier "weed," a verbal and visual nodal point of his character, connects Smallweed back to the central metaphor of mud established in the first chapter as the primordial substance of the London streets, as if he grew directly out of the mud/money/feces/capital association established in the "compound interest" metaphor in the first chapter: in the rainy London streets "tens and thousands of other foot passengers have been slipping and sliding since the day broke (if the day ever broke), adding new deposits to the crust upon crust of mud, sticking at those points tenaciously to the pavement, and accumulating at compound interest" (5). Just as mud breeds weeds and germs, capital breeds usurers and financial parasites, and Smallweed is born out of this metaphor linking mud to money by way of surplus value (money begetting money), or compound interest:

> The father of this pleasant grandfather [Mr Smallweed], of the neighbourhood of Mount Pleasant, was a horney-skinned, two-legged, money-getting species of spider, who spun webs to catch unwary flies, and retired into holes until they were entrapped. The name of this old pagan's god was Compound Interest. He lived for it, married it, died of it. (342)

Smallweed's metaphoric genealogy is traceable to creatures who dwell in holes in the earth and he is repeatedly being reduced to inanimate form requiring reanimation, as if he originated from clay or mud and tended to return to it unless he drew his life-source from others, or from their debt. Even visually Smallweed seems to grow out of the mud/money metaphor, as if his spindly legs were rooted in it: "Under the venerable Smallweed's seat, and guarded by his spindle legs, is a drawer in his chair, reported to contain property to a fabulous amount" (343).[6] As a kind of fetish or symptom-formation within the novel of nefarious social forces, Smallweed's character is a composite of various other images in the novel. His green eyes and long nails reflect those of Crook's predatory cat (as Nabokov notes). He is a weed grown out of the mud/money metaphor of capitalist London. He echoes the signifiers of torsion and extortion that symbolize the extortionary justice-distorting forces of the Jarndyce and Jarndyce suit, the "shirking and sharking" and the "twist and shuffle" that, as the narrator enumerates in the first chapter breed throughout the novel, as Smallweed, for instance, manipulates George "shrilly and sharply" (330) and exclaims, "I'll twist him, sir. I'll screw him, sir. If he won't do it with a good grace, I'll make him do it with a bad one, sir!" (340).

Like the muddy London streets of the first chapter that hearken back to the creation ("as if the waters had but newly retired from the face of the earth") and foreshadow the end of time ("the death of the sun"), there is something insurmountable in the effigy as signifier, something flickering from both within and beyond the logos, and thus Smallweed and his family are in this sense timeless, lifeless, and therefore beyond the reach of human vulnerability, even death, as they sit "fronting one another in their two porter's chairs, like a couple of sentinels long forgotten on their post by the Black Sergeant, Death" (259). By the end of the novel Smallweed ends up inhabiting another hole or well, the grave-like well in Krook's floor that is full of documents likened to decaying corpses, where he sits "in his chair upon the brink of a well or grave of waste-paper; the virtuous Judy, groping therein, like a female sexton" (615). Thus Smallweed himself takes the form of a fetish object that, while its significance is generated by its place in the signifying chain, emerges as haunting and overdetermined, as indestructibly spectralized.

Notes

1 This tendency doesn't even have to be thought of in terms of meaning—think for instance of distortion in the amplification where electrical signals or sound waves can be changed or distorted such that the medium itself begins to emerge as such.
2 *Westminster Review*, July 1856, lxvi 155.
3 The factory worker that Nell and her grandfather encounter at the furnace fire before which they sleep, in fact, sees the fire as a kind of book to be read, which can reflect pathos, otherness, and innerness: "[The fire is] music, for I should know its voice among a thousand, and there are other voices in its roar. It has its pictures too. You don't know how many strange faces and different scenes I trace in the red-hot coals. It's my memory, that fire, and shows me all my life" (343).
4 Dickens even presented Phiz with the absurd difficulty of depicting a stopped clock in one of the illustrations (emphasizing the difficulty of representing time spatially), though he never attempted it.
5 Lukacher goes so far as to say that "*Dombey and Son* clearly reveals why the forces of counter revolution were able to win in England without a fight. For the radicals themselves, like Dickens, did not focus on concrete economic and political changes" (300). One can see, by comparing this with the current work, how the representational framework within which we interpret characters can lead to radically differing conclusions.
6 This image is particularly caricatural: It is as if Dickens were confronted with the challenge of expressing this metaphoric link, or condensation, *visually* rather than verbally, overcoming the logical barrier (or limits belonging to the logos) through visual distortion.

4

Imagos, dolls, and other gazing effigies in *Bleak House*

> For imagos ... the specular image seems to be the threshold of the visible world. (Lacan, "The Mirror Stage" 5)

In considering why Dickens was so fascinated with the idea of effigy and its potential as a mode of representation, we should not forget that the effigy is primarily a visual, rather than a linguistic image, and that it is distinguished from other images by its defining relationship to absence, doubling, and spectrality. Psychoanalysts from Freud to Kristeva have attributed to visual images a unique liminal energy and a special relation to the drive, resulting traditionally from its supposed ontogenetic and phylogenetic primacy and its representational privilege in dreams. Consider for instance Kristeva's interest in the visual language of cinema and her claims that "[t]he specular transforms the drive into desire" (46), and that "the visible [image] is the port of registry of drives" (69). Add to this that the visual image (the imaginary) is bound up with the very constitution of the ego, projected, in its turn, outward onto external images and objects, as captured in the various applications of the term *imago*. Kris, for instance, suggests that "the visual image has deeper roots, is more primitive" than the linguistic, and that the use of the visual image in effigy "presupposes a belief in the identity of the sign with the thing signified" (201).

Freud too asserts the primacy of the visual image in the unconscious, particularly in the fact that dreams are fundamentally a kind of graphic writing, that they translate their signifiers primarily into visual forms of expression. Freud suggests that dream images are a specific *type* of visual image in that they are also signifiers, that they are rooted in a kind of language or syntax, in the same (or a similar) way that words are. These *dream images*, as visually or materially rooted signifiers, which Freud calls "thing-representations," are the representational material of the unconscious, that is, the language of the unconscious ("The Unconscious" 147). Laplanche and Leclaire provide a useful description of these images in their investigation of the ontological nature of unconscious representation and the theory of two "chains" of signification, one preconscious and one unconscious, distinguished by Freud partly in terms of "thing-representations" (*Sachvorstellungen*) and "word-representations" (*Wortvorstellungen*):

> Note immediately that both of these must be taken in all rigor for what they are: elements of language, signifiers. Thing-representations, Freud says, characterize the unconscious; it is these that constitute the language of dreams, concerning which we know that "topographical" regression is accompanied by a requirement of expression in a language of images ... Word-representations, words taken in their most material sense as acoustic traces, characterize the preconscious system. (257)

This distinction leads Laplanche and Leclaire to conclude that each system, preconscious and unconscious, is divisible into signifier and signified, but that "at the level of preconscious language," there is still a "distinction between preconscious signifier (words) and signified (images)," whereas "at the level of unconscious language, there are only images, serving simultaneously and inseparably as signifier and signified" (258). We have obviously reached a certain level of elusive abstraction here, but this idea that the signifiers that make up unconscious language are self-mirrored and specular is a fascinating one and means for Laplanche and Leclaire that they are characterized by a paradoxical and uncanny ontology: they are at once "pure meaning" and yet "open to all meanings" (258), and they display both extreme "fixity" and total "interchangeability" (259). Like Derrida's "image script," or Kris's idea of the *imago*, the unconscious signifier/dream image uncannily eludes and distorts our deep-seated cultural opposition between words and images: the "'words' that compose [the unconscious] are elements drawn from the realm of the imaginary—notably from visual imagination—but promoted to the dignity of signifiers. The term *imago*, somewhat fallen into disuse, corresponds fairly well ... to these elementary terms of unconscious discourse" (Laplanche and Leclaire 259).

The term *imago*, however, alludes not just to *any* image that has been "promoted to the dignity" of a signifier, but to a particular one, one that stands for an I, the ego. As Lacan points out, the mirror stage has to be understood in terms of an identification with an (other) image, or "the transformation that takes place in the subject when he assumes an image—whose predestination to the phase-effect is sufficiently indicated by the use, in analytic theory, of the ancient term *imago*" (*Ecrits* 2). Thus, while from an "intimate" perspective the ego appears as the very core of self-presence, from another perspective, that of the gaze of the Other, or the symbolic Order, the ego becomes an alien thing, an uncanny reflection of an other; that is, from an eccentric viewpoint, the ego becomes *moor eeffocish*, spectralized. The effigy is thus the uncanny zero-degree of the subject/object relation where the ego and the spectral Other becomes specular doubles: "Because of this double relation which he has with himself, all the objects of his world are always structured around the wandering shadow of his ego. They will all have a fundamentally anthropomorphic character, even egomorphic, we could say" (Lacan, *Ego* 166). This "egomorphic" shadowing between the self and others/objects should make us rethink our ontological assumptions about character, since any grounding of "identification" in a primary presence of an *I* can only be understood in an *as if* way, already reflecting the ego's "double relation" with itself.

By now we can see why effigy provided such a fascinating means of representation for Dickens, offering as it did an uncanny otherness both to the mimetic and the logocentric image (which became such signatures of the stability of realism under bourgeois capitalism). Effigy as a *form* is a likeness that is not grounded in the mirror-technology model of mimesis with its one-sided illusion of presence; although a likeness, it is not imitative but uncannily doubled, ontologically spectral like the dream image. Effigy is a threshold (non)object situated in the (non)relation between subject and object. Dickens was endlessly drawn to effigies and they populate his novels from the beginning of his career to the end, from Quilp's effigy of Kit in *The Old Curiosity Shop*, to the Wooden Midshipman in *Dombey and Son*, to Esther's Doll in *Bleak House*, and Jenny Wren the Doll's dressmaker in *Our Mutual Friend*. In *Bleak House*, moreover, as Michael Steig points out, in most of the dark plates, "the only human figures are effigies" (152). The doll, of course, is a particularly good example of an effigy/imago that stands on the threshold between things and persons; and as an object of *play* it occupies that threshold space between fantasy and reality. "With respect to things," says Agamben, "the doll is, on the one hand, infinitely lesser, because it is distant, and beyond our grasp ... but, perhaps precisely because of this, it is on the other hand infinitely more, because it is the inexhaustible object of our desire and our fantasies" (58). Agamben thus defines the doll as a privileged example of the "emblem," an object at once material and fantastic, image and logos, like the "substantial phantom" of the effigy of Kit in the *Old Curiosity Shop*. The doll, and toys in general, as Agamben points out, are genealogically traceable to objects of the more "serious" functions of ritual and memorial, to effigies, things that transgress the rigid limits of subject and object, from ancient statues and statuettes to the miniatures with which the bourgeoisie of the eighteenth and nineteenth century were fascinated. Toys, and the doll in particular, are thus invested with a certain fascination grounded in their liminality, their emblematic status as that which transgresses ontological borders: "Things that to us appear as toys were originally objects of such seriousness that they were placed in the tomb to accompany the deceased during the otherworldly sojourn" (58).

The first effigy in *Bleak House* appears at the very threshold of Esther's narrative in the form of her doll, Esther's first interlocutor in the novel. A kind of domesticated and self-referential effigy, the doll is itself an embodiment of the threshold figure par excellence, the transitional object, which functions to bridge between *Innenwelt* and *Umwelt*, or between identity and otherness. Just as the transitional object functions by *deferring* or delaying the emergence of the subject from primary narcissism, Esther's doll mediates and defers her entrance into the narrative, an entrance marked by a reluctance to record or write, "I have a great deal of difficulty in beginning to write my portion of these pages" (17), being her first words. Anxious about writing herself into the symbolic world of the novel (which begins with such cosmic, sweeping symbolic gestures by the omniscient narrator), having to address an unknown and absent Other, Esther addresses her doll instead, an externalized image of herself onto which she can immediately project a sympathetic and undemanding little other: "Now, Dolly," she says, "I am not clever, you know very well, and you must be patient with me" (17).

The first thing we learn about the doll is that it is an object that can gaze back, and even comfort in its way, but that it still carries that haunting indifference of the Midshipman, as Esther recalls that the doll "used to sit propped up in a great arm-chair, with her beautiful complexion and rosy lips, staring at me—or not so much at me, I think, as at nothing—while I busily stitched away, and told her every one of my secrets" (17). Esther is "born" into the narrative through the doll, as her narrative transitional object, and she is reproduced as a kind of doll or human effigy at the end of the novel, in the form of "Little Esther," Caddy's baby who "lie[s] quiet" all day "with its bright specks of eyes open" (599) and turns out to be "deaf and dumb" (768). That is, the doll is not merely a device used to supplement Esther's character; it inscribes her character from the outset with this representational split between the symbolic (language, writing, subjectivity) and the imaginary (reflection, imago, self as other), just as Daumier's and Grandville's caricatures split the subject between grapheme and logos. For Esther, according to the law of caricature, identifies with a particular character trait, a nodal point of her subjectivity, and this trait is precisely her symbolic reflexivity, as when she says, "I know am not clever," which, as it turns out, is a very clever thing to say in establishing her narrative voice. This symbolic reflexivity is not exactly irony—it could be said to be a kind of unreflective inversion, an irony without agency—but it implies a displacement of her own enunciations. In short, her identifying character trait involves a representational self-displacement and reversal, as if we read her character in a mirror. Far from being a mere detail in Esther's narrative, Esther's doll establishes her effigial presence or shadow in the novel, and appropriately she buries it in a shawl at the loss of her childhood home, and in a sense of her childhood itself (losing her only guardian and being sent away to boarding school) just as Esther herself "had never, to [her] mother's knowledge, breathed—had been buried" (452). Esther, as an I in narrative form, or an I capable of symbolic (self-)representation, is ineluctably linked to her projection of her own desubjectifying imago or ghostly effigy, manifested first in her doll but not buried with it. Like an effigy, the doll's uncanny gaze reflects "nothing," turning Esther into a spectral object like it.[1]

Here we can follow Helena Michie's lead when she discerned a pattern in the scholarship on *Bleak House* and found that most of the readings of Esther's character, as she says, "share a common ground: an assumption of a stable, teleological notion of the self that Esther either fails or succeeds at producing as she reproduces her godfather's house at the novel's close" (201). Michie shows how these readings all hinge upon a concept of the self that assumes an identification, based on gender repetition, between mother and daughter, and her essay opened up new critical potentials by positing a self based not on sameness, but difference: "Refusing to be locked in sameness, Esther chooses difference, even if it ultimately involves ambiguous and sometimes threatening sexual possibilities" (208). Although Michie's reading allows for an unstable self based on difference—even if Michie sees the price of this difference inscribed in the scars on Esther's face and in the dead body of her mother—the underlying teleology of her analysis, which culminates in an integration of some kind, still points to a mimetic and self-present (even teleological) subject. Audrey Jaffe takes this critical development a step further by introducing representation into the consideration of Esther's psychology, showing

Imagos, dolls, and other gazing effigies

that in Esther's character the representation of subject and object are not necessarily teleological or hierarchical, but rather the effect of a "reflexive" linguistic structure ("subject and object exist, suspended, only as reflections of one another," *Vanishing Points* 136). But even Jaffe, in the last analysis, winds up grounding her approach on a traditional notion of self that must either fail or succeed based on autonomy and wholeness, and in her reading, Esther never fully becomes a subject, only ever "the object for whom others are subjects" (*Vanishing Points* 136).

In Jaffe's model, however, Esther fails to achieve the status of an autonomous subject not, at bottom, for plot reasons, but for representational reasons, which in itself is an interesting development in the approach to character in Dickens's novels. In explaining the deficit in Esther's character, Jaffe claims that "Esther comes into existence for herself already structured by what Lacan calls the symbolic: by language, morality, and the law" (*Vanishing Points* 137). But if we are to follow these developments about characterization further, I would suggest, we should do away with the teleological notion of a self altogether, in fact, with any notion of a self that would "fail" or "succeed" as such, which still implies a mimetic principle of subjectivity, and allow for the possibility that Esther's character is grounded in a nonmimetic, and spectral, form of representation. For instance, Jaffe's point about Lacan is very promising here, but the sense of deficiency attached to it is surprising, since Lacan attaches no such implication of failure to symbolic identification. As I have discussed, becoming a subject for Lacan is inextricably bound up with the symbolic order, and there is no other existence for the subject as such but in and through the symbolic order (which Lacan also calls, "the Big Other"): "The unconscious is the sum effects of speech on a subject, at the level at which the subject constitutes himself out of the effects of the signifier," says Lacan; and again, "the subject is subject only from being subjected to the field of the Other ... [T]he subject proceeds from his synchronic subjection in the field of the Other [or the Symbolic Order]" (*FFC* 126, 188). Indeed, in keeping with Lacan's three registers of the symbolic, the imaginary, and the Real, if there is something about Esther that hints at a peculiar subjective structure, it is in fact that, representationally at least, she maintains a certain *resistance* to the symbolic order (as I have suggested above), suspended in an uncanny existence between the symbolic and what Lacan calls the imaginary, the realm of imagos, images, reflections, automata: "Everything of the order of this preverbal thus partakes of what we can call an intraworldly *Gestalt*, within which the subject is the infantile doll that he once was" (*Seminar II* 165).

"Moor eeffocish things"

This is why there is always a split quality to Esther's narrative, so that when she says of her "godmother," for instance, that she is a "good, good woman," we implicitly know she is not, but that Esther has to say she is in order to indicate this to us, as though she were a medium for certain judgments without subjectifying them. In an often unsettling and uncanny way, this ability to reflect without subjectifying can also be turned back on herself, especially regarding the image of her face. For instance, after Esther first meets her mother (to whom she is supposed to show an uncanny resemblance), Ada sees Esther's scarred face for the first time, which of course caused Esther extreme anxiety and self-consciousness, so Esther is relieved to see in Ada's face "the old dear look! All love, all fondness, all affection. Nothing else in it—no, nothing, nothing!" (*Bleak House* 456). On the surface the repetition of "nothing else ... nothing, nothing" seems to emphasize a profound relief that Ada doesn't flinch at the sight of her, but the very idea that she would show some signs of shock at seeing Esther's face, and the fact that looking at Esther and reflecting "nothing" is precisely what her doll does, makes its triple repetition here haunt Esther's representation with an effigial object-like status, a constitutive lack. But this thing-like quality is very different from the failed subjectivity imagined by Jaffe. In fact, it is profoundly reflective of the uncannily object-like status of subjectivity itself, its extimacy—the idea that at the heart of the subject there is something radically other: a lost object.

This is why it is so important to see that the doll is not a "transitional" object in the developmental sense (as in object-relations theory), as something that serves its function in a teleology after Esther has buried her doll, the imago/effigy function it embodied persists throughout the narrative in the forms of mirror images of Esther's face, of her scars, and of her doubles and her deferred relation to her self-image. When, for example, Jarndyce proposes to Esther, bringing the erotic tensions underpinning their history to the surface, she confronts her reflection in the mirror not only as a kind of double but almost as if it were a ghost, a conjured past self that she suddenly recognizes as familiar and with whom she can communicate across a gap of time: "By-and-by I went to my old glass. My eyes were red and swollen, and I said, 'O Esther, Esther, can that be you!' I am afraid the face in the glass was going to cry again at this reproach, but I held my finger up at it, and it stopped" (538). The scars therefore only reveal something that was there in Esther's character all along: a mask-like resistance to returning the gaze, as if Esther somehow has the "visor effect" (of seeing without being seen) with respect to *herself.* Thus Esther refers to her former "old face" after her illness, as if she had been conferred a new face, a mask or effigial self, for it is through the mask-like deflection of the scars that she finally sees herself as from an invisible, spectral position, seeing without being seen: "I felt for my old self," Esther says when she observes Woodcourt's sympathetic reaction to her scarred face, "as the dead may feel if they ever revisited these scenes. I was glad to be tenderly remembered, to be greatly pitied, not to be quite forgotten" (551). It seems evocative that this reunion between Esther and Woodcourt after her illness takes place in Deal, a city whose name strikingly resembles "dead," which may have been the reason for Dickens's choice of place as the working notes show an unexplained emphasis on the name: "Esther to—Plymouth—no—*Deal*" (792, emphasis in original). As Dickens puts it in his working plans for this chapter, Esther is "[g]lad to be thought of like the dead" (792), but I would suggest that Esther's mask-like scars function not like a defense mechanism or protective shield, but as a means of transference for Esther to shift from the kind of disavowal of agency implied in her childhood "cleverness" (in enunciations like "she is a good, good woman") to an ability to appropriate her own trauma, the trauma of subjectivity, the cut of the Real.

Thus whereas Esther at first glance may appear as the realist, monologic voice set off against the romantic, dreamlike, dialogic voice of the omniscient narrator, in fact this seemingly teleological narrative of progressive discoveries about her identity and the secrets of those around her masks an undercurrent of haunting displacements, effigial distortions, and representational transformations, just as "through the placid stream of [Bucket's] life, there glides an undercurrent of forefinger" (626) in a novel in which pointing fingers forge links between such ontologically different characters as Bucket the detective, Jo the illiterate street sweeper, Allegory the ceiling fresco—as well as Esther, the seemingly "failed" subject of the realist *Bildungsroman*.

In the last chapter I discussed the threat of the character of Rosa Dartle, with her expanding scar across her face, to split into two. In fact, in *Bleak House*, she does so. It has often been noted that Dickens carries characters over from one novel to another in transformed roles (Tulkinghorn, for instance, might be seen as a reincarnation of Carker; Volumnia, certainly, of Cleopatra). But in the case of Rosa Dartle, her single self-divided character is split into two separate mutually reflective characters, Rosa (Lady Dedlock's protégé) and Hortense (Lady Dedlock's maid). Hortense, of course, fancies herself to be Lady Dedlock's protégé and Rosa comes to substitute for Hortense as Lady Dedlock's maid. Thus

"Moor eeffocish things"

Rosa Dartle's more complex character is split into two related, seemingly more one-dimensional but mutually rivalrous characters: Rosa, the quiet, submissive, and attractive orphan who (like Ms. Dartle) is taken under the wing of a haughty Lady; and Hortense, the passionate and irascible woman whose beauty (like Ms. Dartle's) is disfigured by her sharpness. Hortense is even given to sarcasm (a simplified form of Rosa Dartle's irony) which is reflected in her sharp features, like Ms. Dartle's: "an enjoyment expressed, in her convivial manner, by an additional tightness of face, thin elongation of compressed lips, and sideways looks" (143). Both of these characters, or each facet of this split character, are now reduced to pure objects of desire; both share elements of effigy and as such are subject to a complex series of displacements of identity. Rosa is likened to a doll by Hortense, who is torn by jealousy by the idea of being being replaced by another *objet a* in her relation to the desire of the big Other— "this doll, this puppet, caressed—absolutely caressed—by my Lady on the moment of her arriving at the house!" (143). As a substitute for the object of Lady Dedlock's motherly affection and a narcissistic projection of her (younger) self—Lady Dedlock having lost her only child (Esther) as well as her own youth—Rosa is not only an uncanny return of Esther's doll but also a *displacement* of Esther herself in the place of her mother's affection. Thus Rosa is to Lady Dedlock as the doll is to Esther and as Esther should have been to Lady Dedlock, an uncanny parallel Esther herself registers when she says that "I knew that I had brought no joy, at any time, to anybody's heart, and that I was to no one upon earth what Dolly was to me"—a double parallel, that is, in which Esther stands in the absent place of both "dolly" (daughter) for "no one" (mother) and "anyone" (mother) for Dolly, since Rosa displaces her in this identifying symbolic relation. But since Rosa cannot ultimately fulfill the role of protégé, she is only another in the series of displacements: Esther, Hortense, Rosa ... It is interesting, then, that Hortense's anger at being displaced by Rosa is itself interrupted (displaced) by a long digression about the infinite substitutability of parliamentary figures from "Lord Boodle, Coodle, Doodle, down to Noodle," and "Lord Buffy, Cuffy, Duffy, down to Puffy." Hortense, displaced, attempts to reinsert herself in the chain of substitutes by becoming for Esther what she had been for Lady Dedlock (offering herself to Esther as a maid), but her rejection is affirmed, and at the end of this same chapter, the place she hoped to occupy is filled by Charley, a present from Jarndyce and one in a series of returns of Esther's buried doll (although, unlike the doll, Charlie can speak, she can't learn to write, and she is the childish adult in whom Esther confides all her secrets): "I am

Imagos, dolls, and other gazing effigies

a little present with his love, and it was all done for the love of you," says Charlie of herself, as though the doll in which Esther's lack of desire was buried returned from beyond the grave as pure affirmation of desire and desirability. But if Charlie is the double/effigy that mediates the desire between Esther and the fatherly Jarndyce, the Hortense–Rosa complex is a split effigy of Esther's conflicted desire for her mother: love and submissiveness (Rosa), or passion and erotic aggression (Hortense).

Hortense plays a central role in this strange allegory of effigy, perhaps secretly providing the very key to the whole representational mystery, as it were, and it is Bucket who literally unveils her part in this allegorical theater during his surreptitious investigations attempting to penetrate the secret of Lady Dedlock for Tulkinghorn in the chapter titled "Mr Bucket." As a key chapter reflecting, perhaps more explicitly than any other in the novel, the centrality of effigy and specters to characterization in *Bleak House*, this chapter warrants a closer look. The chapter "Mr Bucket," the first word of which is "Allegory," and which begins with an extended personification of the painted Allegory on Tulkinghorn's ceiling, is composed of three central scenes that link two unlikely locations: Tulkinghorn's chambers and Tom-All-Alone's. The two dramatic centers of the chapter are the journey to the London slums to find Jo so he can confirm Tulkinghorn's suspicions about Lady Dedlock's secret associations, and the rather uncanny scene in which Mr. Bucket brings Jo to Tulkinghorn's chambers to gaze upon Hortense, whom he has mysteriously planted there like a veiled statue, so that Jo could bear witness to her uncanny referentiality to Lady Dedlock, that "it is her and it an't her," as he concludes (283).

In this Hamlet-like, allegorically framed "play" or dumb show that he stages for Tulkinghorn and Jo, Bucket transforms Hortense into an effigy as a key to revealing secrets about the identity of Lady Dedlock. Bucket orchestrates the scene so that when they enter they confront a kind of spectral entity: "A female figure, closely veiled, stands in the middle of the room, where the light falls upon it. It is quite still and silent. The front of the figure is towards them, but it takes no notice of their entrance, and remains like a statue" (283). This "figure"—Hortense disguised as Lady Dedlock disguised as Hortense—seems, as if conjured by Bucket, to speak and act only according to subtle cues by him and in order to evoke reliable testimony from Jo. It is worth quoting the dialogue at length here.

> "Now, tell me," says Bucket aloud, "how you know that to be the lady."
> "I know the wale," replies Jo, staring, "and the bonnet, and the gownd."

> "Be quite sure of what you say, Tough," returns Bucket, narrowly observant of him. "Look again."
>
> "I am a-looking as hard as ever I can look," says Jo with starting eyes, "and that there's the wale, the bonnet, and the gownd."
>
> "What about those rings you told me of?" asks Bucket.
>
> "A-sparkling all over here," says Jo, rubbing the fingers of his left hand on the knuckles of his right without taking his eyes from the figure.
>
> The figure removes the right-hand glove and shows the hand.
>
> "Now, what do you say to that?" asks Bucket.
>
> Jo shakes his head. "Not rings a bit like them. Not a hand like that."
>
> "What are you talking of?" says Bucket, evidently pleased though, and well pleased too.
>
> "Hand was a deal whiter, a deal delicater, and a deal smaller," returns Jo.
>
> "Why, you'll tell me I'm my own mother next," says Mr Bucket. "Do you recollect the lady's voice?"
>
> "I think I does," says Jo.
>
> The figure speaks. "Was it at all like this? I will speak as long as you like if you are not sure. Was it this voice, or at all like this voice?"
>
> Jo looks aghast at Mr Bucket. "Not a bit!" (283)

Jo, who instinctively recognizes—perhaps his illiteracy here gives him the advantage of not being misdirected by the signifier—that this figure cannot be the same Lady Dedlock he encountered even if in the same disguise, can only fathom this uncanny staged encounter as a dreamlike repetition of identities, or a conjurer's trick: "It is her and it an't her," he says perplexedly, just as later he will say when he sees Esther, "Is there *three* of 'em then?" (383).

And indeed Jo's interpretation is in a way truer than the realist one, since the veiled effigy, here performed by Hortense, establishes a series of identifications between characters and effigies throughout the novel, such as Esther's buried doll, Jenny's dead baby whom Esther covers with a handkerchief, Lady Dedlock hidden behind her veil, and Esther peeking through the veil of her hair to see her disfigured face reflected in the mirror. This theatrical scene, in fact, sparks a chain of events that leads eventually to Tulkinghorn's murder, since Hortense considers him indebted to her for her involvement and seeks revenge when he brushes her aside instead of compensating her with his personal recommendation to a wealthy family. Moreover, it is the symbolic function of effigy dramatized here that overdetermines the whole murder-mystery plot respecting Lady Dedlock, Hortense, and Tulkinghorn: playing the role of Lady Dedlock's effigy that exposes her identity and subjects her to Tulkinghorn's blackmail, Hortense is compelled to pursue that symbolic

Imagos, dolls, and other gazing effigies

role to its conclusion by taking revenge for her in effigy and murdering Tulkinghorn in her place. The social guilt for that murder which releases Lady Dedlock from Tulkinghorn's power is, from another perspective, assumed in effigy by Hortense. In short, the symbolic role of effigy completely subsumes Hortense's character. This use of effigy to displace and channel retribution will be discussed in more detail shortly in relation to Esther and Tom-All-Alone's.

The journey from Chancery to Tom-All-Alone's to fetch Jo, which occupies much of this chapter leading up to the veiled effigy scene, centers on another, more subtle but related use of effigy. In the process of this crossing over into the Dantesque underworld of the London slums, while waiting for Jo in a dark collapsing hovel, Bucket stumbles (almost literally) upon Jenny, Liz, and Liz's newborn baby sleeping among the vagrants. It will be remembered that Esther had witnessed the death of Jenny's baby upon a charitable visit to her home with Mrs. Pardiggle and had laid her handkerchief (which will eventually turn up with Lady Dedlock) over the little corpse.[2] The muted emotional loss of that earlier scene finds displaced expression in possessive affection for the infant in this scene but transferred from Jenny's dead baby to Liz's living baby, as if it were a double or effigy of the dead one: "I was the mother of one like it, master, and it died," says Jenny, explaining her intense attachment to Liz's baby. As the baby becomes the focal point of the scene it is first allegorized—"Mr Snagsby is strangely reminded of another infant, encircled with light, that he has seen in pictures" (279)—and then immediately compared by its mother to Jenny's dead infant: "Much better to think of dead than alive, Jenny! Much better!" (279). Esther's childhood suffering and loss of her mother are thus also transferred, as social and existential crisis, onto this infant effigy poised between a mother who lost her infant and a mother that clings to hers under the most precarious of prospects of survival. This transference resonates throughout the entire dialogue: Liz's claim that she would "stand between [her child] and death ... as true as any pretty lady," evokes Lady Dedlock's (apparent) failure to do so for Esther, and Jenny's attempt to justify her fear "of its being taken away from [its mother] now" in its infancy (279, 280) echoes Esther's family story. That is, the infant's body here becomes an effigy of loss itself—for what effigy more universally represents the social pathos of loss than the infant body of Christ?—an "effigy of the absent" (to use Jean-Luc Nancy's phrase) that crosses the threshold of living and dead, and of singular identity and the symbolic Other.

"Moor eeffocish things"

If effigy here has the paradoxical function in *Bleak House* of exposing rents in the social fabric by weaving unlikely nodal points between subjects (and objects) across social antagonisms, it does so by embodying a gaze-beyond-death, or beyond the signifier, as a potential to render absence visible, and thus to bear witness—the potential for a subject to be the bearer of social witnessing or the gaze. Death is "brought into [Liz's] head," she says, as she "look[s] down at the child lying so" (280). The thought of the baby never opening its eyes inspires an appeal to "look at" and bear witness to the state of existence that engulfs it: "If [my child] was never to wake no more," Liz exhorts Bucket, "you'd think me mad, I should take on so. I know that very well. I was with Jenny when she lost hers ... But look around you, at this place. Look at them [the poor sleeping on the ground] ... Look at the boy you're waiting for" (280). Bucket hadn't intended to "look at" Jo; he had intended to engage Jo as a witness to the duplicity of Lady Dedlock's character as constructed in Tulkinghorn's covetous fantasies. But the effigial (living/dead) infant he stumbles upon unexpectedly reconfigures the scene for him (and thus us), as this detour from his intended purpose suddenly makes *Bucket* the unwitting witness to a metonymic chain of social effects and ontological disparities, and his authorial association draws the reader into this effigial gaze as well. A "realistic" or objective description of a London slum would not capture the Real here, only the particular social conditions of a dramatic scene—as it would merely be another means of bourgeois representation or symbolic inclusion and thus lack access to the trauma of subjectivity itself that gives the scene its universality. This is exactly Žižek's point when he criticizes the realist desire to "[describe] the world, reality, the way it exists out there, independently of us, observing subjects," rather than the position of Lacanian materialism that aims to represent "as if we are observing ourselves through inhuman eyes" in order achieve "something much more uncanny, a radical shift in the subjective attitude by means of which we become strangers to ourselves" (*Disparities* 328–9). This is also precisely what Jaffe misses (the opportunity to explore) in her distinction between realism and the Real. The Real of Tom-All-Alone's, in other words, becomes visible only through a kind of stain in the scene, an impossible gaze of an absent dead infant that distorts the fantasy of a coherent social whole, made possible by a series of uncanny displacements—the uncanny effigial links from Esther to the dead infant to the living infant to Bucket (with his hints of omniscience) to the reader. Through associations with the dead baby Esther covered with her shawl, with Esther's buried doll (and all of its associations with Esther's subjectivity), and with Esther herself as child lost at birth to her mother, Liz's

Imagos, dolls, and other gazing effigies

baby links Esther to Tom-All-Alone's in a kind of *effigial gaze*. Looking at Liz's living child Jenny sees not what is present before her, but an effigy of the absent: "'It's my dead child,' says Jenny, walking up and down as she nurses, 'that makes me love this child so dear, and it's my dead child that makes her love it so dear too'" (280). That pause punctuating what could for a moment seem to be a shocking deictic statement, "It's my dead child," delaying its predication, breaks with mimetic reference in positing the dead in the place of the living so that the baby, by being at once present and effigial, dead and alive, itself and other, in short, spectral, forges a link between the perspectives of "us two mothers," as Jenny says, while also making Esther a spectral (absent) presence in both scenes, in the form of the dead gaze of the effigial infant in Tom-All-Alone's and in the veiled figure of the lost mother in Tulkinghorn's chamber.

As in the case of the other novels I have discussed so far, the function of effigy in *Bleak House* could only be partially understood without a close analysis of the illustrations and their enigmatic relation to the narrative. Steig does a remarkable job of discovering many of the connections—iconographic, thematic, and compositional—between the illustrations of *Bleak House*, revealing (for the first time) the complex way in which these plates parallel, reflect on, and anticipate one another. Yet somehow Steig doesn't quite seem to capture the eerily uncanny quality of the dark plates, a quality, I would argue, that comes in part from a certain liminality inherent to them, a play of presence and absence at work in and between the illustrations and the text, embodied particularly in their use of effigy. Steig himself points out that in most of the dark plates, "the only human figures are effigies" (152). The most frequent of these effigies in the illustrations throughout the novel is that of the doll. The doll, as mentioned above, is introduced in the text at the threshold of Esther's narrative, and is introduced in the illustrations on the threshold of Esther's entrance into the world of Chancery (though as a device used by Phiz, it dates at least back to Brogley's pawn shop from *Dombey and Son*, in very a similar milieu) in "The Lord Chancellor Copies from Memory" (Figure 16). In this illustration, Esther and Krook face the wall, on which Krook traces the letter "J," with their backs to us, and in the right corner, hanging in a frame (a doorway or a window frame) is a small doll next to a large key and a demonic mask, as if to show in effigy that Esther is entering into a world of mystery and of dark forces. As does not seem to have been noted by Steig, or anyone else for that matter, neither Krook nor Esther are looking at the writing on the wall, but rather Krook is gazing at Esther and Esther is staring down into an open pit,[3] "a kind of well in the floor"

"Moor eeffocish things"

16 Phiz (Hablot K. Browne), "The Lord Chancellor Copies from Memory," etching for *Bleak House*, 1853.

(as the narrator explains), through an open trap door, filled with packets of waste paper, in which, towards the end of the novel, after Krook's combustion, Smallweed will "dig and delve" and Judy will grope "like a female sexton" and from which Smallweed will disinter the key to the mystery of the Jarndyce suit—but too late—the lost will.

There have, of course, been numerous readings of this almost maddeningly allegorical scene of writing that seems to dangle an ever elusive "key" to its own deciphering before our eyes and that in its gestural dumb show of inscribing/erasing teases our gaze with the opacity of even the most elementary signifiers. Yet in all of the interpretations of this illustration and this scene that Dickens criticism has produced, has the most *literal*

Imagos, dolls, and other gazing effigies

one even been considered?—that perhaps Krook is writing "Jarndyce" on the wall because he has *just now* tossed the will in question into the well in the floor into which Esther is gazing, before her very eyes? Since Krook can't read, we might assume his copying "from memory" would be from rather short-term memory. And in fact, later in the novel, just before Krook's spontaneous combustion, Guppy tells Jobling, when asked if he has any documents of real value, that "[h]e is always spelling words from them, and chalking them over the table and the shop-wall, and asking what this is, and what that is; but the whole stock from beginning to end, may easily be the waste paper he bought it as" (401). Are Esther and Krook looking directly at traces of the tragic mystery that eludes them, missing the signs right before their faces?—or looking directly at the key to that mystery without seeing it because of their fragmented perspectives, just as Krook writes letters on the wall without being able to read the meaning of the words they form? If this reading is correct (and it is at least suggested by the positioning of the gazes in the illustration and details of the text), there is certainly something demonic in the Kafkaesque joke of tossing the one key to end the suffering of everyone involved (Esther's sickness, Richard's death, Ada's solitude and widowhood, to mention only those in the present scene) down a well right in front of them, or of concealing it most effectively by pointing it out in plain sight, and yet it would accord with the Kafkaesque hilarity at the end of the suit when all the lawyers are doubled over with laughter at the ridiculousness of its all ending in a pointless joke. But of course the joke itself is not without allegorical implications. And it is a particularly uncanny joke at the expense of the reader as well, as Dickens shows us the cards he holds openly in order best to conceal them: our gaze is evoked and elided in the same sleight-of-hand gesture. In any case the doll/mask/key cluster of images hanging in the corner of the room resonates in elusive ways as specters of both Esther's past and future. John O. Jordan provides a wonderful discussion of the many specters that haunt the novel and its illustrations, noting in particular how "after [Krook] has disappeared, Krook's room is described as 'ghostly with traces of its dead inhabitant, and even with his chalked writing on the wall'" (Jordan 115).

After its visual introduction in "The Lord Chancellor Copies from Memory," The doll appears in two more illustrations, "The Appointed Time" (Figure 17), depicting the remnants of Krook's spontaneous combustion, and the famous "Tom-All-Alone's" (Figure 19), depicting an empty street in the abandoned London slum as Woodcourt wonders though at dawn. But I will first address the former illustration, from

"Moor eeffocish things"

17 Phiz (Hablot K. Browne), "The Appointed Time," etching for *Bleak House*, 1853.

chapter 32 in the novel, in relation to another, much later plate, "A New Meaning in the Roman" (Figure 18) from chapter 68. In "The Appointed Time" the doll appears hovering above the smoking residue of Krook's spontaneous combustion, only this time with a facial expression of surprise and eyes aghast as though it had witnessed the ghastly event, which links it to the pointing Allegory, the "paralyzed dumb witness" in "A New

Imagos, dolls, and other gazing effigies

18 Phiz (Hablot K. Browne), "A New Meaning in the Roman," dark plate etching for *Bleak House*, 1853.

Meaning in the Roman" that witnesses Tulkinghorn's mysterious death. And in fact, if we look closely at the doll that witnessed (the only witness) Krook's spontaneous combustion, we realize that not only is it in a compositional position similar to that of the effigy of Roman Allegory in the latter plate, but it also points down at the spot on the floor where Krook's smoldering remains lay, just as the Roman Allegory points at the traces of Tulkinghorn's murder on the floor. Both effigies, Allegory and the doll, that is, are near the ceiling (slightly left of center top), pointing down below (slightly right of center bottom) at the absent subject in each image, a missed death, or better, the traces of an absent corpse haunting an empty room with its effigial gaze, at the presence of *nobody*—not unlike Dombey gazing at the reflections in the dining room table.

If the pointing doll in "The Appointed Time" thus points us to a new meaning in "A New Meaning in the Roman," by way of gazing effigies, the Roman's connection to the doll points us in turn to another new meaning in "The Lord Chancellor Copies from Memory," in which a giant key appears next to the doll associated with Esther. The Roman Allegory is of course associated with Tulkinghorn, and by the time of Tulkinghorn's death, the signifier *key* becomes associated with Tulkinghorn's character and his symbolic concealment (like allegory) as well, as Tulkinghorn holds the "key" to a great many homes of wealthy families along with all their invaluable secrets. He also has a dazzling array of keys of his own, which seem to exist in metonymic relation to each other, like partial clues in a narrative leading to darker mysteries: "Not humoring [the Roman Allegory] with much attention, Mr Tulkinghorn takes a small key from his pocket, unlocks a drawer in which there is another key, which unlocks a chest in which there is another, and so comes to the cellar-key, with which he prepares to descend to the regions of old wine" (57). Of these, Tulkinghorn flourishes a large phallic key at Hortense when she comes to his chamber, which, far from putting her under his power, helps incite her to murderous rage: "Look, mistress, this is the key of my wine-cellar. It is a large key, but the keys of prisons are larger." Keys are an overdetermined symbol in the representation of Tulkinghorn's character: they signify his own symbolic opacity and deliberate secrecy, and the many secrets others entrust in him, but they also suggest the more guarded psychic dimensions of his character, such as the repressed eroticism of his pure will-to-power, and his uncannily erotic enjoyment of concealment itself. Keys are also suggestive of allegory in general (allegory always requires a key), and the fact that his largest key opens the door to his wine cellar where he stores his stash of "radiant" old port, gives him the mythical

Imagos, dolls, and other gazing effigies

aspect of a vampire. Thus the key hanging next to the doll in "The Lord Chancellor Copies from Memory" symbolizes not only Esther's entrance into the dark mysteries of the suit, but the dangerous secrets about her own identity (of which she herself is still unconscious) Tulkinghorn will soon come to possess through his erotic drive to plumb the secret mysteries of Lady Dedlock.

In a sense, then, the key in the mask–key–doll cluster of images/objects in the corner of the illustration gives Tulkinghorn a retroactive presence in the scene through the pointing doll–pointing/Allegory–key–Tulkinghorn cluster of associations. This helps account for the darkly haunting impression of many of the illustrations in *Bleak House*. Similarly, in "A New Meaning in the Roman" we seem to see only an empty room, but dead center and taking up much of the scene is an old press—presumably the press from which Bucket seemed to emerge on that former occasion when he observed unseen while Snagsby revealed information to Tulkinghorn that would lead them to seek Jo as a witness in the quest to unravel Lady Dedlock's mystery. With that in mind, the object itself seems to channel into the empty unsolved crime scene a potential to be seen even when there seems to be no subject present to do the seeing.

Perhaps the most well-known, as well as the most elusive plate from *Bleak House* is "Tom-All-Alone's" (Figure 19). Steig makes some wonderful observations about the composition of this plate, most importantly that "Browne has framed the upper edge of the plate with a horizontal brace between the two houses so that the very sky seems to be held up by this untrustworthy support, a brilliant way of underlying the relation between the condition of Tom-All-Alone's and the rest of society" (151). Steig's observation is quite suggestive; moreover, by internalizing the frame in the form of a wooden "brace" (a sign of collapse), which is further internalized and echoed in the various wooden beams and braces repeated throughout the image, Phiz's illustration raises some crucial questions about perspective, in effect offering the acts of looking and framing themselves as gestures of omission, editing, cropping—gestures that evoke both the limits and potentials inherent in perspective. But there is another question imbedded in this image that does not seem to have been expressly articulated and that stems from its unexpectedly elusive relationship to the text. That is, most novelistic illustrations have a narrative function, but this illustration appears to be oddly torn out of its narrative context, to represent the empty streets of the London district Tom-All-Alone's as a *setting*, rather than as the unfolding or even aftermath of a particular drama (for example, the moment after Krook's combustion or Tulkinghorn's murder). Yet if we pay close attention to the iconographic details in the illustration, we can see that the plate in fact suggests *two* possible narrative scenes. The title of the chapter, "Stop Him," refers to the central action of the chapter, Woodcourt chasing Jo through the streets of Tom-All-Alone's (thinking he may be a thief) and capturing him, so one might therefore have expected Phiz to have chosen this chase scene, a "grimly ridiculous pursuit" that Dickens depicts in detail, as a more dramatic subject matter than an empty street. Yet, of course, there are no living characters at all in this illustration, let alone any action taking place. On the other hand, one might assume that the plate illustrates the streets of the slum from the perspective of Woodcourt who in the opening of the chapter wanders through them in the early dawn to escape the pains of insomnia (a habit, of course, for which Dickens himself is well known), "stroll[ing] hitherward at this quiet time," when "nothing is to be seen but the crazy houses, shut up and silent" (*Bleak House* 553). Yet Woodcourt is at this point wandering through the streets leisurely and in the illustration we stare straight down a no-thoroughfare whose way is blocked by the wooden beams, which would seem a very odd iconographic incongruity. I would suggest, then, that this illustration can be properly placed only if we assume that the illustration *does* depict the chase scene, only not from the perspective of Woodcourt, but from the first-person perspective of the fleeing *Jo* the moment before he is caught, as if we are seeing through Jo's eyes like a camera lens. Dickens's description of the moment when Jo is caught would accord perfectly with this reading: "At last the fugitive, hard-pressed, takes a narrow passage, and a court which has no thoroughfare. Here, against a hoarding of decaying timber, he is brought to bay, and tumbles down, lying gasping at his pursuer" (556). Indeed we see that in the illustration the way is blocked by a mound of dirt and barred by the crossbeam that holds up a crumbling house, and that the court leads only to a cemetery (a nothoroughfare in more senses than one). If we look on the right we see the "hoarding of decaying timber" into which Jo will momentarily collapse. Giving the viewer the direct point of view of Jo would put this plate in a unique relation to the other dark plates. While the other dark plates depict effigies that are mute witnesses of events that have been missed by human observers, Tom-All-Alone's gives us the perspective of this effigial gaze itself in the form of the quasi-mute "rejected witness" Jo, looking down at no thoroughfare that will "stop him" momentarily. This gives the illustration a strange déjà vu effect, linking it (and Jo's perspective) with an earlier plate, "The Ghost's Walk," which shows an empty scene from

19 Phiz (Hablot K. Browne), "Tom-All-Alone's," dark plate etching for *Bleak House*, 1853.

the perspective of Esther, just before she enters it only to be met with the uncanny feeling that her destiny had brought her there, that the steps on the Ghost's Walk prophesied her own all along: "it was I, who was to bring calamity upon the stately house; and that my warning feet were haunting it even then" (497).

But does the fact that these details can be explained by assuming the plate illustrates Jo's point of view clear up the apparent ambiguity in perspective, the fact that it seems to be linked to Woodcourt and is simply titled "Tom-All-Alone's" rather than given a more dramatic title? I suspect that many readers simply see this illustration as a "setting," or a peek at Tom-All-Alone's—a curious place we have "seen" in the narrative but not yet in the illustrations—thereby linking it with Woodcourt's perspective, and this is certainly justified since the narrator adopts Woodcourt's point of view for the chapter's opening description of Tom-All-Alone's and hovers about his point of view throughout the rest of the chapter. The answer then is no, not only is the ambiguity not cleared up, but seems deeply embedded in the illustrations itself. For instance, despite the invitation to see the illustrated scene from Woodcourt's viewpoint, most of the iconographic images in the illustration are associated directly or indirectly with Jo, via allusions to icons from other illustrations featuring Jo, so there is an unconscious force of visual association supplementing the apparent narrative association and reinforcing the split in perspective between the two viewpoints. The post that sticks up from the dirt in the foreground reproduces exactly the post on which Jo is leaning with his broom in "Jo, the Crossing-Sweeper." The sign with a small animal to the right also appears, and in the same compositional position, in the plate "Consecrated Ground" next to Jo who points through the bars of a grate at Nemo's remains, paralleling in turn the Roman pointing at Tulkinghorn's remains and the doll pointing at Krook's remains, and in the far background of "Tom-All-Alone's" is a gate and a cemetery, looming above which is what Steig points out are the "pawnbroker's three balls, symbol of decline into poverty" (151). The perspective of this plate somehow manages, in an empty scene, to implicate two very different points of view, that of Woodcourt and of Jo, and perhaps another as well, as I will discuss shortly. But in any case there is a social antagonism played out in the *perspective itself* in this plate: between the apparent point of view of Woodcourt and the implied point of view of Jo. We *look at* this scene from a split viewpoint, both from that of the "good" bourgeois that can't see its gaze, and from that of the poor waif who is its gaze.

But I have still yet to address the detail in "Tom-All-Alone's" that is most relevant to this discussion, the one iconographic detail not clearly linked in some way to Jo: the doll hanging above a doorway on the left side of the street. Perhaps the doll suggests, for one thing, Esther's unfortunate connection to Jo (the infection Jo brought from Tom-All-Alone's that caused her illness and scarred her face), of which he is unaware, and that is partly the motivation for Jenny to track him down in this scene. But it also has, I would argue, another significance altogether in this plate, by way of importing a visual allusion from an unexpected source. Steig sees the inspiration of this plate in Hogarth's "Gin Lane," "probably by way of the novelist's own knowledge of that engraving" (150). Surely Dickens and Phiz get some iconographic inspiration from "Gin Lane" here, but even a glance at that illustration's composition (which is teeming with people) will show they are radically different in style, and it might even be said that this dark plate—with its haunting shadows and dreamlike use of gloomy shading—is among the least Hogarthian of Phiz's work. Moreover, the illustration is clearly not concerned with the vice of drunkenness or its moral relation to poverty here, so if we are looking for a more symbolic or stylistic (as opposed to iconographic) source of inspiration, we would have to look elsewhere altogether.

There is, however, another possible source of inspiration for this plate in a lithograph by Daumier titled "Ah! His! ... Ah! His! Ah! His!" ("Heave-Ho! ... Heave-Ho! Heave-Ho!" Figure 20), which first appeared in Philipon's *La Caricature* in 1832 and was reproduced for sale as an independent print thereafter. This wonderfully dreamlike illustration depicts a darkened and shadowy barn in which three faceless figures heave the taught cord of a pulley that hangs a huge ponderous pear—Louis-Philippe's ominous effigy—from the barn's lofty rafters, which also frame the scene. Phiz's use of darkness for tone through his dark plate-etching technique (probably inspired by the dark tonality of the lithograph and in particular those of Daumier) is quite similar to Daumier's, and the compositional similarity is particularly striking in both artists' use of beams and supports to frame the scene; also, the mound of earth on the bottom in both images subtly suggests a grave. Though there are three human figures in Daumier's scene, they are faceless and condensed together in the shadows in a rather conglomerate fashion (more like a single shape with several legs and heads, not unlike the crowd of vagrants that flits through Tom-All-Alone's). And both plates seem to construct a kind of metonymic enclosure, a closed off, claustrophobic space that uncannily

"Moor eeffocish things"

20 Honoré Daumier, "Ah His! ... Ah His! Ah His!" ("Heave-Ho! Heave-Ho! Heave-Ho!"), lithograph published in *La Caricature*, July 19, 1832.

Imagos, dolls, and other gazing effigies

exposes a larger social antagonism in its air of suspense, especially in the immensely ponderous collapse looming above: the enormous pear barely suspended by the tiny rope and the teetering heavers in Daumier's illustration; the slanting propped-up houses and "the very sky" barely held up by the old wooden braces in Phiz's.

Beyond the visual composition, there is also a symbolic connection between these two illustrations: although it may not at first be apparent, the central parallel is that each plate depicts a hanging effigy in the midst of its desolate scene, Daumier's pear and Phiz's doll. Of course, the doll does not expressly represent hanging in the same sense as the pear does, but the ominous mound of earth beneath, the cemetery in the background, and the cross beams looming above the doll all subtly suggest a darker subtext here (not to mention the relations of dolls and effigies to murder and strange deaths in the other illustrations). Moreover, this thematic parallel of social retribution or revolutionary violence symbolized in effigy is mirrored in the text of this chapter as well. The striking analogy here is that in Daumier's plate the entire system, up to its highest representative (the king), is threatened to be torn down by the lowest, by the undifferentiated faceless workers in a barn, precisely via the symbolic power of effigy. Dickens puts this subversive mechanism of effigy to similar use in his description of Tom-All-Alone's in the chapter "Stop Him," with one sentence in particular capturing the sweeping symbolic gesture from bottom to top, from "an atom of ... slime" to the "highest of the high," reflected so perfectly in Daumier's image: "There is not an atom of Tom's slime, not a cubic inch of any pestilential gas in which he lives, not one obscenity or degradation about him, not an ignorance, not a wickedness, not a brutality of his committing, but shall work its retribution, through every order of society, up to the proudest of the proud, and to the highest of the high" (553). To make the comprehensiveness of this social retribution chillingly intimate, we see the doll associated with Esther, Esther who has suffered severe illness and near death due to her indirect connection with Tom-All-Alone's, hanging in effigy in the slum's streets—no one, good or bad, is outside the reach of the effects of social iniquity or its retribution. Just as one of the foreboding names Jo was called by in Tom-All-Alone's, at Bucket's earlier trip there, was "Gallows" (278), Tom-All-Alone's haunts bourgeois English society with the spectral trace of an effigial gallows. The use of the inhabitants of Tom-All-Alone's to represent the poor in general, which is then condensed into the single personification "Tom," to represent that symbolic retribution, is akin to Daumier's visual condensation of the group of workers into a single anonymous composite acting as a person to hang the effigy of Louis-Philippe. As Kerr points out, "[t]he invention of the pear marked a step in the increasing vehemence of *La Caricature*'s campaign against the king, for it allowed Philipon to publish caricatures of an altogether more violent nature" (85). It is the same mechanism of effigy itself, just as Dickens's gets retribution on the Chancery legal system for the injustices to society by *exploding it in effigy* in the spontaneous combustion of the other "Lord Chancellor," Krook.

I have called the illustration "Tom-All-Alone's" dreamlike, which depends on seeing it in the context of the rich texture of symbols woven throughout the text and the other dark plates and that makes it a good example of what Derrida calls the "polycentrism of dream representation" (*Writing and Difference* 217). In it, hanging in effigy is everywhere and nowhere, and, like a dream image, it is haunted by absent signifiers. In fact, the doll effigy hanging in the streets of Tom-All-Alone's echoes other images of Esther as a revenant, or as hanging in effigy, that resonate throughout *Bleak House*. Esther's words that end the chapter immediately preceding "Stop Him," just before we see the doll associated with her hanging in the dark empty streets of Tom-All-Alone's, are: "I felt for my old self as the dead may feel if they ever revisit these scenes" (551). After meeting her mother, Esther considers that "it would have been better … if indeed I had never breathed" for Lady Dedlock, "against whom," like Jo, "[she] was a witness" (453). We can now look back at "The Lord Chancellor Copies from Memory" (Figure 16) and see that the "J" of Jarndyce that Krook traced on the wall behind him twists up like a noose, and that the cat's tail dangles above his head like a rope, and that the doll hangs from a string in the corner, and that the well full of wills and other deathly documents at Esther's feet could as easily be imagined as a gallows' trapdoor. But as the prevalence of letters, writing, and documents constantly reminds us, this theme of effigy and hanging is always bound up with representation, with the signifier and its symbolic order. It is even tempting to see Dickens allegorizing this symbolic dimension of effigy in a little scene involving writing and the one double in the novel that seems to reflect Esther, Esther's doll, and (through her name at least) Dickens himself, Charley: when she tries to teach Charley to write (or imitate her writing), Esther tells us that "every pen appeared to become perversely animated" in Charley's hand, and when trying to copy an O "the pen wouldn't join Charley's neatly, but twisted it up into a knot" … and occasionally a "pear-shaped" knot, of all things (378).

Imagos, dolls, and other gazing effigies

Before concluding this chapter I would like to return to what I called earlier the use of effigy to "displace and channel retribution" in relation to Hortense and Jenny's infant, but here in relation to Esther and the doll in the illustration of Tom-All-Alone's. It is precisely here that I think the concept of effigy and the gaze can be so useful in thinking through the difference between the form of the realist novel and Dickens's form of spectral representation. I say this because the idea of effigy being used as a symbol for social antagonisms can, when applied to character, easily be confused with the idea of the scapegoat. This is precisely the argument Audrey Jaffe makes in her discussion of Esther in *Vanishing Points: Dickens, Narrative, and the Subject of Omniscience*:

> Esther's story "contains" the anxiety about knowledge that the other narrative displays; as personal history, her secret can be known, contained, expunged. But if an answer to supposedly objective conditions can be localized in the individual subject, it is also the case that the subject has been constructed to serve precisely that function: to fall ill and be cured, in a process that keeps society from seeing itself as needing a "cure." (147)

I would point out here that one can only see Esther as a scapegoat for social "ills," or antagonisms, if one first posits that Esther's character must be understood as a representation of a realist bourgeois subject, an "individual subject," and then determines that her character fails in precisely that function. This seems to be both circular and counterproductive, to be closed-minded to the idea that there are *other forms* of characterization at work here. The spectral character does not serve to "localize" or "contain" social antagonisms—in fact, I would say, the concept of the realist character is all too often itself an attempt to reify, to particularize the universal as a kind of defense mechanism against it. Whereas the idea of the imago, for instance, incorporates the idea of negativity or lack precisely as a representation of something that can't be "contained" or symbolized. Jean-Luc Nancy describes this quality nicely in *The Ground of the Image*: "The word *imago* designates the effigy of the absent, the dead, and, more precisely, the ancestors: the dead from whom we come, the links of the lineage in which each of us is a stitch. The *imago* hooks into the cloth. It does not repair the rip of their death: it does less and more than that. It weaves, it images absence" (67). The idea of a (lacking) signifier that "hooks into," weaves, and "images" absence, the past, death, into a universal, without repressing or repairing or "curing" the whole or text in which it appears, can serve as a good metaphor for what distinguishes spectral characterization from realist representation, since by the very laws of its form realism needs to resolve itself or make present its subject in some way. On the other hand, it doesn't at all accord with my experience of reading *Bleak House* to see it ultimately as a work that conserves, that contains anxiety and distracts from "social ills." The effigial gaze allows us to see social antagonisms precisely by resisting the temptation to particularize them in individual subjects. We can see the *Real* of Tom-All-Alone's, in its universal dimension, only because it is inscribed, haunted from within, by an effigial gaze that transcends the particular subject. The effigial gaze does not "expunge" anxiety and antagonism; like the doll, or the infant displacing another dead infant in Tom-All-Alone's, it haunts us with their promised return. The effigial or spectral character does not assuage social trauma by substituting a social antagonism with a "personal history" to be repaired—it offers *subjectivity itself* as the trauma, the cut in the big Other or the symbolic network.

Notes

1 John Carey points out that "this is the final element in the spell which effigies cast over [Dickens] … They turn you into an object, because their stare acknowledges nothing human in you" (103).
2 See Carolyn Dever's excellent analysis of this strand of the plot, especially relating to the handkerchief, in *Death and the Mother from Dickens to Freud: Victorian Fiction and the Anxiety of Origins*.
3 Though the faces are rather obscured in this print, it is quite clear from the position of Esther's head and the height of the letter on the wall that Esther is looking not at the letter but down the well. Remarkably, most critics who address this plate seem to see Esther looking at the writing on the wall and few seem to note the well on the floor at all.

Part III

Beyond the realism principle: spectral materiality

5

Dream as spectral form in *Bleak House* and the comic surplus of Micawber in *David Copperfield*

What we have, in short, is something rather new and spectacular. Such a breakthrough in literature would in the nature of the case have to be largely unconscious; it could not at first have been understood by the person who was the bearer of such a force. For Dickens has committed himself at the outset of *The Pickwick Papers* to something like pure writing, to language itself. No novelist had, I believe, ever done this in such a measure before—certainly not Sterne. (Marcus, "Language into Structure" 137)

I am no longer anything. My ambition was greater than I ... And precisely to the extent that I desired it too much, that I partook in this action, that I wanted to be, myself, the creator, I am not the creator. The creator is someone greater than I. It is my unconscious, it is the voice which speaks in me, beyond me. (Lacan, *Ego in Freud's Theory* 170–1)

In his seminal essay "Language into Structure: Pickwick Revisited," Marcus himself makes a breakthrough in Dickens criticism—one that, however, has yet to make itself fully felt, has yet to be confronted in all its implications. Marcus points out something crucial and unequivocal: there is a change in the history of English literature; something unique, something that hadn't existed before, comes into being at a certain moment in history, through Dickens. The novel, he says, with *The Pickwick Papers*, "becomes ... airborne" ("Language into Structure" 136). Marcus isn't the only one to note a change in the course of the novel precipitated by Dickens, but he *is* the first to name so explicitly this "breakthrough":

> Dickens was able to abandon himself or give expression to what Freud called the primary process in a degree that was unprecedented in English fictional prose; he was able to let the fundamental and primitive mental processes of condensation, displacement, and equivalence or substitution find

their way into consciousness with a minimum of inhibition, impedence, or resistance. ("Language into Structure" 137)

This is a tremendous claim, yet in it one is confronted with a kind of ambiguity, inasmuch as this breakthrough is expressed by Marcus in mainly passive terms: Dickens "abandoned himself" and "let" other forces (the primary processes) "find their way" into his writing. So why this passive position of the "creator" or author of this breakthrough, of the very subject who should lay claim to it? And how are these fundamentally linguistic processes (condensation, displacement, and substitution) to be distinguished so radically in Dickens's writing from presumably more conscious processes in other authors on merely linguistic grounds? If the author is only a medium for the breakthrough that could "not at first have been understood by the person who was the bearer of such a force," is not some extra-linguistic principle necessary to explain it? In this section I attempt to answer these questions and explore the full implications of Marcus's development, but in order to resolve some of the difficulties it gives rise to I will recast this development in terms of what has been called the "materiality of the signifier," or what I call *spectral materiality*, to bring the issue of representation into the foreground. In formulating a comprehensive theory of this radical change in literary representation, I will reconsider the contributions of three invaluable critics in the history of Dickens scholarship: Marcus, in relation to narrative, Kucich, in relation to character, and Trilling, in relation to the question of ontology.

Although Marcus declares Dickens the site of the breakthrough of the primary process into the novel, he never provides a theory of how these processes are translated into the writing; they are, in fact, only mentioned to specify what makes Dickens's prose distinct from anything that came before it. His essay is everywhere alive to Dickens's linguistic genius, in a way only to be matched, perhaps, by Chesterton's affinity for Dickens's imagination for character, and in order to bring to light this breakthrough of the primary process into Dickens's novels, Marcus manages to keep his critical eye on something rather elusive and slippery, something about the way, in Dickens, language "writes itself," becomes the subject of itself, even the subject of its own writing of itself. But then self-reflexiveness is clearly not the salient issue here (there would be no uniqueness in the history of literature in this), nor does Marcus mistake it to be. How, then, can we go about theorizing more rigorously this rather abstruse idea of language "writing itself"?

Marcus does so by means of two (very different) concepts: the "dramatiz[ation] of the fundamental activities of the logos" and the "doodle" ("Language into Structure" 133). Dramatizing the logos entails tapping into the power of language to call objects into being, to let them be in the manner of a kind of self-generative deixis (in a Heideggerian sense), and the doodle refers implicitly back to the surrealist notion of "mechanical writing" and beyond that to Freudian "free association" (though Marcus doesn't discuss these antecedents). The idea of the doodle is also, interestingly enough, alluded to by Ernst Kris in relation to the origin of caricature, which highlights its visual bent, and calls upon the creative importance of play, on the implicit idea that play can be a form of distraction that loosens the restriction of logic and social censorship, allowing unconscious structures to find external expression. Marcus unites these two concepts wonderfully in an explanation of what it means for language to be "Pickwickian":

> It is the world, language, writing, as these exist in each other, as a complex process that is self-generating—so that beginning, so to say, either with the name Pickwick, or the word or title Pickwickian, the world, the language, and the writing implicit in or unfolded by such words appears to generate itself. It is language with the shackles removed from certain of its deeper creative powers, which henceforth becomes capable of a constant, rapid, and virtually limitless multiplication of its own effects and forms in new inventions and combinations and configurations. ("Language into Structure" 136)

Provisionally, at least, this passage defines well what I am referring to as "spectral materiality," the property of the signifier to generate "its own effects and forms" as the effect of its internal structure, of the signifier's internal drive and "presencing" effect. But this definition is still only descriptive and we shall have to turn to Lacan to theorize the nature of the signifier's structure and its ontological status. To anticipate a fundamental alteration to Marcus's approach, I will simply say that the "fundamental activit[y] of the logos" for Marcus is a positive and creative one, one of presencing, while in the Freudian ontology the more primary drive is characterized by lack, by what Freud calls the death drive.[1] There is also the question of how this phenomenon relates not just to language, but to character, a question that remains quite open in Marcus and to which I shall return shortly.

The idea that Dickens's novels tap into the primary process of the unconscious must inevitably be compared with the more common observation that Dickens's novels are dreamlike. Of course, this observation can often name only a vague impression, but to the extent that it is a more fundamental hypothesis about representation the two ideas are certainly linked. After all, it is through dream interpretation that Freud is led to name the primary processes in the first place, and it is in the elaboration of these primary processes that Lacan discovers the structure of the signifier as constitutive of the subject. It is in this sense that we could say that Marcus's insight also amounts to the premise that Dickens's novels *use representational material in the same way as the dream does*. In order to illustrate this and to illustrate the implications of spectral materiality in this chapter, I will turn to Lacan's reading of a particular dream, Freud's dream of "Irma's injection," which he uses to demonstrate the effect of the letter in the unconscious.

The dream of Irma's injection and beyond ...

To begin with I will provide the text of the dream as Freud presents it, for context:

> A great hall—a number of guests, whom we are receiving—among them Irma, whom I immediately take aside, as though to answer her letter, and to reproach her for not yet accepting the "solution." I say to her: "If you still have pains, it is really only your own fault"—She answers: "If you only knew what pains I have now in the throat, stomach, and abdomen—I am choked by them." I am startled, and look at her. She looks pale and puffy. I think that after all I must be overlooking some organic affection. I take her to the window and look into her throat. She offers some resistance to this, like a woman who has a set of false teeth. I think, surely, she doesn't need them—The mouth then opens wide, and I find a large white spot on the right, and elsewhere I see extensive grayish-white scabs adhering to curiously curled formations, which are evidently shaped like the turbinal bones of the nose—I quickly call Dr M, who repeats the examination and confirms it ... Dr M looks quite unlike his usual self; he is very pale, he limps, and his chin is clean-shaven ... Now my friend Otto, too, is standing beside her, and my friend Leopold percusses her covered chest, and says, "She has a dullness below, on the left," and also calls attention to an infiltrated portion of skin on the left shoulder (which I can feel, in spite of the dress) ... M says: "There's no doubt that it's an infection, but it doesn't matter; dysentery will follow and the poison will be eliminated" ... We know, too, precisely how the infection originated. My friend Otto, not long ago, gave her, when she was feeling unwell, an injection of a preparation of propyl ... propyls ... propionic acid ... trimethylamin (the formula of which

Dream as spectral form

I see before me, printed in heavy type) ... One doesn't give such injections so rashly ... Probably, too, the syringe was not clean. (*Interpretation of Dreams* 139–40)

Lacan breaks the dream down into two parts: the first culminating when Freud looks into Irma's mouth and sees strange patches of "turbinate bones" (linking the dreams to Freud's conversations with Fliess and his infamous obsession with noses); the second culminating in the introduction into the dream of the symbol of the chemical formula for trimethylamine, which Freud sees before him "printed in heavy type." In Lacan's hands the dream becomes a kind allegory for the search for the meaning of the dream, and the two parts of Irma's dream reflect a double search for the meaning of dreams in general: the search for the latent content beneath the manifest content that leads to the desire, or "wish," which motivated the dream (on the level of the fantasy here, in Lacan's terms), and the search for the laws that govern the very form of dreams, the language that structures the dream's content (Lacan's *symbolic*). For Lacan, Freud's dream represents a passing through, a breakthrough, and at the same time a *staging* of that breakthrough in the revelation of a *solution*. The dream of "Irma's injection," then, is for Lacan not just another example of a dream, but the dream of dreams, as it were, and moreover stages a representation of his categories of the imaginary, the symbolic, and the Real—at least, insofar as he has developed the last category in this early seminar.

In the first sequence of the dream, the figure of Irma is already caught up in the signifying chain: she represents the whole "feminine series, sketched out behind her" (Lacan, *Ego in Freud's Theory* 137), for instance, and is also identified by her role in Freud's dialogues with Fliess, but the symbolic does not ontologically ground the imaginary here and so the whole drama is staged at the level of the imaginary, at the level of the ego and its (little) others, its eerily simulacra-like neighbors. When Freud peers into Irma's open mouth, however, he is confronted with the limit of the imaginary, the remainder that exceeds the imaginary field but is somehow not mediated by the symbolic:

> There's a horrendous discovery here, that of the flesh one never sees, the foundation of things, the other side of the head, of the face ... the flesh in as much as it is suffering, is formless, in as much as its form in itself is something which provokes anxiety ... the final revelation of ... *you are this, which is so far from you, this which is the ultimate formlessness*. (Lacan, *Ego in Freud's Theory* 154–5, original emphasis)

Lacan points out (following Erikson) that when confronted with such a threat to the ego in sleep, the threat to its imaginary boundaries, the usual reaction is to awaken. But Freud pushes through, as it were, and on the other side of the flesh, the "other side of the face," he finds the second revelation, a symbol, the chemical formula for trimethylamine. This second part of the dream, dramatized at the level of the symbolic, rather than producing anxiety, provides a fundamental "solution" to the question of the secret of the dream, for the structure of the signifier itself (the chemical formula for trimethylamine) seems to structure the whole imaginary form of the dream. This symbol that expresses itself in triplication (tri-methyl), is reflected in the groupings of threes (three women condensed in the figure of Irma, three of Freud's colleagues, etc.) in the thematic content of the dream. Moreover, the formula is *itself* the key to the sexual content of the dream, the *solution* in every sense of the term: it is the nodal point of all the dream's associative links, the symbolic representative of the flow of sexual substance that is blocked or corrupted in its aim (the dirty syringe), and it is the structure that by splitting off into threes inscribes a series of displacements that generates the dream itself, the fact that the desire could not be represented in its "pure form" in the Real. Thus the chemical word for trimethylamine is itself the "solution" to the problem of dream formation, inasmuch as it embodies the relation of the imaginary to the symbolic in a signifier whose material ambiguity generates its signifying surplus/lack as drive, the drive generative in itself as the structure of the signifier: as Lacan says, following the "Islamic formula—*There is no other God but God.* There is no other word, no other solution to your problem, than the word" (*Seminar II* 158). The dream, like the symptom, is generated by this spectrality of the signifier, its uncanny spectral materiality: "The important thing, and this dream shows us it, is that analytic symptoms are produced in the flow of a word which tries to get through" (Lacan, *Seminar II* 159).

But perhaps what is most enticing about this dream, and the interpretations has generated, is the question of the beyond to which it gives rise and seems to dramatize so graphically. In Freud's dream of Irma we confront the questions: What does it mean to ask what lies beyond the dream, beyond the symbolic, beyond the drive? It therefore embodies that fundamental question at the heart of our rethinking the dynamic of fictional character: the relation of language to reality, and why the Real is precisely the dimension that makes it impossible to think the two realms in terms of an opposition. The formulation the dream poses, therefore, speaks to exactly what makes the "solution" to the problem *spectral*, as it is here that Lacan is, in this early seminar, hinting at the concept that he will ultimately call the Real considered as the (lacking) "beyond" of the imaginary and the symbolic, as the strange "stumbling block" of Being, as Alenka Zupančič calls it, to which psychoanalysis leads us. In the first part of Freud's dream, at the level of the imaginary, this beyond takes the form of something like the Freudian Thing, the "other side of the face," the very proximity of which provokes ontological anxiety as the proximity, as Lacan explains, "of the real lacking any mediation, of the ultimate real, of the essential object which isn't an object any longer, but this something faced with which all words cease and all categories fail, the object of anxiety *par excellence*" (*Seminar II* 164). The dream thus dramatizes the idea that the approach to this Thing beyond the imagery stages a beyond to the ego, where "there is no longer any Freud, there is no longer anyone who can say I" (Lacan, *Seminar II* 164). And yet it is precisely in this place of the Thing, the anxiety-producing object, that in the second stage of the dream, in the dramatized symbolic, the mysteriously material signifier appears, the signifier in the Real, and thus, as Lacan says, "If the ego as such rediscovers and recognizes itself, it is because there is a beyond to the ego, an unconscious, a subject which speaks, unknown to the subject" (*Seminar II* 171). So how can we think this signifier in the Real and its strange materiality, so well pictured in the uncanny materialization of a symbol appearing "printed in heavy type" before the dreamer's eyes?

Alenka Zupančič explains quite concisely why Lacan's *materialism* is precisely what distinguishes his linguistic model from the Saussurean/structuralist model that sees language as a system of pure differences in which signifiers have only an "arbitrary" relation to things or concepts of things. For Lacan, "what pins the dimension of language to the gap of the unconscious" is the fact that signifiers "are never pure signifiers" but "are ridden, from within, by unexpected surpluses" that throw the "pure" system of difference off kilter and generate lack, and therefore *desire*: "It is precisely through this surplus meaning (bound up with surplus enjoyment) that signifiers are intrinsically bound to the reality to which they refer; it is in this way that they 'enter the signified'" (Zupančič 61). This materiality is of course not a simple one, but is exactly what is at stake in our discussion of Dickens's spectrality, since what is at stake is the materiality of the drive and its relation to the Real: "The signifier enters the signified (in a form 'which is not immaterial,' as Lacan adds), and thus takes its place in reality, in the form of this surplus which creates, as well as complicates, the signifying relations, twisting and 'driving' their logic" (Zupančič 61–2). This model of psychoanalytic or Lacanian materialism (what I am here calling spectral materialism), gives us, I believe, a more well-defined and specific way of theorizing Dickens's breakthrough, his ability to tap into both the creative powers of the unconscious and the generative "force" of the "logos," as Marcus puts, which in the psychoanalytic model characterizes a dimension that is precisely the (missing) link, or common lack, between the signifier and the unconscious: Lacan sometimes refers to its structure as *"glissement,"* which plays upon its signifying autonomy (language writing itself) in the pun between "sliding" (of signifiers) and "slip" (as in a slip on the tongue, a Freudian slip). The question thus becomes not one of the author's "ego," or even one of individual psychology, but a question of ontology, or more specifically, hauntology, where there is a "short-circuit" (as Zupančič puts it) between epistemology and ontology, between representation and the real:

> The true materialism, which ... can only be a dialectical materialism, is not grounded in the primacy of matter nor in matter as first principle, but rather in the notion of conflict or contradiction, of split, and of the "parallax of the Real" produced in it. In other words, the fundamental axiom of materialism is not "matter is all" or "matter is primary," but relates rather to the primacy of a cut. (Zupančič 76)

Materialism is concerned with the spectral (ontologically) in-between (non)space of *glissement* and the Real. Considering the question in terms of psychoanalytic materialism, understood as the (hauntological) primacy of the cut, radically reconfigures the problem we faced with Marcus that if by tapping into the primary process we refer solely to metaphor, metonymy, and substitution, it becomes very difficult to maintain the idea of a breakthrough on the part of Dickens, as opposed to many other novelists. This is partly because in these terms Marcus's articulation of a breakthrough always risks becoming wholly quantitative (as if there are merely *more* of the rhetorical tropes in Dickens's prose). Instead, what is at stake in Dickens's tapping into the "primary processes" of the unconscious should be understood as a new *form*, a form of symbolic materialism, of tapping into this "sliding [*glissement*] of the signified under the signifier," this drive or cut inherent to the split structure of the signifier. The primacy of this contradiction or antagonism inherent to the Real is what gives the sense that there is a kind of doubleness to Dickens's prose, as there is in the dream as a *form*, the "primary" or unconscious form of the *Real* always being in tension with the "secondary" discourse of logic and mimesis. We could do no better to find an example of this than to look to the opening pages of *Bleak House*.

Dream as spectral form

In the narrative of *Bleak House*, this *glissement* (to slide/let slip) or drive is not simply an element of the text, then, but its very form, its structuring principle; it imprints itself in the narrative form, in other words, like the material signifier in the dream of Irma's injection, and this is what marks the nature of Dickens's breakthrough in the novel form. Though there has been much discussion and many close readings of the opening passage of *Bleak House*, this concept of the structuring principle of the *cut* (as its uniqueness) that underlies it casts it in new light. In order to get a sense of what this means, let us confront this famous first paragraph:

> LONDON. Michaelmas term lately over, and the Lord Chancellor sitting in Lincoln's Inn Hall. Implacable November weather. As much mud in the streets, as if the waters had but newly retired from the face of the earth, and it would not be wonderful to meet a Megalosaurus, forty feet long or so, waddling like an elephantine lizard up Holburn Hill. Smoke lowering down from chimney-pots, making a soft black drizzle with flakes of soot in it as big as full-grown snowflakes—gone into mourning, one might imagine, for the death of the sun. Dogs, undistinguishable in mire. Horses, scarcely better; splashed to their very blinkers. Foot passengers, jostling one another's umbrellas, in a general infection of ill temper, and losing their foot-hold at street-corners, where tens of thousands of other foot passengers have been slipping and sliding since the day broke (if this day ever broke), adding new deposits to the crust upon crust of mud, sticking at those points tenaciously to the pavement, and accumulating at compound interest. (13)

Immediately one is confronted with something striking: a tone that is at once breathless and imposing and that has remained rather elusive to critics. Robert Newsome remarks that "*Bleak House* begins like a newspaper story, with a dateline" (15). It is a suggestive question here whether this is an observation about the voice or the typography. In any case, it would seem to me more accurate to say that there is an echo, a *trace* of the journalistic dateline here. But what is even more telling is what *distinguishes* this opening sentence from a newspaper dateline. A dateline is appended as the signifier of a discourse, the discourse of journalism, to fix its sliding, anchoring it in historical event and place. The dateline must therefore formally "precede" the text, remain without in order to fix it, to "quilt" it, to conceal the *glissement* (drive/sliding/slip) of ordinary discourse (the ambiguity of "lately over" for instance already implies a shifting that would be out of place in a dateline). But here the first word, "LONDON," is included in the text not as a dateline, nor as a framing/fixing point, but as a signifying cut that inscribes an ambiguous, unstable reference point, both in place and time, initiating but also dependent upon a series of displacements throughout the first paragraph, the first chapter, the novel (when/where exactly does that signifier LONDON cease and stop resonating?). It is at once inside and outside from the start, and as such radically structures the images at work in this first chapter not by concealing but by unmasking and thus enlisting the narrative's *glissement*.

LONDON—a fragmented, cut-off signifier, a dangling noun, so to speak, left floating in the realm of metonymy, yet pervading the following fragmented predicates; being detached from them grammatically, it slides beneath them and echoes in their silent reference back to that first signifier—"LONDON." In this first paragraph, we are confronted with a chaos of images: mud, horses, dogs, carriages, pedestrians, umbrellas, chimneys, soot, rain, etc. Yet it has been overlooked just how *structured* this chaos is on another level. Not only does "Michaelmas lately over" refer back to that first word (London and the courts are from the first, then, mutually implicative) but so does "implacable November weather" and "[a]s much mud in the streets" and "dogs, undistinguishable in mire" and the "foot passengers," and, in the next paragraph "fog everywhere," etc. down to the "warning" (or curse) at the threshold of the Court of Chancery, echoing the inscription over the gates of hell in Dante's inferno, barring access to their justice: "Suffer any wrong that can be done you, rather than come here!" Not only does this signifier pervade them, that is, not only do all the images retroactively determine the content of the first signifier, but the first signifier anticipates the *syntax* of all the following clauses: "London. Michaelmas term lately over" repeats its structure in the sentence fragments with modified "dangling nouns" that follow, as in "Lord Chancellor sitting," "smoke lowering," "dogs, indistinguishable," "horses, scarcely better," "foot passengers jostling," etc. The signifier LONDON is itself an initiation, or a performance of itself as a signifying initiation.

We can see what in these first paragraphs marks a radical break from novelistic discourse up to this point. As Marcus points out, the novel is itself a discourse that tends to be at home at the level of the secondary processes: "The novel had been built primarily on the secondary, logical processes, processes that develop ontogenetically at a later state of mental existence and form the essential structures of consciousness" ("Language into Structure" 137). We could say that novelistic discourse tended up this point to paint its imaginary layer rather liberally or perhaps, that the novelist's brush, dipped in the paint of the imaginary, tended to touch up

Dream as spectral form

the gaps in the real. But in this first chapter of *Bleak House* there is an altogether different use of the imaginary illustrated in Dickens's prose. The picture it paints does not cohere according to the internal structure of the images. There is, for instance, a lack of logical relations between these images in the opening of *Bleak House*—*because of, however, instead of, without which*, are notably lacking in these first few paragraphs. Rather, the images seem to speak themselves rather than just to speak *of* themselves; beneath these images there is a structure, a symbolic cut at work, as is the case in dreams, which, as Freud says, "disregard all these [logical] conjunctions, and it is only the substantive content or the dream-thoughts that they take over and manipulate" (*Interpretation of Dreams* 347). We can think again of Freud's dream of Irma's injection here: images are themselves substantive, signifying material structured according to the order of a signifier that eludes them.

For instance, it has often been pointed out that the metaphor of the fog seems to structure the novel thematically, which is certainly true from one perspective, but what has not been noted is that this image functions at the level of the imaginary and as such provides a key to the more primary symbolic structuration of images at work in the novel, its symbolic "latent content," as it were. From this perspective we can distinguish between imagistic signs, at the level of the *imaginary*, and structuring metaphors, at the level of the *symbolic*. Thus, under the former category we have the concrete images *mud* and *fog*, while under the latter category, "taking over and manipulating them" (like the dream image), we have the symbolic abstractions *money* and *law*. Here again we can see the *glissement* or signifying surplus/lack at work in the narrative form. The image of the fog, for instance, does not function, in the usual way of metaphor, on a representational level *standing in* for the law (the law is foggy); rather, it is a concrete image that *fills the place of* the law in the imaginary, almost literally diffusing the social obfuscation and alienation it initiates in atmospheric form. In this way the fog itself as an image can also form symbolic connections with other images as a source of myriad associations, displaced from *property* law, throughout the novel. Mud is likewise introduced not simply as a metaphor for money, but as a concrete image that substitutes for money, displacing the qualities of the absent symbolic onto itself: in the image that first unites mud to money, for instance, the foot passengers "have been slipping and sliding since the day broke ... adding new deposits to the crust upon crust of mud, sticking at those points tenaciously to the pavement, and accumulating at compound interest" (*Bleak House* 5). When the image of mud or fog (or both) appears throughout the novel, then, it is as though it expresses a "dream thought," a latent idea that expresses itself only formally or through the links between these images; for example, the name Smallweed seems to "root" this money lender and hoarder's essence in the image of mud, which on a symbolic level makes him a very revenant or effigy of "compound interest" or capital, various expressions of money in its form of slipping and sliding.

Thus the "the dense fog is densest, and the muddy streets are muddiest" at the *threshold* of the Court of Chancery where property law and the draw of property meet in the big Other, and where "at the very heart of the fog, sits the Lord High Chancellor" (5–6). The court and the chancellor, therefore, like the dream symbol for trimethylamine, are not merely metonymic precipitates of the abstract law/money connection, but signifiers that have already "broken through" to register at the imaginary level an unapproachable Thing at the level of the Real. Law and Money meet in the Court of Chancery since this is where disputes over property are tried, and the whole first chapter stages an approach to this symbolically liminal space, rather remarkably like the staging of the approach to the unrepresentable Real in Freud's dream of Irma's injection. That an ultimately unrepresentable signifying surplus/lack lurks beyond this symbolic nodal point of money and law is reflected at the imaginary level in the otherworldly overtones of magic, allegory, repetition, and visionary prophecy. The approach to the courts crystalizes the incantatory tone of the opening passages of the novel, and repetition takes shape beneath the flux of images as a sign of something having already eluded them. There are thus four approaches to the court: in the first three, as a particular element of the Court of Chancery is evoked, the language seems to split into its functions of the modal and the deictic (e.g., "ought to be" *vs.* "here he is"), ending in the fourth approach, a simple declarative, "this is the Court of Chancery." In each of the first three cases, around this split in language, the concrete images of mud and fog (imagistic metaphors of money and law) cluster in various implicit metaphoric forms, never stated but made present in their mystical imagery and effects: "The Lord High Chancellor ought to be sitting here—as here he is—with a foggy glory round his head"; "the High Court of Chancery bar ought to be—as here they are—mistily engaged in one of the ten thousand stages of an endless cause, tripping one another up on slippery precedents, groping knee-deep in technicalities"; and, "the various solicitors in the cause … who made a fortune by it, ought to be—as are they not?—ranged in a line, in a long matted well (but you might look in vain for Truth at the bottom of it" (50). Inasmuch as it is around these slips or breaks in the

Dream as spectral form

tenses, marked off by dashes, that these associations cluster, the narrative *glissement* expresses itself in the dream logic that structures these images, in the *form* itself, the mystical repetitions that echo the mystical cycles of the endlessly proliferating Chancery suits.

The signifier driving (by exceeding) all these associative links and images makes its initial appearance at the heart of a very structured cluster of accumulating clauses and repetitions. The deictic declarative, "This is the Court of Chancery," that is, comes after four (three short and one very long) parallel conditional clauses beginning with the repetition of "well may" (expressing possibilities) and is followed by five (four short and one very long) parallel relative clauses beginning with the repetition of "which" (expressing completed positive properties) as though tracing an ontological circuit from (opaque) potentiality to being to afterlife:

> *Well may* the court be dim, with wasting candles here and there; *well may* the fog hang heavy in it, as if it would never get out; *well may* the stained-glass windows lose their colour, and admit no light of day into the place; *well may* the uninitiated from the streets, who peep in through the glass panes in the door, be deterred from entrance by its owlish aspect, and by the drawl languidly echoing to the roof from the padded dais where the Lord High Chancellor looks into the lantern that has no light in it, and where the attendant wigs are all stuck in a fog-bank! *This is the Court of Chancery*, *which* has its decaying houses and its blighted lands in every shire; *which* has its worn-out lunatic in every madhouse, and its dead in every churchyard; *which* has its ruined suitor, with his slipshod heels and threadbare dress, borrowing and begging through the round of every man's acquaintance; *which* gives to monied might the means abundantly of wearing out the right; *which* so exhausts finances, patience, courage, hope; so overthrows the brain and breaks the heart; that there is not an honorable man among its practitioners who would not give—who does not often give—the warning, "suffer any wrong that can be done you, rather than come here!" (50–1, emphasis added)

The first set of clauses (being conditional) trace a hypothetical approach to the court's threshold that emphasizes its resistance to representation, its dimness, its fogginess, its opacity to light (un)seen from the point of view of the supposed "uninitiated" deterred from admission to the big Other of the legal system; while the second set of clauses traces a movement radiating outward from the opaque (lacking) "light" of the court throughout the nation's property and lost propriety, exposing its muddy and fog-inducing effects of decay, corruption, and decomposition, the effects of (in yet another displaced condensation of money and law in a signifier) not muddied but "*monied* might" on the "right" of the little others shut out from their own fate with Kafkaesque indeterminacy. At the "center" of these clauses, rhetorically but also as a kind of dramatized symbolic, is the only unqualified un-metaphorically deictic statement thus far, "this is the Court of Chancery," as if what lay beyond these highly figurative and linguistic approaches to the threshold of the court were ultimately impervious to anything but its own name, a signifier marking a (lacking) place where language and the real should meet—*there, there it is; look at that thing*. In the last and most dreamlike of the clauses leading up to this representational threshold, the sense of approaching a mysterious, and even demonic (in the ritualistic sense) *beyond* is heightened:

> well may the uninitiated from the streets, who peep in through the glass panes in the door [who echo those "chance people ... peeping over the parapets" at the fog-smothered Thames] be deterred from entrance by its owlish aspect, and by the drawl languidly echoing to the roof from the padded dais *where the Lord High Chancellor looks into the lantern that has no light in it*, and where the attendant wigs are all stuck in a fog-bank! (51, emphasis added)

The mystical and mystifying ontology of the court is formally reflected, for instance, in the almost trance-like repetition of the lulling "l" sounds that draws the triple "ls" of the Lord Chancellor's title into his "drawl languidly echoing" to the rooftop and echoes them back in the Chancellor's lightless lantern. And where the Lord High Chancellor sits on his "padded dais," prophet-like, blindly reading the lightless destinies of hapless suitors, the novel's structuring signifiers and their imaginary forms— mud/money, law/fog—are most compressed in the single phrase that immediately precedes the deictic threshold to the court, referring to the (metonymic) wigs as being "all stuck in a fog-bank!" In these few words, which mark the destiny of our linguistic excursion into the mud and fog, we find metaphor, metonymy, displacement, and condensation all together ("bank" is another metonymic condensation of mud and money, displaced from "stuck in the mud" by the metaphorical fog).

Just as, for Freud, words in dreams are part of the "material of the dream thoughts" (*Interpretation of Dreams* 348), words in Dickens's prose are broken up, condensed, combined, distorted, and proper nouns particularly are frequently composite (consider just some of the examples from *Bleak House* alone, such as Turveydrop, Skimpole, Boythorn, Woodcourt, Dedlock, Summerson, Tulkinghorn, Smallweed, Pardiggle, Chadband, etc.). The materiality of words, or the material treatment of words that subjects them to distortions such as condensation and displacement, forges previously inexistent connections, forming strands of associative links between various ideas that are signified by those words, centering on nodal points. "The work of condensation in dreams," Freud tells us, "is at its clearest when it handles words and names. It is true in general that words are treated in dreams as though they were concrete things, and for that reason they are apt to be combined in just the same way as presentations of concrete things" (*Interpretation of Dreams* 330). A highly overdetermined nodal point of the novel with respect to names would thus be the name most linked to the novel's most elusive signifier, the Court of Chancery, the name/names being, of course, "Jarndyce and Jarndyce."

Jarndyce and Jarndyce, as Newsome points out, is "itself a repetition;" but it is also a composite, which doubles it within as well. And is it two names or one? A unifying concept, the family name, split into a unity divided against itself, a repetition of a split. This overdetermined name and nodal point in the novel is, as would be expected of a nodal point of a dream, introduced into the novel in an offhand, parenthetical manner as "JARNDYCE AND JARNDYCE (the cause in hand)," yet the words that combine to form Jarn-dyce bring together images that symbolize the courts and repeat themselves in motifs threaded throughout the text: "yarn" and "dice," metonymic and metaphoric images of the pure chance and gamble of being entangled in the web of a Chancery cause that can never be unraveled. "Dice," for instance, a metonymy for gambling, finds its metonymic role in the pun on *Chance*ry, where members of the bar run "their goat-hair and horsehair warded heads against walls of words and [make] a pretense of equity, as players might," and becomes a running metaphor for the occult-like draw of equity law with its prospects of windfall property (*Bleak House* 50). This trope plays itself out most tragically in Richard, who takes "rather too much to Billiards" (376), has a "better luck next time" attitude toward the court system in general (401), and of whom Jarndyce felt "that the uncertainties and delays of the Chancery suit had imparted to his nature something of the careless spirit of a gamester, who felt that he was part of a great gaming system" (205). Richard too might make "a pretense of equity," but in the universal gaming system of London, "the great tee-totum [that] is set up for its daily spin and whirl," ones destiny seems determined in the a roll of the dice (199).

Similarly, the signifier "yarn" of Jarndyce, as a metonymy for weaving, metaphorically entangles suitors in the endless ravel of a case that spins increasingly "unfinished connections," so that throughout the novel there develops a running joke-like pun on the meaning of the word "suit," as in Richard's confession, "I was born into this unfinished connection with all its chances and changes, and it began to unsettle me before I quite knew the difference between a suit at law and a suit of clothes." This pun runs several bleak courses as it manages to enlist the sartorial metaphor (in a Carlylean way) interweaving clothes and destiny as when Richard himself says his half-hearted attempts at employment are "suited to my temporary condition—I may say, precisely suited" (376) and of course the suit always ends up "wearing out one's right" in the end. The weaving metaphor also draws in Esther and her doll, a woven double, an effigy, and the theme of her shawl that draws her into still tighter connections with her mother and the legal suit. The image of yarn, then, is an imaginary metaphor for the connection between the court cases and the people involved, between the suits and the suitors, a connection that draws closer and closer all the time and even blurs the ontological distinction between the two, as a wonderfully displaced observation by Esther, when going to meet Richard in a sea-side town (where Woodcourt's ship comes in), reveals: "The sea" she describes, "was heaving under a thick white fog; and nothing else was moving but a few early rope makers, who, with yarn twisted round their bodies, looked as if, tired of their present state of existence, they were spinning themselves into cordage" (544).

Thus the signifier that links the cause of the Chancery to characters' names, "Jarndyce and Jarndyce," quilts together, on the one hand, the novel's larger metaphors and their imaginary expression—money→mud and law→fog—and on the other, the signifier's material associations in weaving (yarn) and gambling/chance (dice). To this I would even add the word "jar," with its connotations of repetition and strife, and *dis*cord, as in Richard's observation about "the *jar and dis*cord of the law-suits" (461).[2] The introduction of the suit as "JARNDYCE AND JARNDYCE (the cause in hand), which was squeezed dry years upon years ago" (51), echoes the "crust upon crust" of mud that links it to *money* (through the compound interest metaphor), which, like the "newly retired waters" whose trace is that mud upon the dried-up earth, leaves only the traces of its absence in the "squeezed dry" suit. These traces of money or interest make their presence felt only in the chance or gamble of the suit into which Richard will soon sink deeper than any of those foot passengers slipping in the mud, a rather fluid but fatal transition, much as the expression "cause *in hand*" provides the offhand metonymic link that leads smoothly from monetary lure to moral infection: "How many people out of the suit, Jarndyce and Jarndyce has *stretched forth its unwholesome* *hand* to spoil and corrupt, would be a very wide question" (53, emphasis added). And from the lure of chance through dissipation we are led back to moral entanglement as "the very solicitor's boys" who accept petty bribes "may have got," in remarkably esoteric and caustic pun on *yarn* and *dice*, "an extra moral *twist* and *shuffle* into themselves out of Jarndyce and Jarndyce" (53, emphasis added). Since "twist and shuffle," true to the law of gambling, soon become "shirking and sharking" (Nabokov has noted the echo here of "slipping and sliding," which, moreover, links it back to mud and money), the cause in hand has its influence even on the hand of fate, insofar as those concerned share "a loose belief that if the world go wrong, it was, in some off-hand manner, never meant to go right" (53).

If there be anyone to tie up the warp and woof of entanglement, enticement, and entropy enwound in the very words Jarndyce and Jarndyce, then it must be Mr. Tangle, who first introduces the three central children of *Bleak House* into the confusion, violence, and deathliness of the suit. Mr. Tangle's first word in the novel, "Mlud," concisely condenses "my Lord," he who presides over the Court of Chancery, with the "mud" of the milieu of London forming a distorted allusion to "blood," or the cold violence concealed in the court's formalities, as we find confirmed in Mr. Tangle's next phrase, "begludship's pardon—dead" (10).

Mr. Tangle, moreover, gives us in intensified form the same stylistic techniques of the narrator of these opening passages—the extreme condensations, the elliptical grammar, the distortions, even the cool irony set against powerful forces—and can thus help us answer the question we raised above about the ineffable tone of these opening pages. Dickens's linguistic style, here, we may say, has something in common with the pictorial style of caricature, particularly with that dark sublime of the more "serious" caricature of, for instance, Daumier. That is, just as Daumier's style cuts through the long-entrenched structural laws of mimetic portraiture—the laws of imitation—in order to allow for another structure altogether to emerge—the laws of the signifier—and take precedent over the "realistic" arrangement of parts (exaggerating, distorting, rearranging them, etc.), Dickens has dropped the necessities of mimetic realism in order to allow other structuring principles to order and arrange the "parts" or material of representations, principles or processes we could call "primary," such as condensation and displacement, but that ultimately draw upon the spectral structure of the cut. The tone, then, may be compared to a dark caricature as well: there is simultaneously a sense of penetrating a dark, absurd, dreamlike profundity beyond reality, and also a breathless, exhilarating sense of having broken free of the strictures of secondary (censored) logic, of enjoyment or release, even of a sense of ease and rapidity, as with the caricatural image that seems to have been "tossed off" in a few effortless strokes.

From mechanical to material through Micawber

This discussion of tone (and its doubleness) leads us naturally to the idea of "voice," and, having addressed the idea of spectral materiality, or the cut of the Real, in relation to the narrative, I will carry over this discussion into voice and characterization. Since Marcus leaves these issues open, particularly that of character, which seems to interest him most only when characters can be seen as referring to Dickens himself, I will resituate the problem of characterization in terms of representation or form. To review some of the conclusions drawn thus far about what characterizes this "breakthrough": Dickens's prose makes use of the ability to take signifiers apart and play with them like material things, to break them up and recombine them, to condense together different words that make use of the same phonemes or sounds, to invest by this means particular words and phrases with discrete meanings that are thus joined together through associations. As Freud says of dream representation: "words, since they are the nodal points of ideas, may be regarded as predestined to ambiguity; and the neuroses (e.g., in framing obsessions and phobias), no less than dreams, make unashamed use of the advantages thus offered by words for purposes of condensation and disguise" (*Interpretation of Dreams* 376). And as Lacan emphasizes, the possibility of such representational transference presupposes the principle of *glissement*: "*Entstellung*, translated as 'distortion' or 'transposition,' is what Freud shows to be the general precondition for the functioning of the dream, and it is what I designated above, following Saussure, as the sliding of the signified under the signifier [or *glissement*], which is always active in discourse (its action, let us note, is unconscious)" (*Ecrits* 160). A signifier is not fixed to a certain thing, not even, as Saussure suggested, arbitrarily: meaning flows through the signifier as a kind of motion created by its split structure, the effect/affect of its intrinsic signifying surplus/lack. The word "*glissement*," more than distortion, gives a sense of this drive, this propulsion of the signifying chain effectuated by the cut of the Real (the "beyond" that signification always both creates and lacks), while also designating its unconscious dimension, its relation to *jouissance*. Dickens's prose, I am suggesting, is characterized by a remarkable ability to bring us up against, or into a kind of uncanny proximity with, the *lack* or cut, this (signifying) limit to discourse that is the unconscious, to what Lacan calls the "letter" of the unconscious. As Lacan points out, the dream brings us into a proximity of this signifying lack, the cut of the Real, even, or perhaps especially, when it draws on speech, since that speech is always merely more material for the "laws of the signifier":

> That the dream uses speech makes no difference since for the unconscious it is only one among several elements of representation. It is precisely the fact that both the game [charades, for instance] and the dream run up against a lack of taxematic material for the representation of such logical articulations as causality, contradiction, hypothesis, etc., that proves they are a form of writing rather than of mime. (*Ecrits* 161)

This idea of speech as a form of writing, so to speak, or of a split between discourse and the unconscious cut (or the law of the signifier), proves fruitful for an understanding of Dickens's narrative voice and especially of his form of characterization. The chapter "Mechanical Style," from John Kucich's book *Excess and Restraint in the Novels of Charles Dickens*, provides an extended and rigorous analysis of the strange (almost nonhuman, as his metaphor of mechanical suggests) duality to Dickens's writing style, so I will take up his argument as a means to pursue this idea of the cut as fundamental to Dickens's form.

First, it is worth remembering that, in the history of criticism, Dickens's style is itself something more of a problem than the style of most other novelists either earlier or later. The description "mechanical" proves an excellent example of this. Kucich is by no means alone in using this adjective, and many of Dickens's contemporary critics saw his characters as resembling automatons, yet as many notable critics (Chesterton for one comes immediately to mind) claim just the opposite, that Dickens's style is the most "vital" and "animated" of any novelist, that this is what distinguishes his voice, his characters, etc. In any case, this observation is complicated somewhat by the fact that if Kucich attempts to define Dickens's style as mechanical, it is really in order to emphasize a paradox in this claim: "In a paradoxical way, Dickens's narrative style allows him covertly to achieve a kind of excess by extravagantly pursuing the mechanical quality of human beings, and of language" (*Excess* 197). Two of the most extended (book-length) modern studies on Dickens's narrative *style* have this focus on paradox or contradiction in common: Kucich's study on "excess" and "restraint" and Rosenberg's on "contradiction" and "conflict" in *Little Dorrit's Shadows: Character and Contradiction in Dickens*. It is no coincidence that both of these critics, among others, detect a doubleness rather difficult to define in Dickens's voice; to begin with, then, a closer look at the subtleties of Kucich's argument will be helpful in relating this doubleness to our discussion of spectral materiality.

The first thing that directs Kucich's discussion of the mechanical here is the idea of "energy," whose "unchanging laws" bridge "the gap between the organic and the inorganic" (199). In a close reading of the style of the opening of *Oliver Twist*, Kucich notes that the prose "whirs along inhumanly fast" such that its "regular cadence ... approaches the inhuman energy of a machine" (*Excess* 208). In fact, this term "energy" is anything but unique to Kucich: it has been used to describe Dickens's novels and characters from their earliest criticism and probably appears in relation to Dickens's novels with more frequency than to those of any other writer in the English language. Kucich is only the first (to my knowledge) to link it explicitly with the idea of the machine and in relation to style (it is more frequently attributed to characters). Yet this combination of concepts allows Kucich to make a very interesting observation. This energy, says Kucich, which drives Dickens's prose, also does something all its own; it "splits off" from its object and produces a kind of "doubleness" in the narrative voice. This doubleness is translated in Kucich's language in terms of restraint and excess, here in the form of work and play, or "satire" (which like work is put to use and directed towards an object) and "parody" (which is a pure "verbal game" that breaks away from the object and, like play, has no use beyond its own excess or transgression of the work of satire, *Excess* 209). Strangely enough, the machine metaphor appears not on the *work* side of the opposition, but on the *play* side: this is because, like the machine, which is "free of human purpose," parody manages to "turn mechanicalness into a vehicle for the nonuseful, purposeless—and in this sense both mechanical and nonhuman—energy of play" (Kucich, *Excess* 209). It is interesting that Kucich should be led to make this twist in his argument (although his argument leads there logically), since one might normally consider that machines do work, are created to do work (and thus not "free from human purpose" at all), while humans play. Nevertheless it is precisely the energy of the machine that allows him to make this step, since this energy, the argument runs, is not internally regulated by consciousness, or we could also say by an ego, but is prior to it.

If energy, or even "energy of play," seems an appropriate yet common enough description of Dickens's style, we might then ask what exactly the metaphor of the mechanical contributes to this intuition. What is unique and invaluable in Kucich's approach here is none other than his descriptions, which are the fruit of his best close readings, of the narrative *glissement*, the inscription of spectral materiality in Dickens's prose. What Kucich describes as this "excess" of language or voice, this "splitting off" from its object that allows the signifier to generate a kind of "energy" of its own, by its very nature, is analogous to what I have been describing as *jouissance*, the drive of *sense* generated in the cut of the signifier. It is for this reason that Kucich's argument, in my opinion, is at its most convincing when he describes not the "whir" of the narrative, nor the dialectic between useful and playful prose (satire and parody)—which in itself seems overly subtle and not tenable in many cases, such as in the opening of *Bleak House*—but the sheer mechanical autonomy of the language, the free-play of the signifier. Kucich says that Dickens's prose, for instance, is "inhumanly mechanical, since it takes its impetus not from a desire to communicate, but from the sheer ability of language to elaborate itself endlessly, meaninglessly" (*Excess* 212). This last description, in fact, applies to the opening passage of *The Pickwick Papers*, appropriately enough, since it leads us back to Marcus's claim with which I opened this chapter, that language "writes itself," that the opening of *The Pickwick Papers* dramatizes the presencing activities of the logos. But what Kucich contributes here is a shift in focus from the conscious/unconscious split onto the split inherent to language itself; Kucich, that is, unwittingly provides a model that supplements and to a certain extent advances Marcus's theory. It is interesting that Kucich refrains from attempts to contextualize this "meaningless" excess—maintaining that the excess is always "nonsense," as such, energy "that consumes itself before our very eyes" (Kucich, *Excess* 232)—which I commend, but I would suggest that rather than label it as "nonsense"[3] and be content with that, we could push still further on this intuition that there is always a certain *nothing* ("meaninglessness," an excess, a self-canceling "energy") pinned to the *something* of Dickens's narrative voice or prose style.

In this case, the doubleness in Dickens's voice would not consist of a voice with purpose (such as satire for moral or political ends) and one without a purpose (parody for purposes of pure nonsense), in tension merely with each other. What gives Dickens's style this sense of surplus, on the one hand, and this sense of a "split" or "splitting off," on the other, is the (unconscious) drive of the signifier; the "nonsense" sustained in/by his prose, in other words, is not (just) nothing in itself, but always *brings us up against* this "nothing," this limit-point/beyond of representation (the Real)—which is also the lack or gap of the unconscious, or subjectivity.

But in order to achieve this, there must be a *formal* element of the text that registers its relation to lack. This is where the analogy of the dream is so useful, since it illustrates for us that, as Lacan emphasizes, speech can be a form of writing, or discourse can point beyond its own content to the laws (or form) of the signifier—one can indeed only express this lack through form.

In making this observation about dream representation, Lacan was drawing on Freud's discussion of speech in dreams as being repeated material traces taken from memory:

> Where spoken sentences occur in dreams and are expressly distinguished as such from thoughts, it is an invariable rule that the words spoken in the dream are derived from spoken words remembered in the dream material. The text of the speech is either retained unaltered or expressed with some slight displacement. A speech in a dream is often put together from various recollected speeches, the text remaining the same but being given, if possible, several meanings, or one different from the original one. (*Interpretation of Dreams* 339)

Freud thus distinguishes between two levels of representation here; between the "text" on the one hand, which, as remembered "spoken words," is part of the *representational material* to which the dream has access, and, on the other hand, its expression in the dream, or its "manifest content." But neither "level" gives us the "latent" content, its interpretation. It is only in the *process* of being transposed from one text to the other (where *form* manipulates content), when language undergoes either symbolic transformations (i.e., condensation and displacement), representational transformations ("consideration of representability"), or both, that interpretation can be generated. Similarly, the traces of the cut, the symbolic limitations or "doubleness" of discourse, are always only discernable in the form, or style, of a work. This may give us a better handle on Kucich's theory of the "double" voice and how it can bring us into proximity with the cut, as I will try to show with the help of a particularly overdetermined character when it comes to voice and style, Mr. Micawber.

It is, perhaps, rather rare that we should literally have a primary "text" with which to compare the speech of a character in a novel as if it comprised a "manifest content," but in the case of Mr. Tangle's single word, "Mlud," for instance, we can see traces of an *other* discourse precisely in its distortions: we recognize that the words on the page condense signifiers from a "manifest" discourse (plot, context), "My Lord," with signifiers from another, more formal discourse (structuring metaphors of the novel), "law," and "mud," to form a nodal point, like the punch line of a joke, that conveys a surplus meaning, "blood" (or systemic violence). Moreover, there *is* a particular case, and a rather crucial one at that, where we do have a primary "text" for a character's speech—the case of Micawber's farewell speech to David Copperfield. It is well known that Micawber's words at this point are an echo of Dickens's father's words to him around the time he was imprisoned for debt. Dickens recorded the incident thus: "He told me, I remember, to take the warning by the Marshalsea, and to observe that if a man had twenty pounds a year, and spent nineteen pounds, nineteen shilling and six pence, he would be happy; but that a shilling spent the other way would make him wretched" (Forster 13–14). These remembered spoken words are transposed into the novel *David Copperfield* in two forms. First, in the words of the narrator, David, they are reproduced, in words and tone very closely resembling the actual words of Dickens's father (or Dickens's record of them), as a paraphrase of Micawber's parting wisdom to him: "He solemnly conjured me, I remember, to take warning by his fate; and to observe that if a man had twenty pounds a year for his income, and spent nineteen pounds nineteen shillings and sixpence, he would be happy, but that if he spent twenty pounds one he would be miserable" (147). The second time, the remembered words are given in Micawber's voice, spoken by Micawber himself, but quite changed in form. That this speech appears first, only minutely altered, in the voice of David (the figure analogous to the young Dickens, the speech's recorder) and later, more dramatically transformed, in the voice of Mr. Micawber (the figure analogous to its speaker, Dickens's father) seems to encourage us to pay more critical attention to the changes it undergoes in form (as if Dickens were supplying us in the novel with traces of another discourse). If we compare these two "texts" then, we should begin to hear in *Micawber's* voice that doubleness of which Kucich speaks, but now in terms of the function of the cut and the surplus nonsense "energy" or drive of the signifier—and "beyond" that the spectral dimension of the trace of the father:

> "My other piece of advice, Copperfield," said Mr Micawber, "you know. Annual income twenty pounds, annual expenditure nineteen and six, result happiness. Annual income twenty pounds, annual expenditure twenty pounds ought and six, result misery. The blossom is blighted, the leaf is withered, the god of day goes down upon the dreary scene, and—and in short you are forever floored. As I am!" (154)

The first thing we notice is that the same text is now full of what we would call "Micawberisms" (excessive rhetorical flourishes, the inimitable "in short," etc.); that is, the text has been reshaped so as to capture in caricatural strokes Micawber's character or key characteristics, his verbal tics. The exaggerated use of parallelisms and antithesis, for instance, makes the advice seem even more like a reliable maxim, but simultaneously, even more comically like a "real" formula, almost mechanically so in its nonhuman, pseudo-mathematical calculations. In fact, the implicit *fantasy* behind the absurdly acute logic of his father's statement (childlike in both simplicity and incisiveness) finds expression in the grammatical *form* here, which seems at once to break its own rules (throwing out logical conjunctions) in favor of a more mimetic structure reflecting the mathematic logic behind the advice, and at the same time to play fast and loose with numbers, translating them effortlessly into emotional states ("happiness" and "misery") as simply part of the equation. That is, this repeated bit of text, transferred from Dickens's father to Dickens to David to Micawber, embodies the way in which repetition compulsion can transform loss into excess. This comic-objective, formulaic way of rattling off his own fatal flaw gives us the impression that Mr. Micawber has repeated and will repeat this phrase many times over, just as he will repeat the tragicomic flaw itself over and over, despite its harmful results. So these formal transformations are not simply comic; they reflect the darker aspect of Mr. Micawber's comic psyche, such as his compulsion to repeat this altogether masochistic behavior (consider his "making motions at himself with a razor," 141), which in turn finds expression in the compulsion *to play the role* of the fallen "hero" as a source of pleasure. Thus the perfectly balanced rhetorical use of parallel and antithesis in the first part of his speech gives way to the overly and overtly theatrical mock-Shakespearean language in the last part: "The blossom is blighted, the leaf is withered, the god of day goes down upon the dreary scene." Dickens's father had, in actuality, spoken of the day setting on him forever, but that in Mr. Micawber's mouth this trope is displaced onto an imagined "scene" gives the whole passage a melodramatic and theatrical quality, almost a self-referential or even meta-fictional quality regarding his status as a character, which paradoxically seems to raise Micawber to the level of the (comic) universal in the very idiosyncrasies of his speech.

For example, the full force of the overdetermined formal transformations of this speech falls on the two words that most concisely capture Micawber's key character trait, in the form of a verbal tic, his infamous "in short." In this short passage Micawber's speech moves effortlessly from

Dream as spectral form

excessively objective legalese, with the addition of such words as "expenditure" and "income" to the original, to excessively romantic theatricality with emphasis on his typical comic pretenses to genteel eloquence. But this formal display of grandiloquence only sets Micawber up for his (linguistic/theatrical) fall: the language builds towards a climax in its culmination of melodramatic hyperbole and (comic) piling up of tropes and poeticisms, only to *fall* short in the "in short" that reveals Micawber's inability to maintain the linguistic pretense, or discursive "act," of gentility he repeatedly adopts. Thus, in this overdetermined little speech bemoaning the seemingly arbitrary and austere existential consequences of exceeding limits, the "in short," Micawber's trademark, translates *formally*, in a single speech mannerism, Micawber's repetition compulsion to exceed his own means financially into his compulsion to exceed them *linguistically*. Micawber's character thus takes on this universal quality not as an excess but precisely as a lack or *subtraction*, as in the "in short" that registers language's failure or limit. It is true, as Kucich suggests, that the prose here generates excess for its own sake, producing nonsense and even "pure sounds," but the "in short" speech mannerism demonstrates how this is also a *lack* of sense, a drive or desire—that Micawber's linguistic failure is the failure of language that brings us into contact with the cut/the Real.

But in order to better understand Micawber's role in the novel we must see him in relation to another father substitute for David, Mr. Dick (whose doubling with Micawber Phiz emphasizes in the illustrations). Though both Micawber's and Mr. Dick's characters revolve around repetition compulsions that express themselves in terms of language, there is an even more literal (and regressive) emphasis on materiality in the language of Mr. Dick, who, after all, compulsively turns his memoirs into kites and flies them with the schoolboys. Mr. Dick spends his days attempting to write his autobiography ("for upwards of ten years"), but can never keep out the radical anachronism of the decapitation of King Charles I, at which point the pages become material for kites and he must begin again. One can't help but think of Freud's analogy between castration anxiety and political panic in his essay on fetishism, when he says that, "In later life grown men may experience a similar panic, perhaps when the cry goes up that throne and altar are in danger, and similar illogical consequences will also follow them" ("Fetishism" 205). With all the latent implications of the Oedipal complex here in the play on names (from Dickens to Dick, and with reference to Charles I), Mr. Dick's repetition compulsion finds expression above all in his language, which is truncated and repetitive both in writing and in speech. Thus Mr. Dick—pathetically entrapped in

Beyond the realism principle

his repetition compulsion—exists in a childish state of language wherein he "diffuses" the "facts" of his history by turning them into playful objects of imaginary flight, as if his words themselves were freed from the weight of authority only to leave them all the more ineffectual. Of course, this doesn't do much for the plight of poor Mr. Dick, whose real name is Richard Babbly (diffused language) and who, Aunt Betsy tells David, "can't bear his name" (176). Indeed, he cannot bear his name in a more fundamental way because he cannot finally grasp himself, his own history, in language, there always being some displaced past trauma that he "can never make perfectly clear" (177). If Mr. Dick's words are finally ethereal and incommunicable, however, Mr. Micawber's have substance and give sensual pleasure. Moreover, if Mr. Dick takes refuge in literally tossing his words to the winds, Micawber finds refuge from trauma *in* words and their material value.

Thus both Mr. Dick and Mr. Micawber dramatize a certain tension or struggle between the pleasure principle and the reality principle, specifically in their respective repetition compulsions. For what reader does not, at some level, sympathize with Micawber's childlike view of the world that it should satisfy the demands of the pleasure principle without extracting fiscal, familial, social, and other dues. But whereas Mr. Dick maintains his purely childish domain of reality-free pleasure at the *expense* of the symbolic, Micawber seems to circumvent the demands of the reality principle by obtaining pleasure *in* symbolic play or performativity at the *very place where reality demands a limit*. In this sense there is a price to pay for the innocence of each. Mr. Dick's more ethereal words may find imaginative freedom in fleeting flights, but their material value is completely expended in this pleasure ("I never know where they may come down," he says, and when they do come down he "seemed to wake gradually out of a dream," 179, 189). The worldly Aunt Betsy, whose job it is to give currency to his airy language ("it's not a business-like way of speaking," she says of his "allegorical" articulations, "nor a worldly way," 179) must *literally* pay for Mr. Dick's linguistic innocence, at first by "bargaining" for him and then through compromising blackmail. The two form a pair, then, in each other's lacks, Aunt Betsy's calculated expression paying for his extravagant flights.

As for Micawber, it is clear that he translates worldly suffering into linguistic gratification, that whatever his material losses may be, the linguistic pleasure generated by transforming them into words is his payoff.[4] Thus whereas the conflict between the pleasure principle and the reality principle for Mr. Dick is settled through linguistic foreclosure,

Mr. Micawber manages largely to circumvent the conflict by transforming pain in reality into pleasure in language, an exchange facilitated by a fixation on the signifier's materiality as appealing to the drive (i.e., the ability to cathect words). Partly this is reflected in terms of oral gratification, as the word used most frequently to describe Micawber's linguistic indulgence, "relish," suggests: after he proclaims his "Ignominy, Want, Despair, and Madness," for instance, David says "the relish with which Mr Micawber described himself, as prey to these dismal calamities, was only to be equalled by the emphasis with which he read his letter" (630). This "relish" of language, as it were, has the effect of de-cathecting reality, of depriving the reality principle of its bitter iniquity by transferring that cathexis onto language. Language is thus, at least partly, associated with food, or with oral satisfaction, and in fact Micawber is said to expend much of his insufficient credit on delicacies he can't afford, and is even said to be best at relishing food, just as he is with language—"Mr Micawber (who could do anything of this sort to perfection) covered [the mutton] with pepper, mustard, salt, and cayenne" (351). All this gives Micawber's character the sense of manifesting the indefatigable force of the drive in the face of overwhelming prohibition. In fact the way in which Micawber plunges into the despair inspired by his situation is invariably counteracted by the spontaneity with which he bounces back:

> It was nothing at all unusual for Mr Micawber to sob violently at the beginning of one of these Saturday night conversations, and sing about Jack's delight being his lovely Nan, towards the end of it. I have known him come home to supper with a flood of tears, and a declaration that nothing was now left but a jail; and go to bed making a calculation of putting bow-windows to the house, "in case anything turned up," which was his favourite expression. (145)

Micawber seems in fact to depend on both parts of the equation, as much on the financial destruction as on the ability to transform it into melodramatic outpourings, which seems at first approach to suggest an indestructibility to Micawber's ego.

But as I have indicated above, Micawber's speech at these moments of linguistic compensation is always already "other" in that it is performative and borrows from language radically dissociated from its context, and in this sense his speech is fundamentally fragmented (freely patched together from various discourses). In this case we might wonder where the "I" of Micawber lies, and in fact we find that Micawber's references to himself are frequently marked by logical involutions and absurd metaphors, that is, that his identity is subjected to all kinds of distortions—rather than localized—in his speech. Thus Micawber's crazy circumlocutions often interpose themselves between his personal pronoun and its predicate, and references to his body seem particularly objectified and dispersed, as when he says in a letter to David that "my feet will naturally tend towards the King's Bench Prison" (591), or in his roundabout signatures, e.g., "such ruined vestiges as yet / Remain, / Of / A / Fallen Tower, / WILKINS MICAWBER" (591), or "The / Eye / Appertaining to / WILKINS MICAWBER, / Magistrate" (734). This last pun on "eye" and "I" is an excellent example of Micawber's comic dissociation of self/body/identity in speech: we would normally assume a much clearer, immediate relationship between a body part, or a pronoun, and a person, but the phrase "appertaining to" allows for a much broader, vaguer, more mediated relation, and is, moreover, borrowed from legalese, which doesn't rationally belong here but finds its way in through the common notion of ownership that implicitly underpins that relation. The idea of an eye or an I "appertaining to" a person is highly amusing not only because of its absurdity, but because it reveals the implicit difficulty of these logical connections that we normally cover over, ignore, or are unconscious of. This loosening of logical connections in comic linguistic constructions—particularly in relation to the forms of ownership of self, body, and money—is indeed one of Micawber's most profound characteristics.

So in a sense Micawber may be said to pay for the triumph of the pleasure principle through language by loss, or fragmentation, of ego, but the difficulty with this view is that Micawber seems to "relish" this loss of ego as well. Indeed, if Micawber's language is fragmented from the start in its otherness and materiality, this latent quality is brought more and more to the surface as the tensions engaging Micawber's character are pushed to their extreme—tensions brought into play particularly in his being paired with the character of Uriah Heep. Thus there is a tendency in Micawber's fragmented language to split apart, to explode or shatter. This tendency is implicit from the beginning even in his character tic "in short," which is invariably referred to as a "burst" of confidence (the phrase is used three times in the first few paragraphs describing Micawber's entrance into the novel), as if Micawber were about to burst into language literally. But as Micawber is increasingly subjected to Uriah's oppression, the tendency finds increasingly literal expression, for example when, upon reunion with David to tell him of his plot to overthrow Uriah Heep, he refers to himself as "a shattered fragment of the Temple once called Man"

Dream as spectral form

(594). And when he finally reveals that plot to David, Aunt Betsy, and Mr. Dick, he bursts into broken fits of syllables piled up and poured forth in an irrepressible gush:

> "I'll put my hand to no man's hand," said Mr Micawber ... "until I have—blown to fragments—the—a—detestable—serpent—HEEP! I'll partake of no one's hospitality, until I have—a—moved Mount Vesuvius—to eruption—on—a—the abominable rascal—HEEP! Refreshment—a—underneath this roof—particularly punch—would—a—choak me—unless—I had—previously—choked the eyes—out of the head—a—of—interminable cheat, and liar—HEEP!" (599)

Moments like this and the final denouement of the Uriah/Wickfield mystery plot reveal a latent tendency governing Micawber's character: he gains a certain power over language precisely by shattering himself in it, by allowing it to distort and fragment his ego as means of *jouissance* (we might even point out the relevance here of "punch" being his favorite drink, with both its intoxicating effects and its association with the invulnerable marionette of that name). This self-shattering in language, moreover, is a fundamental aspect of Dickens's comic genius, which is introduced at the very start of his career in the form of Jingle in *The Pickwick Papers* whose first speech is similarly fragmented and eruptive:

> Terrible place—dangerous work—other day—five children—mother—tall lady, eating sandwiches—forgot the arch—crash—knock—children look round—mother's head off—sandwich in her hand—no mouth to put it in—head of a family off—shocking, shocking! Looking at Whitehall, sir?—fine place—little window—somebody else's head off there, eh, sir? (78–9)

This association, moreover, is not just formal as we see in the fact that the body, here as well, is subject to violent distortion and fragmentation, the figurative use of "head" serving to condense the group and the individual, "dismembering" both. Even more notable is the common reference to the beheading of Charles I, suggesting that there is a violence to the paternal metaphor at the root of Dickens's comic use of language. We could compare Dickens's linguistic innovations with what Žižek describes as Hegel's concept of the fundamentally negative power of the imagination:

> Ultimately, imagination stands for the capacity of our mind to dismember what immediate perception puts together, to "abstract" not a common notion but a certain feature from other features. To imagine means to imagine a partial object without its body, a color without its shape, a shape without a body: "here a bloody head—there another ghastly white apparition." (*Ticklish Subject* 30)

The linguistic genius at the root of both Jingle and Micawber, in other words, not only taps into the primary processes, but does so in the service of the death drive as a generative lack, a relation to the (hauntological) *structure of the cut*. Micawber's "relish" of language, then, which leads us to discover his pleasure in linguistic self-shattering, both conceals and reveals a *jouissance* of the death drive at work in spectral materiality.

But Micawber's explosive energy would be ineffective if there were not some external force to oppose it, and that force, which is initially reflected in financial dilemmas, is ultimately embodied in the character of Uriah Heep, who is as self-consuming as Micawber is self-expansive. That is, beyond the various obstacles that oppose and oppress Micawber—his financial dilemmas, his imprisonments for debt, familial duties, etc.—we can see the common denominator of a restriction on *jouissance* itself, or more specifically a taboo on an enjoyment of transgressing the self-contained economy of pleasure within a bounded ego/body, a restriction that is ultimately symbolic. Uriah is oppressive *in this very respect*, confining Micawber's communications even with his family and friends and keeping him, as Micawber himself says, "under a Taboo" (598); he embodies a prohibition on language. It is not just chance, therefore, that Micawber and Uriah become nemeses in a struggle over the articulation of a secret that imposes silence on a whole group of characters, including David. Uriah represents a kind of uncanny form whose power over language co-opts it into selfhood, swallows it, as it were, into itself in attempts to capitalize on its potential excess *jouissance*, and he constantly reveals this role in his absurdly tortuous dumb shows, for example he "sucked in his cheeks until they seemed to meet inside" his face (513), he sleeps with his mouth "open like a post-office" (as if to devour letters, 327), and he "hovers" around like a vulture "gorging himself on every syllable that [David] said to Agnes, or Agnes said to [him]" (327). He also repeatedly tells his mother to "hold [her] tongue," and wants to see David's tongue "cut out" (637). Even his laughter seems consumed in self-gratification: when he thinks he has gotten the upper hand of David and imposed a silence on him as well, he "stopped short, put his hands between his great knobs of knees, and doubled himself up with laughter. With perfectly silent laughter, not a sound escaped from him" (514).

Uriah's energies are thus directed towards and mediated through writing, as we see when he takes control over Mr. Wickfield's documents and imitates his signature in order to steal his identity and gain control over his affairs. When David and Uriah first meet at Wickfield's home, Uriah appears literally on the other side of writing (the papers hanging over his desk) where he is copying legal documents or contracts and gazing at David as if from the other side of a mirror, like an uncanny double materialized in David's autobiography, a distorted self-reflection that assumes a dark volition of its own:

> Though his face was towards me, I thought, for some time, the writing being between us, that he could not see me; but looking that way more attentively, it made me uncomfortable to observe that, every now and then, his sleepless eyes would come below the writing, like two red suns, and stealthily stare at me for I dare say a whole minute at a time, during which his pen went, or pretended to go, as cleverly as ever. I made several attempts to get out of their way ... but they always attracted me back again; and whenever I looked towards those two red suns, I was sure to find them, either just rising or just setting. (193)

As a double of David, Uriah is another writer; but as an uncanny, external return of David's fantasy of himself, Uriah is a kind of sham writer (his pen may have only "pretended to go") using his writing to conceal himself and his intentions, relishing the strangely silent power that *copying* procures, and he seems in this uncanny, doubly reflexive scene to be copying *David* into his writing just as David (as narrator recording his history) is "copying" Uriah into his. So the *two sons* of the novel gaze at each other *through* the medium of writing, commencing a conflict that only the claim over words will settle.

This overdetermined status gives Uriah's character, despite his frail frame and his "umble" refrain, a strangely elusive, effigial power. In fact, Uriah's body seems indestructible precisely *because* it is so mutable and abject. Uriah has a bodily presence that is uncannily fluid and protean, as if his regressive bodily transformations mocked or parodied David's "progressive" transformations of identity. His face, for instance, is frequently likened to a mask or gargoyle and undergoes all sorts of distortions and disfigurations (for instance, "he made his face very lantern-jawed, for the greater convenience of scraping" and then "slowly restored his face to its natural form," 513), and at times his body almost seems, like that of some Ovidian villain, to be about to metamorphose into some lower-life form,

> as he sat on my sofa, with his long knees drawn up under his coffee cup, his hat and gloves upon the ground close to him, his spoon going softly round and round, his shadowless red eyes, which looked as if they had scorched their lids off, turned towards me without looking at me, the disagreeable dints I have formerly described in his nostrils coming and going with his breath, and a snaky undulation pervading his frame from his chin to his boots, I decided in my own mind that I disliked him intensely. (322)

Uriah's uncanny, deathly body and his linguistic antagonism are not unrelated: Uriah represents the "other side of the face" that we confronted in the dream of Irma's injection as the imaginary image of the body beyond the symbolic, "the flesh in as much as it is suffering, is formless, in as much as its form in itself is something which provokes anxiety," that "something faced with which all words cease and all categories fail" (Lacan, *Ego in Freud's Theory* 154–5). His threat to David is thus precisely his elusiveness to the signifier, and as David's double, struggling for the same object of desire, he seems to embody what Lacan terms (in his later work) the "lamella," that undead asexual thing that is at once object and nonobject, like *das Ding*, intimate to and alien to the subject. Thus David is "oppressed … with a leaden dread" of him yet "attracted to him in very repulsion" as he can't help watching him asleep, "lying on his back, with his legs extended to I don't know where, gurglings taking place in his throat, stoppages in his nose, and his mouth open like a post-office" (*David Copperfield* 327). It is appropriate, then, that the conflict between David and Uriah is never directly played out in "reality": David imagines, in a semi-dream state, that he runs him "through the body" with a hot poker,[5] he slaps him across the face with dreamlike lack of effect, but it is Micawber who must ultimately defeat him in David's place.

But before there is confrontation between these two characters—Micawber and Uriah—who stand at the extremes of language, Micawber notably withdraws from the narrative and his absence is accompanied by an unmistakable loss of momentum in the novel. The chapter "Domestic" in particular sees David's life reduced to a kind of domestic farce, a dreamlike submersion in the interminable struggle with the quotidian: unruly pages, household bills, overcooked dinners, etc. At this point in the novel, David's development, and thus his narrative, seems to have dwindled to a slow eddy, and this paralysis stems from a failure to communicate with Dora, his "child-wife" whose development has also been curtailed, a failure, that is, of language. After an attempt to appeal to Dora in the figurative terms that they "infect every one about" them, David finds "it was of no use repeating this kind of effort" and asks himself: "What other course was left to take! To 'form her mind?' This was a common phrase of words which had a fair and promising sound, and I resolved to form Dora's mind" (583, 585). The result of this (obviously misguided) effort is to turn them even more into creatures of mindless and ineffectual repetition: "I found myself in the condition of a schoolmaster, a trap, a pitfall; of always playing the spider to Dora's fly, and always pouncing out of my hole to her infinite disturbance" (585). He finds, of course, that he "had effected nothing" (585), and this chapter turns into a lesson for David in the necessity of conceding to the reality principle, which is not so readily pliable to our wishes and desires, the lesson that in order for the ego to meet with loss, it must give up a certain part of its being, of its *jouissance*: "What I missed," he says, in an attempt to bring his narrative's "secrets to light," "I still regarded—I always regarded—as something that had been a dream of my youthful fancy; that was incapable of realisation; that I was now discovering to be so, with some natural pain, as all men did" (587). This forfeiture of desire entails maintaining a lack in language, a "shadow" that resists linguistic expression in the narrativization of his life: "it was undefined as ever, and addressed me like a strain of sorrowful music" (587). But strangely enough, as soon as David accepts Dora as she is and concedes to the reality principle as the restriction of libidinal pleasure, two interesting things happen: Dora becomes deathly ill, and Micawber explodes Uriah's plot to subdue David's real (unconscious) object of desire, Agnes. This chapter ends with a phrase that implicitly unites these two seemingly disparate events, a phrase foreshadowing Dora's death, which has (rather shockingly) more than a little of the mark of Micawber's rhetoric in it: "O what a fatal name it was, and how the blossom withered in its bloom upon the tree" (590). The "name" to which this sentence refers is Dora's nickname, Little Blossom, but names will play a more symbolic role in the unraveling of this symptomatic complex that unfolds in the next chapters.

It is here that Micawber steps in and achieves the "explosion" in which David only "assists" but that frees him from his narrative freeze by a symbolic displacement of linguistic *jouissance* onto Micawber. This "explosion" and the whole resolution of the David–Uriah–Micawber plot (and ultimately the continuation of the narrative) can be explained, I will argue, in terms of two implicitly prosopopoetic passages. The first is a letter from Micawber to David that effectively announces to the reader his re-entrance into the narrative:

> Circumstances beyond my individual control have, for a considerable lapse of time, effected a severance of ... intimacy ... This fact, my dear sir, combined with the distinguished elevation to which your talents [i.e., renown as a writer] have raised you, deters me from presuming to aspire to the liberty of addressing the companion of my youth, by the familiar appellation of Copperfield ... It is not for one ... who now takes up the pen to address you ... to adopt the language of compliment, or of congratulations. That, he leaves to abler and to purer hands. (590)

Although the "you" "address[ed]" in this passage refers on the plot level to David, one could almost as easily read an implicit apology *to the reader* on *behalf* of David, wondering, in Micawber's rhetoric of self-effacement, "if your more important avocations should admit of your ever tracing these imperfect characters thus far—which may be, or may not be, as circumstances arise—" and foreseeing that "you will naturally inquire by what object I am influenced, then, in inditing the present missive," promising that he will "defer to ... that enquiry; and proceed to develop it" (590). Reading "characters" in both senses, in other words, one can hear in Micawber's words an address to the reader of the novel, apologizing for Dickens's necessity of delving into David's sluggish domestic life with its "imperfect characters" and promising a more Micawberesque turn of events. Thus Micawber's "latent" role of author is couched in terms of a mythical overthrow as he suggests "without more directly referring to any latent ability that may possibly exist on my part, of wielding the thunderbolt, or directing the devouring and avenging flame in any quarter" (591). There is thus a sense in which Micawber has usurped the narrative as the means by which the motive that is repressed in David's narrative, unable to find linguistic expression (the "dream of [his] youthful fancy"), will find its release, and the language of this letter, as Micawber "now takes up the pen to address you," becomes almost uncannily self-conscious in doing so, as if the words/characters were *rising up against their author*. If the repressed unnamable lack that paralyzes David's narrative relates to the blindness of David to his own desires ("blind, blind, blind" repeats Aunt Betsy) then the personification of the disavowal of those desires is Uriah. Thus Uriah (in his present form) must be written out of the text before David can have access to his desire in the form of Agnes, upon whom Uriah has also placed a taboo.

The other implicitly prosopopoetic passage is spoken by David as an aside to the reader and is even more explicitly admonishing towards Micawber than Micawber's is to him. It should be noted here that Micawber has nearly always been read as an ambiguous character ("The case against Micawber is certainly ambiguous" says Stewart), someone to be both appreciated and resisted by both the reader and by David (*Dickens and the Trials*); though he provides a certain amount of humor, the argument runs, he also provides an example of a linguistic style that is to be strictly rejected as a model for David. Garrett Stewart, for instance, goes so far as to say that Micawber is a "powerful enemy" of David's style, and his "grandiose clap-trappings" represent a "rhetorical style that is 'infectious' in the worst sense" (*Dickens and the Trials* 138). Stewart uses the

Dream as spectral form

following passage from the novel—which is the second prosopopoetic passage to which I refer here—to exemplify this stylistic threat to David:

> Again, Mr Micawber had a relish in this formal piling up of words, which, however ludicrously displayed in this case, was, I must say, not at all peculiar to him. I have observed it, in the course of my life, in numbers of men. It seems to me to be a general rule. In the taking of legal oaths, for instance, deponents seem to enjoy themselves mightily when they come to several good words in succession, for the expression of one idea; as, that they utterly detest, abominate, and abjure, or so forth; and the old anathemas were made relishing on the same principle. We talk about the tyranny of words, but we like to tyrannise over them too; we are fond of having a large superfluous establishment of words to wait upon us on great occasions; we think it looks important, and sounds well. As we are not peculiar about the meaning of our liveries on state occasions, if they be but fine and numerous enough, so, the meaning and necessity of our words is a second consideration, if there be but a great parade of them. And as individuals get into trouble by making too great a show of liveries, or as slaves when they are too numerous rise against their masters, so I think I could mention a nation that has got into too many great difficulties, and will get into many greater, from maintaining too large a retinue of words. (*David Copperfield* 633–4)

Among the various critical responses to this passage, two things seem to be of general consensus: that Dickens, more or less explicitly, ventriloquizes himself into the text here through David, and that he does so in order to indicate that Micawber has gone too far in his linguistic eccentricities. Of this passage Stewart says that "David, speaking for Dickens" gives "the most detailed piece of stylistic criticism to be found in any of the novels" (*Dickens and the Trials* 141), and McGowan nicely concludes from this passage that "Micawber's use of language, marvelous as it is, is finally seen as abusive, and he is banished to Australia" ("Bankruptcy" 75). These readings take the intrusion of Dickens into the text at face value, but if we push a little farther in our inquiry into this passage some further subtleties will be revealed.

For one thing, the issue of repetition and proliferation in this passage, itself repetitious and wordy, is ambiguous to say the least. If, as we have suggested, David is trapped in an ineffectual repetition revolving around an unspoken "secret," Mr. Micawber's linguistic repetition roots out and purges the cause of his repression which is in itself the result of a blockage or obstruction of language embodied in Uriah, who represents a menacingly elusive Thing-beyond-the-writing. This Micawber would be incapable doing if he did not take a "relish in this formal piling up of words" that David complains of in the passage quoted. Thus David's protestation about the undue enjoyment of words for the sake of pure sound or surplus, despite their intended authority (all the metaphors to describe which, such as liveries, slaves, retinue, etc., involve the discourse of the master) may also be taken as an implicit or masked *celebration* of Micawber in reverse form, of which he cannot be (or is not meant to be) consciously aware. For Micawber's use of language here is not dry and bureaucratic (as David's examples suggest) but performative and meta-representational: he reads the entire speech from a "foolscap document," he wields his ruler like a sword, he makes several references to *Hamlet*, and *Macbeth*, and the letter from which he reads is likened to an array of forms of representation—a "sermon," a "performance," an "Act of Parliament," a legal document—which have all been comically exploited by Micawber. Micawber almost dissipates into a proliferation of texts here in an over-the-top "explosion" of language that translates the materiality of signifiers into *jouissance* ("Mr Micawber read on, almost smacking his lips," says David, 634), while David gazes on, silent and demure. *David's* prosopopoetic passage, then, with its anxiety over words/characters rising up like "slaves" "against their masters," can be read as a masked response to *Micawber's* prosopopoetic passage, in which the character of Micawber "takes up the pen" with the intention "of wielding the thunderbolt, or directing the devouring and avenging flame" in the stead of the supposed hero/autobiographer (590).

This passage, though a ventriloquistic intrusion by Dickens, is thus apparently marked by David's "blindness" to what Micawber is doing with language, since Micawber clearly is using words like a "large retinue" in order to effectively overthrow Uriah Heep and his taboo. Stewart points to the fact that David gives the example of stating things in legalese "in triplicate," but he neglects to note the fact that Micawber also takes his triplicates from Shakespeare, as in "to dwindle, peak, and pine" (*Macbeth*). In an even more sublime parody, this time of *Hamlet*, he soliloquizes about "the contest within myself between stipend and no stipend, baker and no baker, existence and non-existence" (632), an uncannily self-referential bit of criticism on the part of Micawber whose existential crisis would clearly have to be framed in the terms "money," "food," "being." Appropriately, then, what David seems to misrecognize most in this prosopopoetic passage is Micawber's formal use of repetition, the use of "several good words in succession, for the expression of one idea," as David sees it, which is really at the heart of his "stylistic criticism." However, what David is blind to is that Micawber's use of repetition is not merely high-flown style, but a means of tapping into a nonmimetic, transformative play or drive inherent in the relationship between signifier and signified, as indicated by his ritualistic punctuation of each phrase with the name HEEP (which David calls "the magic word," 599) as if he had made an effigy of the word itself: "the scoundrel's name is—HEEP!" Micawber repeats and Uriah "fell back as if he had been struck or stung" (628). Micawber makes an effigy of the name Heep by formally subjecting the name itself to material/symbolic distortions, by *heap*ing masses of words on Uriah, and reducing him to a "HEEP of infamy," thus drawing on the potential of the sliding of sense in the signifier, its intrinsic drive, to have a *real effect* (631). Accordingly Micawber's use of the *name* as an effigy unmasks *Heep* as the "atrocious mass" already latent in the signifier, a horrifying undead pre-linguistic "matter" ("I now saw him with his mask off," says David, 629): "Villainy is the matter; baseness is the matter; deception, fraud, conspiracy, are the matter; the name of the whole atrocious mass is—HEEP!" (598).

But if David's stylistic criticism of Micawber is really a mark of (momentary and necessary) linguistic blindness, why should it appear to be given as an apparent ventriloquism of the authorial voice (as prosopopoeia), as so many critics agree? The answer to this question is suggested in a play of naming/un-naming disguised at the heart of this prosopopoetic passage—a passage inserted into a scene of unmasking though names—which points to a certain castration metaphor at the heart of the text.[6] Preceding the scene of Micawber's "explosion," for instance, Micawber renames Mr. Dick "Mr Dixon," bringing the truncated name Dick ("you think Mr Dick a short name, eh?" asks Aunt Betsy, 176) in even closer association with that of Dickens by condensing the last syllable of Dickens with the homophonous phoneme "son," thereby relegating Mr. Dick [son] (the autobiographer haunted by the intrusion of the dead father) to the role of the son instead of the father (of the text/symbolic) and relieving him of a metaphor he cannot lay claim to; accordingly, in response to his new name, Mr. Dick "laughed rather childishly" in relief (623). Furthermore, a more masked instance of unmasking through the act of naming/un-naming can be found in David's prosopopoetic address to the reader. In his complaints about Micawber's abuses of language, David compares Micawber's circumlocutions to the practice of disguising anathemas, saying that "the old anathemas were made relishing on the same principle." Anathemas—accursed things, or more precisely, the names for these things that were prohibited—were made "relishing" (that is, not just pronounceable but pleasurable) by substituting them with more appealing euphemisms or circumlocutions. We know that "relishing" is Micawber's key signifier, but the reference to it in relation to these anathemas may seem strange, until we realize that the name Dickens itself—which in the OED is described as "substituted for the devil," as in "the Dickens take you" or "go to the Dickens"—is an example of an anathema made relishing. Mrs. Micawber provides an example in the text of this particular anathema when she claims in a letter to Traddles that "Mr Micawber asserts that he has sold himself to the D" (she could just as easily have said, "sold himself to the Dickens") (592). But Mrs. Micawber's statement turns out to be more than a cliché, since Mr. Micawber has in fact literally sold himself to Uriah, who is repeatedly likened to a serpent and a devil ("as if I had some meaner quality of devil for a lodger," 326), and whose mysterious taboo prevents Micawber from addressing David "by the familiar appellation of Copperfield." In this sense, then, David, in a masked allusion to naming the un-namable (anathema), unmasks Micawber as the usurper of—the one who, as a mask of the voice, disfigures or effaces—the authorial voice of Dickens himself. But it is only by doing so, by effacing himself in the signifier/character who assumes the *jouissance* of language, that Dickens can make the unsayable (symbolic castration) not only sayable but relishing, can become not Mr. Dick but Mr. Micawber (or better, Heep-Micawber–Copperfield).

This play of naming/un-naming between characters and on the borders of the text (between inside and outside), then, can be seen as a formal expression within the text of a link between the entrance into the symbolic order and symbolic castration, particularly the castration of the father or what Lacan calls the "Name-of-the-Father." References throughout Micawber's speech, for instance, repeatedly indicate violence to the father—*Macbeth*, *Hamlet*, Arnold's "The Death of Nelson"— implying that the voice behind these masks is always already split and self-divided between the oppositions father/son, enjoyment/restriction, author/character. Mr. Dick, for instance, is overburdened by his castration complex because he cannot *name* the violence to the father in such way as to symbolize it ("there was that sort of thing done to me somehow? Eh?" he asks David, gesturing with his hands to indicate both his "confusion" and the decapitation of Charles I, 550), and thus he remains somewhere between psychotic and childlike. Micawber, on the other hand, is able to name Heep, the Thing, as a signifier for symbolic castration in the text and distance David from his unconscious ambivalence about language and/ as enjoyment (*jouissance*), through a symbolic play on the name *Heep* that unmasks the name and the identity it signifies as a referential/ontological play of the signifier, its spectral materiality, which had eluded David (and others) who saw the name as a fixed signifier for a real person. That is, the unnamable, anxiety-producing Thing beyond the symbolic, in the form of the uncanny and primal "matter" of Heep, is given a place in the symbolic precisely through symbolic castration, giving up one's lost object to the symbolic Other, just as Dickens has given up his childhood trauma and life narrative to the Other of the text in the Micawber's translation of his father's parting "text" and in the novel *David Copperfield*. Consequently, the "snaky" villain Uriah is rendered impotent, or, as Welsh so intuitively put it "the villain suddenly goes limp and ceases to be a threat to anyone" (154). Thus Micawber, a surrogate of Dickens's father, is linked to the Name-of-the-Father/Author precisely through the signifier "to relish"—not only to relish language, but to enjoy/embellish the act of making the unsayable sayable through the signifier's (death) drive, the *jouissance* of desubjectification that is the very act of (being a) speaking (subject).

Finally, we should further note here, in this ironic reversal of self-reference on the part of Dickens, that what David is observing with disapprobation is precisely what lies at the source of Dickens's genius: to take the ridiculous "clap-trappings" of Members of Parliament, journalists, lawyers, etc., and transform them into sublime humor of the likes of Shakespeare and Joyce. Thus when Micawber is "shipped off" to Australia I don't think it should be taken as a pronouncement on Micawber's rhetorical style ("'infectious' in the worst sense"): though by the end he has fulfilled his role in the *Bildungsroman* plot, there is still no repressing his *writing*, and his letters still come "by the ream." We might even say that Micawber himself, the character of Micawber, is structured like a joke—as the absurd distortion of conscious logic that lets the unconscious wish-fantasy irrupt into consciousness.[7] David's narrative may regain its impetus only after the castration of Heep, but this can only be achieved by the *symbolic* castration of the position of the author/autobiographer, that is, by Micawber's self-shattering and perilously nonsensical linguistic excess/lack. Thus Dickens's representation of Micawber works to overcome, to return to Marcus's terms of the primary and the secondary processes here, the "resistance" of consciousness, and here we can recall "that analytic symptoms are produced in the flow of a word which tries to get through" (Lacan, *Seminar II* 159). The threat of Micawber is not rooted in his stylistic influence over David's more controlled and deliberate narrative voice, as many critics have supposed. Nor is it that he is not a threat at all; rather, his threat runs much deeper, like the threat of Master Bates from *Oliver Twist*: it is the threat that he will cause you to laugh your head off.

Notes

1 Marcus seems aware of this problem on some level, as his essay moves towards a dialectical resolution in appealing to Hegel. But this still leaves the problem of the primary process untouched since *his* Hegelian response seems to posit an external dialectical force (social injustice) both negating and bringing into being a primarily creative energy (presencing logos). Moreover, this dialectic emerges in rather *deus ex machina* fashion at the end of the essay.

2 As *Johnson's Dictionary* points out, the word "jar" resonates with both repetition and justice "to strike ... to repeat the same sound or noise ... to clash, to interfere ...[Shakespeare] ... to quarrel, to dispute ... [Milton]" and "clash of interests [Shakespeare]."

3 The idea of "nonsense" in Kucich's book, however, which seems to me both central and somewhat ambiguous, has at bottom a certain deconstructive function that makes it very suggestive in relation to my thesis about *jouissance* here.

4 In *David Copperfield*, the materiality of language enters into the discourse of the novel metaphorically in relation to oral satisfaction, with its ambiguous moral implications. Words in *David Copperfield* are repeatedly treated as things to be ingested, inhaled, or even tasted. Peggotty, for instance, refers to her nephew as "Am," and David comments that she "meant her nephew Ham, mentioned in my first chapter but she spoke of him as a morsel of English Grammar" (30). Doctor Strong, David tells us, was always "engaged in looking out for Greek roots; which in my innocence and ignorance, I supposed to be a botanical furor on the Doctor's part, especially as he always looked at the ground when he walked about—until I understood that they were roots of words, with a view to a new Dictionary, which he had in contemplation" (206). And Micawber (to whom we will return momentarily) is often said to "relish" words.

5 That this gesture suggests violence to an uncannily fantastic double is confirmed in a similar scene from *Little Dorrit* in which Flintwinch confronts his sleeping self, his "double," in Affery's supposed dream and "looked about him for an offensive weapon, caught up the snuffers, and ... lunged at the sleeper, as though he would have run him through the body" (82).

6 We can also note at this point that the name Copperfield has a special significance in relation to castration as well: "copper" being a play on the Old French verb "coper" meaning "to strike a blow" or "to chop off," and "field" suggesting regrowth. As one whose progress in life is repeatedly broken off and yet yielding new beginnings, David is the one who endures and integrates repeated castrations.

7 Or as Todd McGowan posits in *Only A Joke Can Save Us: A Theory of Comedy*, where lack and excess come together—a better example than Micawber, at least in terms of novel characters, it would be hard for me to imagine.

6

The "as if" hauntology of *Little Dorrit* and the uncanny dream of the three fathers

Having explored the role of *glissement*, or *jouissance*, in relation to narrative voice and of "spectral materiality" in relation to character, in this chapter I will focus on a particular narrative trope that most highlights that spectral space between representation and reality, and especially its relation to character: the Dickensian *as if*. Dickens's use of what has been called his "favorite descriptive device" (Rosenberg 60), has frequently been noted and commented on, but there is still much to be explored in this, his most spectral of formal traits. I will therefore sketch out a few aspects of this trope that give it an ontological significance and explore its use in *Little Dorrit*, where, I will argue, it finds its fullest hauntological expression.

Probably the most rigorous and fascinating analysis of the *as if* trope in Dickens's prose is to be found in Jonathan Farina's book *Everyday Words and the Character of Prose in Nineteenth-Century Britain*. Farina makes the important point that the *as if* is in itself, as a form (an epistemological one for him), in some way counter or subversive, as a form of "non-referential, counterfactual knowledge that defied the ascendency of mimesis and the infamous fact" (95). However, where Farina sees the *as if* in terms of its epistemological mediation of knowledge and thought, I see it as having a primarily ontological (or as I have been calling it, hauntological) function, and I find it interesting in this context, especially regarding character, to see how these two frameworks can lead in two opposite directions, since it is the epistemological aspect of this trope that ultimately gives it a subjectifying function for Farina: "*As if* qualifies as a character in the epistemology I am describing because it enables personages to appropriate contingencies and other material conditions of experience as their own" (96). This certainly does seem to be an important part of the trope as it is used in the Victorian novel; but it seems to me rather that the *as if* form, at least in Dickens, does as much to *haunt* the idea of a personage as it does to subjectify it. I will try to show through an analysis of *Little Dorrit* how the *as if* trope can also be, in its *ontological* function, more desubjectifying than subjectifying.

Most discussions of Dickens's *as if*, understandably, see it purely in linguistic terms (Farina, for instance, analyzes it in its rhetorical/epistemological function as "conditional analogy"), whereas it also has a very distinctive *imagistic* function, yet to be fully explored, that introduces an intrinsic *distance*, an otherness or gap, into the typically logocentric structure of analogy. Rosenberg, for instance, says of this trope that "analogies in the form of 'as if' and 'as though' may be Dickens' favorite descriptive device, possibly because they combine the uncertainties of the conditional with the peculiar imagistic juxtapositions of metaphor, allowing comparisons simultaneously to be introduced and rendered doubtful" (60). The two elements of the *as if* trope that Rosenberg highlights—the introduction of conditionals and "imagistic juxtaposition"—seem accurate, but the idea that they are combined in order to render "doubtful" the very comparison introduced seems somewhat ambiguous, at least in these rhetorical terms. One thing I would amend here is that what distinguishes the *as if*, in the way that Dickens uses it, from other forms of analogy or comparison, is that it effects a *shift* in mode from the indicative to the conditional, not just an "introduction" of the conditional, whereby the "imagistic juxtaposition" between the two parts (indicative and conditional, we could say, but perhaps more accurately real and fantasy, or even objective and subjective), seem to exist on two parallel planes, simultaneously. One very interesting point about this is that, far from rendering doubtful the comparison introduced, the conditional image will usually assume more presence than the literal image, since it is used for the purpose of vividness or intensity. For example, early in *David Copperfield*, as David is narrating his own precarious birth, we have the following description of trees during the storm that provides an excellent example of this use of the *as if*:

> As the elms bent to one another, like giants who were whispering secrets, and after a few seconds of repose, fell into a violent fury, tossing their wild arms about, as if their late confidences were really too wicked for their peace of mind, some weather-beaten ragged old rooks'-nests, burdening their higher branches, swung like wrecks upon a stormy sea. (13)

In this, as in many cases from Dickens's prose, the comparison is *already* made before the *as if* is introduced: the wind-tossed trees are like whispering giants. The *as if* modifies the second part of the analogy, the conditional image, and the "imagistic juxtaposition" would not be nearly as striking if the *as if* did not have this surplus value, prepared for by the animating detail that the giants in the comparison were "whispering secrets," which takes us more fully into the realm of the fantasy or the subjective mediation of the real.

There is a syntactical difference here with respect to metaphor, that I can only describe as a kind of *spacing out*, an emphasis on the diachronic, which I will pursue presently. This syntactical difference may be clarified by comparing this example with other forms, such as metaphor, in which the images are usually *condensed* (ex. "the trees whispered secrets and tore their leafy hair"), or analogy, in which the images are presented as *exchangeable* ("the trees were like giants gone mad," etc.). The *as if*, on the other hand, brings about a kind of transformation of that allows a transference of affect from one state to another, not unlike Grandville's metamorphoses. This is precisely why the *as if* structure, as Farina also notes, is in fact another example of what Stewart calls syllepsis, "the undoing of strict sequence by the interplay of disjunction—and its ignited explosion of new meaning" (*Between Film and Screen* 129) and why it can also be seen as a proto-filmic aspect of Dickens's novels. But this affect is often also displaced from the plot level (typically centering on human subjects) to the symbolic level (typically involving objects that take on a symbolic surplus), so that in the *as if* form objects often perform a kind of dumb show. In the last example, for instance, which describes the scene prior to David's birth, the *as if* image punctuates a tension between David's Aunt Betsy and his mother over naming and gender: the Copperfield estate is named Rookery after the rooks' nests, but it turns out that there are no rooks, and Aunt Betsy objects to the inappropriate name. This tension over literal and figurative naming frames this sliding of images in the example, incorporating gestures and images (trees like giants, mad flailing, rooks like ships, treetops like a stormy sea). The tension is of course overdetermined since it relates to David's identity, and Betsy, assuming he will be a girl, wishes him to be named "Betsy Trotwood Copperfield." Of course, David *will* later be named Trotwood by Betsy Trotwood. Thus, this *as if* image is indicative of a larger *as if* structure of the milieu, in which Aunt Betsy (referred to as a "fairy" or "supernatural being") represents another potentiality that both is and isn't negated at David's birth. This fantasy has an effect in the Real. There is something unnamable in David's character that Lacan would call *in him more than him*, a surplus beyond sexual identity that generates an endless sliding of names and pronouns, as I have tried to show, from Rosa to Mr. Dick to Heep and Micawber. The *as if* form, then, is a means for the Real to resist being absorbed into the objective ontological status of reality/realism, since in it the "object resists opposition to the subject and a detail of reality itself gets spectralized" (Žižek, *Disparities* 187); this form is ontological in that it is, as Žižek says, "what introduces the gap that separates the Real from reality—it is on account of this gap that what we experience as external reality always has to rely on a fantasy" (*Disparities* 185). Interestingly enough, I believe Farina would agree with me here, as he points out that *as ifs* mark gaps, they "articulate the gaps between personages and classes, like the 'two nations'; gaps between sensory perceptions and emotional impressions," etc. (97). The difference here would be that for Farina these gaps are epistemological insofar as they are inherent in human consciousness, that "*as if* narrators are only speculating about the putatively real story they purport to tell but to which they seem to have only superficial or limited access" (97)—whereas here I am positing that the function and power of the *as if* is precisely in its ability to show us that this gap is always already inherent in the Real as such.

We can thus break the *as if* down into two particular aspects, a "spacing out" (a playing or "syllepsis") with respect to metaphor, and a "flight of images" that unfolds from this gap (what Garrett Stewart calls "montage thinking" in *Between Film and Screen*). This flight of images tends to be rooted in the visual: in the example from *David Copperfield*, the connection is made from storm-tossed trees to whispering giants by way of visual isomorphism, but once the association has been established, the comparative object becomes imbued with affect, acquires a phantasmic presence (the giants then go out of their minds with the knowledge of their fantastical secrets), or is spectralized. In the opening of *Hard Times*, to use another example, the narrator describes Gradgrind's speaking mannerisms with the repetition of comparisons beginning with "the emphasis" and ends with the particularly protean sentence, "The emphasis was helped by the speaker's hair, which bristled on the skirts of his bald head, a plantation of firs to keep the wind from its shining surface, all covered with knobs, like the crust of a plum pie, as if the head had scarcely warehouse-room for the hard facts stored inside" (7). We see here that the *as if* comes in rather late, but functions to crystalize a form of "montage thinking" that allows a series of metonymic links in a metaphoric chain underlying and enmeshed in the "real" object of description. In this flight of images (or montage), one "objective" image, Gradgrind's head, enters in a single sentence into a quick series of displacements with other "imagined" images: a plantation, a pie, and a warehouse (which returns to metaphor by containing facts like a head). Dickens is at his most absurd here, almost surreal, and also closest to Grandville. We can compare the figurative use of imagery here to Grandville's surrealist flights, such as "Premier Rêve" and "Second Rêve" (Figures 4 and 5). These visual examples are crucial for understanding Dickens's most signature rhetorical trait. What strikes us in Grandville's illustration (and what strikes us as rather "hallucinatory" or even psychotic) is that the images themselves have entered into a kind of radical sliding, they have loosened their anchor in the discursive order that imposes a stability on these endless displacements or associations. This imaginary primacy frees the object of its grounding in the logos and the real and gives it a spectral presence of its own. Images in a way, then, become signifiers, but signifiers freed from the more restrictive laws of logos, discourse, and telos. Part of the energy of these associations comes from the use of metonymy, since, as Laplanche and Leclaire point out, "the metonymic connection establishes a bridge between two (or more) signifiers whose relationship, in form or content, is much less obvious (much more arbitrary and singular) than in the case of metaphor" (249).

Before turning to *Little Dorrit*, I would go a little further along this line of thought to emphasize that the montage thinking that the *as if* introduces into the narrative, in giving images a disjunctive relation to the realist tendency of the narrative, also gives the images or details a kind of symbolic or signifying autonomy of their own. We can see this most notably in the example of Gradgrind in *Hard Times*, where once the details have become spectralized to an almost surreal degree, a *detail* of Gradgrind's own body can channel the implicit (subjective) affect of the author (antagonism or aggression) and almost rise up against him: "his very neckcloth, trained to take him by the throat with an unaccommodating grasp, like a stubborn fact" (7). The point to be taken from this is that when the *as if* applies to characters, the body itself is often treated in the same way that objects are, as material that can be spectralized in a metonymic of associations. A good example of this is found in a description of Twemlow from *Our Mutual Friend*: among a series of other fragmented body images reflected in Veneering's mirror, which, "Reflects Twemlow; grey, dry, polite, susceptible to east wind, First-Gentleman-in-Europe collar and cravat, cheeks drawn in as if he had made a great effort to retire into himself some years ago, and had got so far and had never got any farther" (52). Dickens here uses the *as if* construction to make the body a kind of montage of images in a dumb show of itself, as it were, so that it exists simultaneously on two planes, an "objective" thing in reality and a signifier in a symbolic network, an object of representation but also a form of representational material. Dickens uses the *as if* construction in this way, I will argue, in *Little Dorrit* more than in any other novel, and this is indicative not just of stylistic tendency, but of a deeper structural principle of the novel.

Little Dorrit, that is, *itself* has the structure of the *as if*, and seen from this perspective, certain questions about the novel as a whole will be resolved. There has always been something particularly disturbing about *Little Dorrit*, even among Dickens's dark novels. Chesterton even suggests that the sad tone of *Little Dorrit* is uniquely bleak because it is an end in itself: "In all these other cases of the later books an artistic reason can be given—a reason of theme or of construction for the slight sadness that clings to them. But exactly because *Little Dorrit* is a mere Dickens novel, it shows that something must somehow have happened to Dickens himself" (*Collected Works* 365). And John Wain particularly touched upon something ineffable in the novel when he called it Dickens's "most stationary novel" (175). Wain thought it essentially "plotless" and observed that "for all the scurry of events on its surface, it never for a moment suggests genuine movement" (175). We might simply rephrase this observation a bit and say that all the scurry and motion in the novel happens not on the "surface," but in the realm of the *as if*.

Lionel Trilling touches upon an aspect of the novel that is little emphasized, its existential aspect. For Trilling, this existential sense stems directly from the biographic connection between Clennam and Dickens. Trilling, though he thought this novel one of Dickens's greatest achievements, asks "what The Inimitable has to do with this sad depleted failure" of Clennam's character (289); the only possible association between the two, he finally resolves, is what he calls Clennam's "sickness unto death" (291). Trilling has certainly put his finger on something important here, but there may be even more fundamental questions to ask about *Little Dorrit*. Is there a way to reconcile what have been taken as the major flaws and anomalies of the novel with its haunting force and continued resonance among readers and critics? And what role, if any, does Clennam play in this canonical place of the novel?

I certainly would not go so far as to say that Clennam is a "sad depleted failure," but I do think that his role at the center of the novel is one of the main reasons for the mixed and sometimes unenthusiastic responses to the novel since its publication. As a medium of the narrative (a character who provides the focal point for the narrative), Clennam has none of the quiet humor and passive endurance of a David Copperfield, none of the neurotic complexities or ethical radiance of an Esther Summerson (or even the eccentricities of a Jarndyce), and certainly none of the rueful charm of a Pip.[1] Again, if we were to name Clennam's predominant character trait, we could do no better than to repeat Trilling's "sickness unto death;" but if this were all we could say, we would correspondingly have to admit Clennam to be a "flat" or one-dimensional character, a flat *central* character at that, which would be a serious flaw indeed. But again we can take our cue from this critical disjunction here to consider Clennam not in terms of a mimetic character, but of a spectral character.

If the novel's plot seems to go nowhere, this must be related to the fact that the mystery of Arthur's origin, a mystery that underlies all the other mysteries of the novel (the pocket watch's inscription "Do Not Forget," Affery's dreams, and even the Dorrits' fortune all relate to it), is never answered for *him*: Little Dorrit has Arthur burn the documents that tell the secret of his past (who he really is, his heritage) before he ever reads them. Clennam seems to embody a mystery or a question as such, not an answer to one. To return to Trilling's question about the relation between Dickens and Clennam, we might say that just as the hysteric "asks his neurotic question, his secret and muzzled question, with his ego" (Lacan, *Psychoses* 170), so Dickens asks his existential question *with* the character of Clennam. The hysteric's question "what am I?" (which for the hysteric is embodied in the sexual difference, "am I a man or a woman" or more specifically "am I someone capable of procreating?"), is fundamentally a question of the relation of the subject to the signifier insofar as it appears in the big Other. Lacan's comment in his seminar on *The Psychoses*, alluding to his discussion of the dream of Irma's injection, emphasizes the ontological implications of the role the symbolic order plays in identity: "the word—to be understood with the emphasis this comprises, the solution to an enigma, a problematic function—is located in the Other, through the intermediary of which all full speech is realized, this *you are* in which the subject locates himself and recognizes himself" (162). This question of the fundamental relationship of the subject to the signifier is what gives *Little Dorrit* its uniquely existential status in Dickens's *oeuvre*, and it is the *as if* structure of the novel as a whole that opens up this ontological dimension, this gap, between the two, that gives Clennam his function as a question, since it is the symbolic Other that ultimately situates our being-in-the-world: "The symbolic provides a form into which the subject is inserted at the level of his being. It's on the basis of the signifier that the subject recognizes himself as being this or that" (Lacan, *Psychoses* 179).

Beyond the realism principle

If the word in the field of the Other provides a solution to the enigma of the subject, Dickens formulates the question to the Other with Clennam by giving him, as we will see, an ambiguous status in relation to the symbolic Other, leaving his birth and death at the margins of the signifier. "The question of death, and the question of birth," says Lacan, "are as it happens the two ultimate questions that have precisely no solution in the signifier. This is what gives neurotics their existential value" (*Psychoses* 190).

Clennam's character, then, is structured like a question, and the question he poses is what Lacan designates as the hysteric's question—"*What am I?*, or *Am I?*, a relation of being, a fundamental signifier" (*Psychoses* 170). Every detail of Clennam's character points to this symbolic question, "Am I?" and this is what differentiates him from a mimetically represented character, who might be plagued *by* this question (as part of his "depth") but would not be representational *material for* its articulation. The character of Clennam has no past, no narrative background; though we get some details of his upbringing, they are stark and preliminary, with absolutely none of the Proustian impressions of David Copperfield's narrated childhood, for instance. Clennam's *lack* of past is, rather, a fundamental part of his character; he is partly constituted by this lack that he brings into the narrative present as a gap. He seems, for instance, not to have entered the novel *in medias res*, leaving us to fill in the gaps of his past over the course of the narrative, but rather to have been created *ex nihilo* at the narrative's commencement precisely to bring a gap to bear on the story:

> When he got to his lodging, he sat down before the dying fire, as he had stood at the window of his old room looking out upon the blackened forest of chimneys, and turned his gaze back upon the gloomy vista by which he had come to that stage in his existence. So long, so bare, so blank. No childhood; no youth, except for one remembrance; that one remembrance proved, only that day, to be a piece of folly. (206)

That potential exception, the "one remembrance," moreover, which refers to his youthful love of Flora, is fundamentally characterized by the *as if* ontology of a conditional that has lost all relation to and communication with the real:

> As if there were a secret understanding between herself and Clennam of the most thrilling nature; as if the first of a train of post-chaises and four, extended all the way to Scotland, were at that moment round the corner; and as if she couldn't (and wouldn't) have walked into the Parish Church with him, under the shade of the family umbrella, with the Patriarchal blessing on her head, and the perfect concurrence of all mankind; Flora

comforted her soul with agonies of mysterious signalling, expressing dread of discovery. (196)

As the only potential narrative link to the past of a mimetic character, to a realistic lived past of a fictional personage, Flora only poses her own unreadable "mysterious signalling" to a fantasy reality, throws his existence further into the realm of the *as if*, and the surreal aspect of this fact is only magnified by Flora's uncanny counterpart, Mr. F.'s aunt, whose random remarks, "being totally uncalled for by anything said by anybody, and traceable to no association of ideas, confounded and terrified the mind." True, there *may* be some system to trace this "association of ideas," we are told, but "the key to it was wanted" (199).

Though the novel, in one respect, traces Clennam's return to his past to uncover its secrets, Clennam's past only shrinks further away at every approach. And if the archetype of the hero's return home traditionally evokes repetition as a precondition of progress, Dickens modifies it here in a Kafkaesque way such that it functions only to draw Clennam into an absurd labyrinth of further repetitions. Clennam's return to London, his place of birth, his childhood home—his character's birth, as it were, into the novel—is thus more a nightmarish repetition than a new beginning; in this way he resembles the Kafkaesque subject, who, says Žižek, "is the subject desperately seeking a trait with which to identify, he does not understand the meaning of the call of the Other" (*Mapping* 322). The ontological question of the "call of the Other" lurks palpably around every corner at Clennam's return to London, in the description of which the word "nothing" appears some ten times, and as Clennam immerses himself in the eerily liminal London streets, every detail that confronts him seems to be spectralized into a conditional, like the occasional face that "would appear behind the dingy glass of a window, and would fade away into the gloom as if it had seen enough of life and had vanished out of it" (70). Echoes of, and allusions to, Blake's "London," where all particulars are spectralized into a generalized chain of existential no-thoroughfares—"In every cry of every Man, / In every Infants cry of fear, / In every voice: in every ban, / The mind-forg'd manacles I hear" (26)—resonate throughout the London streets of Clennam's homecoming: "In every thoroughfare, up almost every alley, and down almost every turning, some doleful bell was throbbing, jerking, tolling, as if the Plague were in the city and the dead-carts were going round" (67), and where houses seemed "as if they were every one inhabited by the ten young men of the Calendar's story, who blackened their faces and bemoaned their misery every night" (68). The very name Clennam is very nearly a spectral inversion, a moor eeffocish reflection, of "manacle." And what better representative of Blake's "mind-forged manacles" than Clennam's mother, who "weighed, measured, and priced everything; for whom what could not be weighed, measured, and priced, had no existence" (59)? Clennam is manacled by his existential bind, as the repetition of secrets and mysteries and forgetting throughout the novel emphasizes, an emphasis embodied in the misinterpreted and unheeded warning inside the clock, "Do Not Forget." Like the clock, Clennam's mother embodies the inaccessible secret of Clennam's past, of his identity, of his existence, linking his identity in an unbreakable mind-forged link with his death: "The gloom, and must, and dust of the whole tenement, were secret. At the heart of it his mother presided, inflexible of face, indomitable of will, firmly holding all the secrets of her own and his father's life, and austerely opposing herself, front to front, to the great final secret of all" (597).

Lacan introduces his discussion of the hysteric's question into his seminar on the psychoses in order to shed light on what he calls the "*as if* mechanism," which "is a mechanism of imaginary compensation ... for the absent Oedipus complex, which would have given [the psychotic] virility in the form, not of the paternal image, but of the signifier, *the name of the father*" (*Psychoses* 192–3). The *as if* mechanism in the case of psychosis, in other words, testifies to a fracture between the symbolic and the imaginary, a splitting between the image and the signifier, or, more specifically, a "hole" at the level of the symbolic at the point at which it would have ontologically quilted the imaginary and stabilized its sliding through a paternal signifier. The subject is left only with the "paternal image" (rather than a signifier), which he treats *as if* it were a primordial signifier to compensate for the fact that a primordial signifier (Name-of-the-Father) has been excluded or "foreclosed" ("*Verwerfung*" is Freud's term), which leaves the symbolic wanting in its ontological function of establishing an Other for the other. Since the imaginary is the level, as we have discussed earlier, of the "inmixing" of subjects, the result is, among other things, an "imaginary dissolution," in which the distinction between egos dissipates and individuals seem like reflections or repetitions, as in the dream of Irma's injection when, as Lacan describes, Freud calls upon three colleagues to observe Irma's throat, and "these three farcical characters operate, defend theses, talk only nonsense" (*Psychoses* 193). This *as if* structure in the psychotic serves, in other words, to patch over a kind of failed mechanism in the relation of the unconscious to language (a missing signifier), but it also underlies or highlights part of this structure that is typically invisible, something "that is permanently elided, veiled, domesticated in the life of a normal man—namely, the dialectic of the fragmented body in relation to the imaginary universe, which is subjacent to a normal structure" (Lacan, *Psychoses* 87). This underlying dialectic between the imaginary, in which the body is fragmented and objectified, and the symbolic, which sutures it into a whole, is encoded in the *as if* trope, which forges a gap between the imaginary and symbolic in order to allow for all kinds of expressive distortions in the name of a subjective excess of the objective world. We can see this, for instance, in all the doubling and splitting of characters in Dickens, but especially in *Little Dorrit*.

It is interesting that the *as if* structure of *Little Dorrit* as a whole has yet to be explored in critical terms. The use of the *as if* construction appears at the sentence level prolifically throughout the novel, but it is also fundamental at the level of the plot: William Dorrit enters the debtors' prison *as if* he were "going out again directly" (98), and in fact *does* come out again, many years later, *only in* the realm of the *as if*. He comes out bodily, and lives as if he were a wealthy member of the leisure class, but everything after his release happens in the realm of the *as if*, and he is particularly haunted by the paranoid notion that the servants around him see him for what he "is" (or was), that is, for a person living *as if* he were who he is. As such William Dorrit and his family live out their glamorous life like the subject of the imaginary, who "never enter[s] the game of signifiers, except through a kind of external imitation" (251). The Dorrits' travels, which take up much of the second half of the novel, are represented in the mode of a dream or "delusion," in the mode of the *as if*: "[Little Dorrit's] present existence was a dream," and her travels "all a dream," the tourist sights "unrealities." And Venice, where they finally reside, is the "crowning unreality" of them all (517–19): a world full of reflections that embodies the specular nature of her reality, its being unmoored in from a symbolic ground. It is thus that the scene of Little Dorrit gazing from her balcony into the canal might be compared to the scene of Dombey gazing into the "cold depths of the dead sea of mahogany" in the tabletop (*Dombey and Son* 414–15), in both of which subjective images overwhelm the objective field of vision:

> And then she would lean upon her balcony, and look over at the water, as though [the images of her former life] all lay underneath it. When she got to that, she would musingly watch its running, as if, in the general vision, it might run dry, and show her the prison again, and herself, and the old room, and the old inmates, and the old visitors; all lasting realities that had never changed. (*Little Dorrit* 520)

Beyond the realism principle

William Dorrit, however, is only one of a series of fathers in the novel that exist in the realm of the *as if*. Merdle represents the foremost capitalist of Britain, and the center of what the narrator calls "Society," yet he fills that function only *as if* he belonged there: "he looked far more like a man in possession of his house under a distraint, than a commercial Colossus bestriding his own hearth rug, while the little ships were sailing to dinner" (614), and his chief butler, whom the narrator calls his "oppressive retainer" (613), is more prison guard than servant, reversing Merdle's social role. And the "Patriarch," Christopher Casby, landlord of Bleeding Heart Yard, is another example of a paternal signifier fulfilling a social function based on an imaginary status. He is dubbed "Patriarch" because "with his blooming face, and that head, and his blue eyes, he seemed to be delivering sentiments of rare wisdom and virtue" (188). His patriarchal signs are merely fragmented body parts, his "shining bald head" and his "long grey hair," which as imaginary trademarks place him in the role of Big Other, but as "rumor has it" he is in fact a "crafty impostor" and "seen through [this] medium, Christopher Casby was a mere Inn signpost without any Inn—an invitation to rest and be thankful, when there was no place to put up at, and nothing whatever to be thankful for" (190).

Lionel Trilling may have been the first to note "the remarkable number of false and inadequate parents in *Little Dorrit*" (288). But keeping in mind the pattern of the social function of patriarchy and its false narratives in the novel, it quickly becomes apparent that what is at stake in *Little Dorrit* is not the parent, or even the father as such, but undoubtedly the signifier Name-of-the-Father. Thus these three figures—Casby the Patriarch, Merdle, and the Father of the Marshalsea—are the central paternal *signifiers* of the novel, all functioning in the *as if* mode, and referring to various social aspects of the big Other under capitalism, property, capital, and class. Thus it is that, I would suggest, the *as if* nature of the novel is deeply related to the novel's concern with the growing pervasiveness of speculative capitalism in Europe and globally. This is in fact what connects Clennam's existential status, his hysterical question, to the broader concern with capitalism in the novel as whole: in changing the subject's relationship to desire, the ontological status of the subject is altered under capitalism. And capitalism is precisely a restructuring of the subject's relation to desire. As Lacan points out, in order for culture to function and allow any kind of freedom for the subject, desire must be transferred to the desire of the Other, or, in other words, the symbolic order must intervene by way of a primordially repressed signifier: "there has to be a law, a chain, a symbolic order, the intervention of the order of speech, that is, of the father. Not the natural father, but what is called the father. The order that prevents the collision and explosion of the situation as a whole is founded on the existence of this name of the father" (*Psychoses* 96). But under the structure of capitalism, where desire seems immediate and egoic, the Name-of-the-Father only exists in an *as if* mode, mediating the subject's desire/lack only in an *imaginary* way or in an *image* of the Other rather than quilting it in the symbolic Order via a universal signifier. Put more simply, the subject of capitalism exists in a state of pure particularism (as Lacan puts it, the "aggressive tension of either me or the other is entirely integrated into every kind of imaginary function in man," *Psychoses* 95), existing only *as if* there were a mediating universality to its desire. In *Little Dorrit* Dickens depicts the milieu of global speculative capitalism as a world where the Name-of-the-Father is sham (like Merdle, the Patriarch, and the Father of the Marshalsea) and where therefore the subject is trapped in a narcissistic virtual world of the imaginary devoid of universality and virtually any meaningful singularity of the individual—which is why Clennam is so existentially manacled to a void of desire.

Merdle, the central venture capitalist of the novel, is therefore very appropriately the character most indicative of the failed place of the signifier, the Name-of-the-Father. In Merdle, accordingly, there is especially a kind of uncanny and emphatic fragmentation of the body, a heightened corporeality, at times as if he were an animated corpse, as it were, or inhabited his own body in the *as if* mode. We can see this in Merdle's gestures, which tend to display a comic but spooky dissociation between body and agency, such as when "Mr Merdle, so twisting his hands into what hair he had upon his head that he seemed to lift himself up by it as he started out of his chair" (446), and when he "suddenly [gets] up, as if he had been waiting in the interval for his legs and they had just come" (676), and the moments when he seems completely self-ridden and conflicted, as when he "took himself into custody by the wrists, and backed himself among the ottomans and chairs and tables as if he were his own Police officer" (672). Merdle's strange bodily materiality is thus not spectral but imaginary; and Merdle's name and body, in their imaginary materiality, capture these eerily contradictory and corporeal aspects of *capital*: contagion, expansion, and confinement. The plague metaphor, for instance, born in the abstracted and internalized quarantine of the opening chapters ("to suspect me of the plague is to give me the plague," says Mr. Meagles, 54), spreads throughout the novel as a thematic link between existential imprisonment and global capitalism, especially through the person of Merdle, who gives expression to the global tendency of stock trade mania and market speculation, the forces causing "the British name to be more and more respected in all parts of the civilized globe capable of the appreciation of world-wide commercial enterprises and gigantic combinations of skill and capital" (*Little Dorrit* 445). That "moral infection" of speculation and greed, says the narrator, "will spread with the malignity and rapidity of the Plague," as surely as "we human creatures breathe an atmosphere" (626); and Dickens even provides an eerie fantasy of a kind of hypothetical quarantine for those "infected" by this capitalist mania for speculation and profit to prevent it spreading, a kind of ontological inversion of the debtors' prison: "A blessing beyond appreciation would be conferred upon mankind, if the tainted, in whose weakness or wickedness these virulent disorders are bred, could be instantly ceased and placed in close confinement (not to say summarily smothered) before the poison is communicable" (627). The medium through which this plague-like virulent infection of global capitalism is communicated is the name of Merdle, which itself having an imaginary materiality "was deposited on every lip, and carried into every ear" (627). This name is the perfect signifier for capital, standing as it does for the out-of-control drive capital generates for particularism (as desire, wish, fantasy) to go global: "As a vast fire will fill the air to a great distance with its roar, so the sacred flame which the mighty Barnacles had fanned caused the air to resound more and more with the name of Merdle" (627).

The relation of Merdle the man to Merdle the signifier, in fact, reflects the very structure of fetishism in the money form. The eerie corporeality of Merdle's body is actually materialized out of the associations of the signifier Merdle, with its condensation of muddle and *merde*, obscene matter underlying the spread of wealth he generates. This implicit money/feces metaphor embodied in his name is reflected at the symbolic level of the narrative though images of Merdle's body being associated mud and by extension feces, *merde*. Thus Merdle, who has "that particular kind of dull red colour in his cheeks which is rather stale than fresh," and "was mostly to be found against walls and behind doors" (293) is a *thingly* effigy of capitalist speculation rather than a realistic venture capitalist; hence, rather than, say, voicing the knowledge of complex financial affairs or expressing the agency of a model venture capitalist, he "oozed sluggishly and muddily about his drawing-room, saying never a word" (626). That is, just as with money worthless substance is endowed with symbolic value that both transcends and fetishizes it, the muddy or fecal substance of the man is transcended and fetishized in the symbolic power of the name while at the same time remaining detached and worthless:

> The famous name of Merdle became, every day, more famous in the land ... nobody had the smallest reason for supposing the clay of which this object of worship was made, to be other than the commonest clay, with as clogged a wick smouldering inside of it as ever kept an image of humanity from tumbling to pieces. All people knew (or thought they knew) that he had made himself immensely rich; and, for that reason alone, prostrated themselves before him, more degradedly and less excusably than the darkest savage creeps out of his hole in the ground to propitiate, in some log or reptile, the Deity of his benighted soul. (611)

This image of a "savage" fetishizing a worthless or repulsive object as an effigy of some magic power also links Merdle to the figure of the Wooden Midshipman as an effigy of capital in *Dombey and Son*.

The *as if* structure, then, or the way in which Dickens employs it, provides a particularly apt device in critiquing capitalism from an ontological standpoint, for if the relation between the imaginary and the symbolic is fractured, as the case of the psychotic shows, the very singularity of identity is forfeited, that is, the function of the subject as singular desire becomes ineffectual, people and things are exchangeable, general, elusive, phantasmic. In order to illustrate the fundamental ontological role of the symbolic, Lacan points out the function of certain sentence structures, such as "thou art the one who ..." or simply the deictic "that's it!"—instances of the necessity of the signifier to call a person or thing out of its undifferentiated multiplicity into its (symbolic) being-for-the-Other. The subject is always as such split between these two levels, the imaginary and the symbolic, which by their nature are separated by a gap, but in the dialectic between the two, in the fact of their being "quilted," to use Lacan's term, being emerges as a support in the gap projected *beyond* the solipsistic abyss of the image:

> The former, the other with a small o, is the imaginary other, the otherness in a mirror image, which makes us depend upon the form of our counterpart. The latter, the absolute Other, is the one we address ourselves to beyond this counterpart, the one we are forced to admit beyond the relation of a mirage, the one who accepts or is refused opposite us ... the one to whom we always address ourselves. (*Psychoses* 252)

The theme of the disavowal, or foreclosure, of the Name-of-the-Father in *Little Dorrit* as a metaphor for capitalism, then, gives rise, from the theoretical perspective, to a rather disturbing question about the relation between capitalism and psychosis—and the *as if* structure plays an important role in this question. For the psychotic the primordial signifier Name-of-the-Father is rejected or "foreclosed" (*Verwerfung*) and he finds himself captured by the imaginary, by the realm of the interchangeable little other, the polyphallic subject, in an existence structurally devoid of being. But before the onset of psychosis, the psychotic maintains a more or less functional position in the world (Schreber's judiciary success is a case in point here), which, if we accept Lacan's radically ontological pathology of psychosis, poses a crucial question to the status of the psychotic *before* the onset of his illness. Lacan responds to this paradox with the help of the *as if*: prior to psychosis, the psychotic has already rejected the paternal signifier, but he behaves *as if* he had access to a paternal signifier (through the "paternal image" that stands in for it), and thus lives *as if* he had access to the symbolic Other. This pre-psychotic *as if* phenomenon is the key to our analogy with capitalism: it is not that the symbolic is lost in the capitalist system, but that in order to make the commodity (with its internal division expressed by Marx in terms of use and exchange) the locus of a desire without lack (without Otherness), the *imaginary* status of the object must *stand in* for and displace its symbolic function, and the relation of the subject to the symbolic Other must remain suspended in the realm of the imaginary, the phantasmic *as if*.

In order to make this clearer, we may look at it from another perspective. Žižek explains this function of the *as if* in the capitalist system in terms of the "real abstraction" that comes into play not in consciousness but in the *act* of exchange:

> On the one hand, the "real abstraction" is of course not "real" in the sense of the real, effective properties of commodities as material objects: the object-commodity does not contain "value" in the same way as it possesses a set of particular properties determining its "use value" (its form, colour, taste, and so on). As Sohn-Rethel pointed out, its nature is that of a *postulate* implied by the effective act of exchange—in other words, that of a certain "as if" [*als ob*]: during the act of exchange, individuals proceed *as if* the commodity is not submitted to physical, material exchanges; *as if* it is excluded from the natural cycle of generation and corruption; although on the level of their "consciousness" they "know very well" that this is not the case. (*Ticklish Subject* 302, original emphasis)

In our terms of the imaginary and the symbolic, we could say that once the commodity takes on the function of (appearing to) fill the lack of desire, its symbolic lack (as a nodal point of social relations) becomes disavowed and its imaginary status (as a source of private enjoyment) takes the role of mediating its social status, an imaginary mediation that in turn structures and defines the subject's being-in-the-world. This elision of the symbolic can be compared to what Žižek explains as an ontological "misrecognition": "During the act of exchange, individuals proceed as 'practical solipsists,' they misrecognize the socio-synthetic function of exchange … Such a misrecognition is the *sine qua non* of the effectuation of the act of exchange—if the participants were to take note of the dimension of 'real abstraction,' the 'effective' act of exchange itself would no longer be possible" (*Ticklish Subject* 304). This misrecognition is thus not an element to be pointed out and properly "recognized," but a constitutional condition of its functioning, an *as if* upon which the whole system depends, since the reality it sustains is a "reality *whose very ontological consistency implies a certain non-knowledge of its participants*" (Žižek, *Ticklish Subject* 305, original emphasis).

Little Dorrit, we can say, more than any of Dickens's novels, directs its gaze at this imaginary structure of being or the paternal image, under capitalism as expressed in the sham or illusory nature of the Name-of-the-Father, which effects the very singularity of the individual and is perhaps best embodied in the form of the character Mrs. General. As her name suggests, Mrs. General represents the institutionalization of the very annihilation of the singular, of the proliferation of mere "surface" that obscures singular identity in favor of pure empty generality: "Mrs General had no opinions. Her way of forming a mind was to prevent it from forming opinions. She had a little circular set of mental grooves or rails on which she started little trains of other people's opinions, which never overtook one another, and never got anywhere" (503). Her mental rails that set thoughts in circles and her mindless stringing together of alliterative phrases—in service of the "formation of a demeanor"—such as "Papa, potatoes, poultry, prunes and prism, prunes and prism" (529) are like cultish ritual chants meant to exorcize every trace of singularity. Mrs. General, described as having originated in some Carlylean "transcendentally genteel Mill," personifies what Blake satirizes as "terrible surfaces," referring to a kind of false consciousness that finds self-expression in reducing the universal to the general: "in pride of Selfhood unwieldy stretching out into Non Entity/Generalizing Art and Science till Art and Science is lost" ("Jerusalem" 2:38 153–4). Similarly, Dickens calls Mrs. General's process the "formation of surface" and Mrs. General is its true artist: "In that formation process of hers, she dipped the smallest of brushes into the largest of pots, and varnished the surface of every object that came under consideration" (503).

Mrs. General's "formation of surface" represents not simply the superficiality of social forms, but the very annihilation of difference itself, of the singularity of desire, and the disavowal of the otherness or lack of the Real that capitalist enjoyment introduces. If Merdle represents this foreclosure of symbolic castration in the sphere of speculative capitalism, Mrs. General reflects the analogous way in which this sham value self-generates or "spreads" in the sphere of the capitalist-engendered leisure class of tourists, where the enjoyment of the object as a commodity spreads on the global level to the objectifying world of culture, the making-present without lack or difference of the past itself:

> The whole body of travellers seemed to be a collection of voluntary human sacrifices, bound hand and foot, and delivered over to Mr Eustace and his attendants, to have the entrails of their intellects arranged according to the taste of that sacred priesthood. Through the rugged remains of temples and tombs and palaces and senate halls and theatres and amphitheatres of ancient days, hosts of tongue-tied and blindfolded moderns were carefully feeling their way, incessantly repeating Prunes and Prism in the endeavour to set their lips according to the received form. Mrs General was in her pure element. Nobody had an opinion. There was a formation of surface going on around her on an amazing scale, and it had not a flaw of courage or honest free speech in it. (566)

Mrs. General's "pure element" is the atmosphere of a global cosmopolitan prison-world where all objects exist only insofar as they are available for consumption by zombie-like consumers. It is the element of the psychotic *as if.* "[T]ongue-tied and blindfolded," these "voluntary human sacrifices" seem more like the self-interned undead inmates of a global camp than members of a privileged leisure class. These walking "human sacrifices" devoid of human consciousness (sight and speech) are strikingly similar to what Schreber calls "fleeting-improvised-men" or "cursory contraptions" to describe his delusions that the people of his world are sham, copies, mirror images. Lacan calls this stage of psychosis the "truly imaginary invasion of subjectivity," one of the primary signs of which is that "there is an altogether striking predominance of the mirror relationship, a notable dissolution of the other *qua* identity" (*Psychoses* 97). Mrs. General's cultish chants aim at precisely this "dissolution of the other *qua* identity," and there is more than a touch of dark irony in the fact that, in their mantra of surface, *Prunes and Prism*, Dickens has these "voluntary human sacrifices" hypnotically repeating their own existential committal: pronouncing the incessant *pruning* away of being in a prism of imaginary reflections, the phrase *prunes and prisms, prunes and prisms*, invokes the signifiers' own haunting decree *imprison imprison imprison*.

It is no accident, then, that Mrs. General assumes the position of one who will fill the hole in the Dorrit family, taking the place of the missing mother, since the "formation of a surface" that Mrs. General represents characterizes more and more the world for which the Dorrits have exchanged the world of the Marshalsea, a high-society world that, in fact, turns out to be more its mirror image than its opposite. In fact, to occupy this place would be to substitute for Little Dorrit, since she occupies the paradoxical place of acting as her father's mother, and Mrs. General opposes Little Dorrit in at least this respect. The surface with which Mr. Dorrit surrounds himself and his family, moreover, is not only that of social standing and material wealth, but of the overwhelming necessity of disavowing his past, including his past identity and the past identities of those around him. Little Dorrit herself is the only exception to this, and it is thus clear to her alone that this *as if* world merely reproduces that of the Marshalsea as in a mirror image:

> It appeared on the whole, to Little Dorrit herself, that this same society in which they lived, greatly resembled a superior sort of Marshalsea. Numbers of people seemed to come abroad, pretty much as people had come into the prison; through debt, through idleness, relationship, curiosity, and general unfitness for getting on at home. They were brought into these foreign towns in the custody of couriers and local followers, just as the debtors had been brought into the prison. (565)

Insofar as she is able to maintain a perspective on its *as if* structure, Little Dorrit herself comes to symbolize what must be masked or "obliterated" in order to sustain this world of "terrible surfaces." Thus Mr. Dorrit tells her "there is a—hum—a topic … a painful topic, a series of events which I wish—ha—altogether to obliterate … You alone and only you—constantly revive the topic, though not in words" (531). Thus Little Dorrit symbolically opposes Mrs. General in another way, by being singular and unassimilable, by embodying what we can only call the Blakean "Minute Particular," that particularity that, unlike the specious generality of Mrs. General, sublates the particular itself into/as the universal (and we can think here of Marx's desire to overcome the false social relations of the commodity structure in favor of a true social relation). Little Dorrit's very existence subverts the world of varnished surface by "reproducing" the truth about identity that others, under the "auspices of Mrs General," "blot out":

> I am hurt that [my daughter] should—ha—systematically reproduce what the rest of us blot out; and seem—hum—I had almost said positively anxious—to announce to wealthy and distinguished society that she was born and bred in—ha hum—a place that I myself decline to name ... It is for your sake that I wish you, under the auspices of Mrs General, to form a—hum—a surface ... and (in the striking words of Mrs General) to be ignorant of everything that is not perfectly proper, placid, and pleasant (532–3)

Little Dorrit, in other words, in her very subjectivity, represents the social/ontological conflict that is disavowed by acceptable, "distinguished society." Interestingly, the potential ethicality of Mr. Dorrit's character (which is otherwise quite appalling in most respects) lies precisely in these speech tics, in these gaps and impediments in his language that always stumble upon his disavowal of this contradiction in the form of his own daughter, betraying his unconscious knowledge of it. These coughs and pauses indicate a kind of hole in his speech, the stumbling point of his internality that only emerges after his breakdown; thus his use of such language as "eradicat[ing] the marks," "blot[ting] out," and "form[ing] a surface" takes on an allegorical significance in reference to his own character, the idea that the most traumatic and unnamable thing for Mr. Dorrit is the fulfillment of his desire in the form of presence (name/wealth) without lack. Thus precisely these gaps and impediments reveal the traces of something that saves Mr. Dorrit from ultimately being one of those zombie tourists, his unconscious.

When Mr. Dorrit makes the formation of a "surface" for Little Dorrit herself the condition of the successful blotting out of the past (and thus of his family's identity), it becomes clear that a greater dialectical tension in the novel develops around this opposition between Mrs. General's Surface and Little Dorrit's radical singularity (her ability to avow her own lack).[2] This tension between Surface and Minute Particular pervades the novel in the form of what we have been calling the imaginary and the symbolic. The imaginary realm lacking in its grasp on the beyond of the symbolic Other lies behind the three fathers, the capitalist wealth of Merdle, the leisure class of Mr. Dorrit in Book the Second, and the landlord class of the Patriarch. The novel as a whole is structured around the tearing down of these imaginary structures, and thus each of the worlds of these three fathers comes crashing down by the end of the novel.

If Orwell's famous claim that *Little Dorrit* is a more subversive work than *Das Capital* has any meaning beyond hyperbole, it is surely to be found here. Mr. Dorrit's crash in particular takes the form of a kind of tearing down of the reality principle. In what is perhaps one of the highlights of dramatically "staged" scenes in Dickens's career, Mr. Dorrit, after having painstakingly attempted to "blot out" his past, reclaims his position of Father of the Marshalsea before a party of high-society dinner guests. Mr. Dorrit's crash is the most personal and is presented in terms of a failure of fantasy to serve the purposes of repression, as his dreamlike reality collapses and thrusts him back to the traumatic past that he tried to suppress: "The broad stairs of his Roman palace were contracted in his failing sight to the narrow stairs of his London prison ... When he heard footsteps in the street, he took them for the old weary tread in the yard. When the hour came for locking up, he supposed all strangers to be excluded for the night" (710). Mr. Merdle's crash, however, is central and the most far reaching, since it is at the heart of the capitalist/imaginary identification:

> The Inquest was over, the letter was public, the bank was broken, the other model structures of straw had taken fire and were turned to smoke. The admired piratical ship had blown up, in the midst of a vast fleet of ships of all rates, and boats of all sizes; and on the deep was nothing but ruin; nothing but burning hulls, bursting magazines, great guns self-exploded tearing friends and neighbours to pieces, drowning men clinging to unseaworthy spars and going down every minute, spent swimmers floating dead, and sharks. (777)

And finally, of course, the Patriarch's deposition by Pancks is given as a kind of absurdist castration ritual. Mr. Pancks directly assails the empty signifier that gives the Patriarch his Patriarchal status: "'It's a mighty fine sign-post, is The Casby's Head,' said Mr Pancks, surveying it with anything rather than admiration; 'but the real name of the House is the Sham's Arms'" (871). Pancks thus brings about the most comic, violent, and literal unmasking of the novel on that signpost of a head revealing the sham father beyond the empty signifier:

> Quick as lightening, Mr Pancks, who, for some moments, had had his right hand in his coat pocket, whipped out a pair of shears, swooped upon the Patriarch behind, and snipped off short the sacred locks that flowed upon his shoulders. In a paroxysm of animosity and rapidity, Mr Pancks then caught the broad-brimmed hat out of the astounded Patriarch's hand, cut it down into a mere stewpan, and fixed it on the Patriarch's head. (871–2)

Casby is not merely shorn of his dignity, but of his very signifier, and is therefore transformed almost literally into his own double, his own specter: "A bare-polled, goggle-eyed, big-headed lumbering personage stood staring at him, not in the least impressive, not in the least venerable, who seemed to have started out of the earth to ask what has become of Casby" (872). These three crashes mark a tearing down of the imaginary structures that form the ontology of capitalism, but perhaps we could say more accurately that they represent a "pushing through" or beyond that fantasy, in the same manner as Freud's pushing beyond the imaginary relations in the dream of Irma's injection.

The often criticized collapse of Clennam's house, then, is in this very sense overdetermined; it gives thematic plot expression to the series of abstract symbolic crashes (of the three sham Name-of-the-Father signifiers) in which the novel culminates. Clennam's house crashing down gives a material expression to the collapse of the imaginary, fragmented, specular world of *Little Dorrit*'s milieu. It also links these crashes with Clennam's personal existential plight. After his involvement in economic ruin spurred by Merdle's financial crash, Clennam enters almost willingly (as Trilling also points out) into the Marshalsea prison, as if it were the proper milieu for his existential state near the end of his narrative. The remarkable thing about Clennam's part in the mystery plot of this novel is that his resolution is not a matter of resolving his past, but of *destroying* it, his resolution is to lose everything, including his origin. Little Dorrit, again, the "one weak girl," stands opposed to the extravagant involvement in the Merdle affair, as Clennam sits in prison contemplating Little Dorrit's "self-denial, self-subdual, charitable construction ... Until it seemed to him as if he met the reward of having wandered away from her, and suffered anything to pass between him and his remembrance of her virtues" (787). One should note the important introduction of the *as if* here, which in stark contrast to characters like Merdle, Casby, and Dorrit—who can't see the imaginary or fantastic nature of the *as if* mode of their reality—provides clarity precisely by distancing Clennam from the fantasy of his progress. Little Dorrit herself captures something of the radical desubjectifying potential of the *as if* structure, its ability to bring the excess of the Real to bear upon reality precisely in reality's (subjective) lack itself. As Zupančič puts it, "the subjective excessiveness brings us closer to the truth, as well as to the possibility of engaging with reality's contradictions" (21). In this sense, then, Little Dorrit, to a certain extent like Little Nell before her, can be seen as the driving force in the text representing a kind of radical death drive, a drive to avow one's own

The "as if" hauntology and the uncanny dream

lack, to address one's own symbolic castration (or contradiction)—to tear down and start anew.

We may return now to a final unresolved issue from the beginning of this chapter, an issue that in fact touches upon the very premise of this study of Dickens's characterization, that of the role of the ego in Dickens's "tapping into the primary processes" in his means of representation. This issue is crucial, since the question of ego-psychology enters into the equation as soon as we consider the primary process as a fundamental force in Dickens's work. Both Marcus, in relation to style, and Kris, in relation to caricature, resort in the end to an egocentric model. Marcus makes the implications of this approach for a broader epistemology explicit when he says that,

> Before Dickens, no English novelist had appeared with an ego of such imperial powers and with a sense of reality so secure that he could temporarily abandon those powers without fear of being overwhelmed or of their permanent loss. At the same time, such an abandonment, successfully carried through, marks the opening up of a new dimension of freedom for the English novel, if not for the human mind in general. ("Language into Structure" 137)

Kris makes a similar claim about the impact of caricature for development of art and science, "the birth of caricature as an institution marks a conquest of a new dimension of freedom of the human mind, no more, but perhaps no less, than the birth of rational science in the work of Galileo Galilei, the great contemporary of the Carraccis" (202). The idea of progress as increasing liberation of the ego from repression of the primary processes is an attractive one, but one that is ultimately untenable since it runs counter to the Freudian breakthrough. That is, this ego-psychology re-centers the subject around the ego, making the ego's triumph man's triumph, and foreclosing on the radical nature of Freud's discovery that man's I, his ego, is not where his subjectivity lies, not the point from which he thinks, not where his being lies. The idea of spectrality, or spectral materiality, however, provides us with another model that releases us from this aporia. Dickens has not acquired an ego "powerful" enough to hold its own in the face of the primary processes; rather, he has positioned himself in language more radically than, before him, any subject had done in writing (in the novel form), since such a position is radically *other* to the subject; he has pushed through, in the same sense as in Freud's dream of Irma's injection, to the signifier beyond the symbolic, and has confronted the subject's death and dissolution there, allowing the reader to bear witness as in a dream. Just as in Freud's dream, there is a correspondence with psychosis, in the sense that "the nucleus of psychosis has to be linked to a relationship between the subject and the signifier in its most formal dimension, in its dimension as a pure signifier, and that everything constructed around this consists only of affective relations to the primary phenomenon, the relationship to the signifier" (Lacan, *Psychoses* 250). Were the ego to be "strengthened" by this, our ideological attachment to the fantasy of realism would only be all the greater, our relation to the Real all the more elusive. What Dickens gives us is a relation to the signifier in the Real, as potential, as lack, as specter.

Notes

1 Chesterton contrasts Clennam to David Copperfield pointing out that David "has come from a gloomy childhood; Clennam, though forty years old, is still in a gloomy childhood" (*Collected Works* 369).
2 Interestingly, we could again compare this motif to Blake, who, in "Jerusalem," allegorizes in similar terms the moral imperative of founding an authentic human being-in-the-world on the condition of singularity, linking the General to utilitarianism: "He who would do good to another, must do it in Minute Particulars/General Good is the plea of the scoundrel hypocrite & flatterer:/for Art & Science cannot exist but in minutely organized Particulars/And not in generalizing Demonstrations of the rational Power" ("Jerusalem" 55: 60–5).

Bibliography

Adorno, Theodor. *Aesthetic Theory*. Edited by Gretel Adorno and Rolf Tiedemann, translated by C. Lenhardt, Routledge and Kegan Paul, 1986.
Adorno, Theodor, and Max Horkheimer. *Dialectic of Enlightenment*. Translated by John Cumming, Continuum, 1994.
Adorno, Theodor W., and Rolf Tiedemann. *Notes to Literature, Vol 2*. United Kingdom, Columbia University Press, 1991.
Agamben, Giorgio. *Stanzas*. Translated by Ronald L. Martinez. *Theory and History of Literature*, vol. 69, University of Minnesota Press, 1993.
Austen, Jane. *Pride and Prejudice*. Introduction by Tony Tanner, Penguin Classics, 1972.
Axton, William F. *Circle of Fire: Dickens' Vision and Popular Victorian Theater*. University of Kentucky Press, 1966.
Baltrušaitis, Jurgis. *Anamorphic Art*. Harry N. Abrams, 1977.
Baudelaire, Charles. "On the Essence of Laughter." *The Mirror of Art: Critical Studies*, edited by Jonathan Mayne, Doubleday, 1956, pp. 133–53.
Baudelaire, Charles. "Some French Caricaturists." *The Mirror of Art: Critical Studies*, edited by Jonathan Mayne, Doubleday, 1956, pp. 154–78.
Benjamin, Walter. *The Arcades Project*. Translated by Howard Eiland and Kevin McLaughlin, Harvard University Press, 1999.
Benjamin, Walter. *Illuminations*. Edited by Hannah Arendt, translated by Harry Zohn, Schocken Books, 1968.
Benjamin, Walter. *Reflections*. Edited by Peter Demetz, translated by Edmund Jephcott, Schocken Books, 1978.
Blake, William. *The Complete Poetry & Prose of William Blake*. Edited by David Erdman, commentary by Harold Bloom, Anchor Books, 1988.
Bove, Alexander. "Gender (De)Constructions and 'Disjunctive Montage': Narrative *Telos* and Filmic Play from Dickens' *David Copperfield* to Neil Jordan's *Breakfast on Pluto*." *LFQ*, vol. 46, no. 1, Winter 2018, n.p.
Bove, Alexander. "The 'Unbearable Realism of a Dream': On the Subject of Portraits in Austen and Dickens." *ELH*, vol. 74, no. 3, Fall 2007, pp. 655–79.

Bibliography

Bowen, John. "Dickens and the Force of Writing." *Palgrave Advances in Charles Dickens Studies*, edited by John Bowen and Robert L. Patten, Palgrave Macmillan, 2006, pp. 255–69.

Bowen, John. *Other Dickens: Pickwick to Chuzzlewit*. Oxford University Press, 2003.

Brooks, Peter. *Reading for the Plot: Design and Intention in Narrative*. A. A. Knopf, 1984.

Bryson, Norman. *Vision and Painting: The Logic of the Gaze*. Yale University Press, 1983.

Carey, John. *The Violent Effigy: A Study of Dickens' Imagination*. Faber & Faber, 1973.

Chesterton, G. K. *Charles Dickens: A Critical Study*. Dodd, Mead & Co., 1935.

Chesterton, G. K. *Chesterton on Dickens. The Collected Works of G.K. Chesterton*, vol. 15, Ignatius, 1986.

Christ, Carol T., and John O. Jordan, editors. *Victorian Literature and the Visual Imagination*. University of California Press, 1995.

Collins, Phillip, editor. *Dickens: The Critical Heritage*. Barnes & Noble, 1971.

Crary, Jonathan. *Techniques of the Observer: On Vision and Modernity in the Nineteenth Century*. MIT Press, 1992.

De Man, Paul. *Aesthetic Ideology*. Edited by Andrzej Warminski, University of Minnesota Press, 1996.

De Man, Paul. *Blindness and Insight: Essays in the Rhetoric of Contemporary Criticism*. 2nd revised ed., University of Minnesota Press 1983.

Derrida, Jacques. *Specters of Marx: The State of the Debt, the Work of Mourning and the New International*. Routledge, 2006.

Derrida, Jacques. *Writing and Difference*. Routledge and Kegan Paul, 1978.

Dever, Carolyn. *Death and the Mother from Dickens to Freud: Victorian Fiction and the Anxiety of Origins*. Cambridge University Press, 1998.

Dickens, Charles. *Bleak House*. Edited by Nicola Bradbury, Penguin Books, 2003.

Dickens, Charles. *David Copperfield*. Norton Critical Edition, edited by Jerome H. Buckley, W. W. Norton & Co., 1990.

Dickens, Charles. *Dombey and Son*. Edited by Andrew Sanders, Penguin Books, 2002.

Dickens, Charles. *Great Expectations*. Norton Critical Edition, edited by Edgar Rosenberg, W. W. Norton & Co., 1999.

Dickens, Charles. *Hard Times*. Norton Critical Edition, edited by George Ford and Sylvere Monod, 2nd ed., W. W. Norton & Co., 1990.

Dickens, Charles. *Little Dorrit*. Edited by Helen Small et al., Penguin Books, 2003.

Dickens, Charles. *The Old Curiosity Shop*. Edited by Andrew Sanders, Penguin Books, 2001.

Dickens, Charles. *Oliver Twist, or the Parish Boy's Progress*. Edited by Philip Horne, Penguin Books, 2003.

Dickens, Charles. *Our Mutual Friend*. Edited by Adrian Pool, Penguin Books, 1998.

Dickens, Charles. *The Posthumous Papers of the Pickwick Club*. Edited by Robert L. Patten, Penguin, 1986.

Bibliography

Dickens, Charles. *Selected Journalism: 1850–1870*. Edited by David Pascoe, Penguin, 1997.
Dolar, Mladen. "'I Shall Be with You on Your Wedding-Night': Lacan and the Uncanny." *Rendering the Real*, vol. 58, 1991, pp. 5–23.
Eliot, T. S. *Selected Essays*. Harcourt, Brace & World, 1960.
Farina, Jonathan. *Everyday Words and the Character of Prose in Nineteenth-Century Britain*. Cambridge University Press, 2017.
Flint, Kate. *The Victorians and the Visual Imagination*. Cambridge University Press, 2000.
Forster, John. *The Life of Charles Dickens: The Illustrated Edition*. Sterling Signature, 2011.
Freud, Sigmund. *Beyond the Pleasure Principle*. Edited and translated by James Strachey, W. W. Norton & Co., 1989.
Freud, Sigmund. *General Psychological Theory: Papers on Metapsychology*. Edited by Philip Reiff, Collier, 1978.
Freud, Sigmund. *The Interpretation of Dreams*. Translated by A. A. Brill, Modern Library, 1978.
Freud, Sigmund. *Jokes and Their Relation to the Unconscious*. Translated by James Strachey, W. W. Norton & Co., 1960.
Freud, Sigmund. "The Uncanny." *Writings on Art and Literature*, edited by Neil Hertz, Stanford University Press, 1997, pp. 193–233.
Freud, Sigmund. "The Unconscious." *General Psychological Theory: Papers on Metapsychology*, edited by Philip Reiff, Collier, 1978, pp. 116–50.
Fried, Michael. *Absorption and Theatricality: Painting and Beholder in the Age of Diderot*. University of California Press, 1980.
Frow, John. *Character and Person*. 1st ed, Oxford University Press, 2014
Gissing, George. *New Grub Street*. Penguin Books, 1985.
Glavin, John. *Dickens on Screen*. Cambridge University Press, 2003.
Golden, Catherine. *Book Illustrated: Text, Image, and Culture, 1770–1930*. 1st ed., Oak Knoll P, 2000.
Gombrich, E. H. *Art and Illusion: A Study in the Psychology of Pictorial Representation*. Bollingen Series XXXV-5, Princeton University Press, 1960.
Gombrich, E. H. *The Image and the Eye: Further Studies in the Psychology of Pictorial Representation*. Cornell University Press, 1982.
Harvey, J. R. *Victorian Novelists and Their Illustrators*. New York University Press, 1971.
Higbie, Robert. *Character and Structure in the English Novel*. University Press of Florida, 1984.
Jaffe, Audrey. *Vanishing Points: Dickens, Narrative, and the Subject of Omniscience*. University of California Press, 1991.
Jaffe, Audrey. *The Victorian Novel Dreams of the Real: Conventions and Ideology*. Oxford University Press, 2016.
Jameson, Fredric. *The Political Unconscious: Narrative as a Socially Symbolic Act*. Cornell University Press, 1981.

Bibliography

Jensen, Klaus Bruhn. *The Social Semiotics of Mass Communication.* Sage Publications, 1995.

Jordan, John O. *Supposing Bleak House.* University of Virginia Press, 2011.

Kerr, David S. *Caricature and French Political Culture, 1830–1848: Charles Philipon and the Illustrated Press.* Oxford University Press, 2000.

Kornbluh, Anna. "Reading the Real: Žižek's Literary Materialism." *Everything You Always Wanted to Know About Literature But Were Afraid to Ask Žižek*, edited by Russell Sbriglia, Duke University Press, 2017, pp. 35–62.

Kornbluh, Anna. *Realizing Capital: Financial and Psychic Economies in Victorian Form.* 1st ed., Fordham University Press, 2014.

Kris, Ernst. *Psychoanalytic Explorations in Art.* International University Press, 1952.

Kristeva, Julia. *Intimate Revolt: The Powers and Limits of Psychoanalysis.* Columbia University Press, 2003.

Kucich, John. *Excess and Restraint in the Novels of Charles Dickens.* University of Georgia Press, 1981.

Kucich, John. "Self-Conflict in David Copperfield." *David Copperfield and "Hard Times,"* edited by John Peck, St. Martin's Press, 1995, pp. 141–54.

Lacan, Jacques. "The Agency of the Letter in the Unconscious, or Reason Since Freud." *Ecrits: A Selection*, translated by Alan Sheridan, W. W. Norton & Co., 1977, pp. 138–69.

Lacan, Jacques. *Anxiety.* Edited by Jacques-Alain Miller, English ed., Polity, 2014.

Lacan, Jacques. *Ecrits: A Selection.* Translated by Alan Sheridan, W. W. Norton & Co., 1977.

Lacan, Jacques. *The Ego in Freud's Theory and in the Technique of Psychoanalysis, 1954–1955.* W. W. Norton & Co., 1988.

Lacan, Jacques. *The Ethics of Psychoanalysis, 1959–1960.* 1st American ed., W. W. Norton & Co., 1992.

Lacan, Jacques. *The Four Fundamental Concepts of Psychoanalysis.* W. W. Norton & Co., 1998.

Lacan, Jacques. "The Mirror Stage as Formative of the Function of the I." *Ecrits: A Selection*, translated by Alan Sheridan, W. W. Norton & Co., 1977, pp. 1–8.

Lacan, Jacques. *The Other Side of Psychoanalysis.* W. W. Norton & Co., 2006.

Lacan, Jacques. *The Seminar of Jacques Lacan, Book II: The Ego in Freud's Theory and the Technique of Psychoanalysis 1954–1955.* Translated by John Forrester, W. W. Norton & Co., 1978.

Lacan, Jacques. *The Psychoses.* Edited by Jacques-Alain Miller, translated by Russell Grigg, 1st American ed., W. W. Norton & Co., 1993.

Laplanche, Jacques, and Jean Bertrande Pontalis. *The Language of Psychoanalysis.* Translated by Donald Nicholson-Smith, W. W. Norton, 1973.

Leclaire, Serge. *Psychoanalyzing: On the Order of the Unconscious and the Practice of the Letter.* Stanford University Press, 1998.

Lévi-Strauss, Claude et al. *The View from Afar.* University of Chicago Press, 1992.

Lukacher, Ned. "The Dickensian 'No Thoroughfare.'" *Modern Critical Views: Charles Dickens*, edited by Harold Bloom, Chelsea House, 1987, pp. 281–315.

Lukács, György. *History and Class Consciousness: Studies in Marxist Dialectics.* MIT Press, 1971.
McGowan, Todd. "The Bankruptcy of Historicism: Introducing Disruption into Literary Studies." *Everything You Always Wanted to Know About Literature But Were Afraid to Ask Žižek,* edited by Russell Sbriglia, Duke University Press, 2017, pp. 89–106.
McGowan, Todd. *Only A Joke Can Save Us: A Theory of Comedy.* Northwestern University Press, 2017.
McLaughlin, Kevin. *Writing in Parts: Imitation and Exchange in Nineteenth-Century Literature.* Stanford University Press, 1995.
Malraux, André et al. *Museum Without Walls.* 1st ed., Doubleday & Co., 1967.
Marcus, Steven. *Dickens: From Pickwick to Dombey.* Basic Books, 1965.
Marcus, Steven. *Freud and the Culture of Psychoanalysis: Studies in the Transition from Victorian Humanism to Modernity.* W. W. Norton & Co., 1984.
Marcus, Steven. "Language into Structure: Pickwick Revisited." *Modern Critical Views: Charles Dickens,* edited by Harold Bloom, Chelsea House, 1987, pp. 129–52.
Marx, Karl. *Capital: A Critique of Political Economy.* Penguin Books in association with New Left Review, 1990.
Masschelein, Anneleen. *The Unconcept: the Freudian Uncanny in Late-Twentieth-Century Theory.* SUNY Press, 2011.
Meisel, Martin. *Realizations: Narrative, Pictorial, and Theatrical Arts in Nineteenth-Century England.* Princeton University Press, 1983.
Michie, Helena. "'Who Is This in Pain?': Scarring, Disfigurement, and Female Identity in Bleak House and Our Mutual Friend." *Novel,* vol. 22, no. 2, Winter 1989, pp. 199–212.
Miller, J. Hillis. *The Form of Victorian Fiction: Thackery, Dickens, Trollope, George Eliot, Meredith, and Hardy.* Arete Press, 1979.
Miller, J. Hillis. *Illustration.* Harvard University Press, 1992.
Mitchell, W. J. T. *Picture Theory.* University of Chicago Press, 1994.
Möller, Joachim. *Imagination on a Long Rein: English Literature Illustrated.* Jonas, 1988.
Nabokov, Vladimir. "Charles Dickens: *Bleak House.*" *Lectures on Literature,* edited by Fredson Bowers, Harcourt Brace & Co., 1980, pp. 63–124.
Nancy, Jean-Luc. *The Ground of the Image.* Translated by Jeff Fort, Fordham University Press, 2005.
Newsom, Robert. *Dickens on the Romantic Side of Familiar Things: Bleak House and the Novel Tradition.* Columbia University Press, 1977.
Novak, Daniel Akiva. *Realism, Photography, and Nineteenth-Century Fiction.* Cambridge University Press, 2008.
Panofsky, Erwin. *Perspective as Symbolic Form.* 1st pbk. ed., Zone Books/MIT Press, 2002.
Paris, Bernard J. *Character and Conflict in Jane Austen's Novels: A Psychological Approach.* Wayne State University Press, 1978.

Bibliography

Rabb, Jane M. *Charles Dickens and His Original Illustrators*. Ohio State University Press, 1980.

Ragussis, Michael. "The Ghostly Signs of *Bleak House.*" *Critical Essays on Charles Dickens's "Bleak House,"* edited by Elliot L. Gilbert, G. K. Hall & Co., 1989, pp. 253–80.

Rosenberg, Brian. *Little Dorrit's Shadows: Character and Contradiction in Dickens*. University of Missouri Press, 1996.

Royle, Nicholas. *The Uncanny: An Introduction*. Manchester University Press, 2002.

Sbriglia, Russell. *Everything You Always Wanted to Know About Literature But Were Afraid to Ask Žižek*. Duke University Press, 2017.

Schapiro, Meyer. *Theory and Philosophy in Art: Style, Artist, and Society*. George Braziller Press, 1994.

Schapiro, Meyer. *Words, Scripts, and Pictures: Semiotics of Visual Language*. George Braziller Press, 1996.

Steig, Michael. *Dickens and Phiz*. Indiana University Press, 1978.

Stewart, Garrett. *Between Film and Screen: Modernism's Photo Synthesis*. University of Chicago Press, 1999.

Stewart, Garrett. *Dickens and the Trials of Imagination*. Harvard University Press, 1974.

Trilling, Lionel. "Little Dorrit." *Modern Critical Views: Charles Dickens*, edited by Harold Bloom, Chelsea House, 1987, pp. 71-83.

Vincent, Howard P. *Daumier and His World*. Northwestern University Press, 1968.

Wain, John. "Little Dorrit." *Dickens and the Twentieth Century*, edited by John Gross and Gabriel Pearson, Routledge and Kegan Paul, 1962, pp. 175–86.

Welsh, Alexander. *From Copyright to Copperfield: The Identity of Dickens*. Harvard University Press, 1987.

Wettlaufer, Alexandra K. "From Metaphor to Metamorphosis: Visual/Verbal Wordplay and the Aesthetics of Modernity in Grandville's Caricature." *Word & Image: A Journal of Verbal/Visual Enquiry*, vol. 29, no. 4, pp. 456–86.

Woloch, Alex. *The One vs. the Many: Minor Characters and the Space of the Protagonist in the Novel*. Princeton University Press, 2003.

Ziarek, Krzysztof. "The Global Unworld: A Meditative Manifesto." *Impasses of the Post-Global: Theory in the Era of Climate Change*, vol. 2, edited by Henry Sussman, Open Humanities Press, 2012, pp. 216–32.

Žižek, Slavoj. *Disparities*. Bloomsbury Academic, 2016.

Žižek, Slavoj, editor. *Mapping Ideology*. Verso, 1994.

Žižek, Slavoj. *The Sublime Object of Ideology*. Verso, 1989.

Žižek, Slavoj. *The Ticklish Subject: The Absent Centre of Political Ontology*. Verso, 1999.

Zupančič, Alenka. *What Is Sex?* MIT Press, 2017.

Index

Note: Page numbers that include n indicate notes. Characters are listed by first name.

Ada (*Bleak House*) 134
Adorno, Theodor 53n4, 103
   Dickens as deviating from form of bourgeois Realism 116
   Dickens's "prebourgeois" form *vs.* realism 96–7
   Quilp as material signifier of drive structuring bourgeois fantasy of progress 101
Agamben, Giorgio
   caricature 34, 92
   doll(s) 130–1
   figurehead as "substantial phantom" 131
Agnes (*David Copperfield*) 188
"Allegory" (ceiling fresco) 15, 135
   effigy of 146–7
   extended personification of 137
   point of view in "looking" *vs.* "seeing" 150
anamorphic stain 54
   Sam Weller as 79
anamorphosis 31–53
   as like dream images 57
   as return of the repressed/lost object in visual sphere 49–52
   reversal of perspective 45
   as spectral form of representation 3

antagonism, as focal point of French caricatures 36
artistic vision, *vs.* mimetic representation 33
"as if" 211, 220
   applied to characters 203–4
   critiquing capitalism from ontological standpoint 213
   Hard Times 202
   hauntological function of 199–200
   and identification 130
   Little Dorrit 199–222
   and proto-filmic aspect of Dickens's novels 201
   relation between capitalism and psychosis 213–14;
   and Rosenberg, Brian 199–201

Baltrušaitis, Jurgis, *Anamorphic Art* 43, 45, 49–50
Baudelaire, Charles
   caricature as both drawing and idea 38, 87
   Grandville, J. J. 57, 118
Benjamin, Walter
   Grandville as "tribal sorcerer" of commodity fetish 83–4

Index

Benjamin, Walter (*Cont.*)
  individual *innerness* in bourgeois art forms 89–90
Betsy Trotwood (*David Copperfield*) 60–1, 184, 195, 201
Blake, William 43, 103
  Minute Particular 217
Bowen, John 1, 58, 61, 71, 113
Browne, Hablôt K *see* Phiz (Hablôt K. Browne)
Bucket (*Bleak House*) 135, 137
Bunsby (*Dombey and Son*) 103–4

capital
  jouissance of as spectral embodiment 122–3
  logic of 106
  see also capitalism
capitalism 84, 88, 210–15
  bourgeois 130
  commodity fetishism as central contradiction of 91–3
  M–C–M (money–commodity–money) 105
  ontology of 220
  predatory 122
  stopped clock as linked to debtors 106
  see also speculative capitalism
Captain Cuttle (*Dombey and Son*) 105–9, 118–19
caricature
  Agamben, Giorgio 34
  antagonism between mimesis and distortion 85
  Daumier, Honoré 74
  Dickens and pictorial style of 175–6
  as disruptive and subversive 34
  emergence of as art form 36–8
  genealogy of 84–8
  as playing with visual images 33
  power to transform traditional ideas of representation 43
  signifiers as unwieldy and recalcitrant 66
  as spectral form of representation 3
  splitting of visual image into dual sign 87
  as transforming our vision of victim 36
  Walter Benjamin on 84
  see also Philipon, Charles; Phiz (Hablôt K. Browne)
Caricature, La see illustrated journals
caricaturist
  Dickens seen as 31
  French lithographers 36
  see also caricature
Carker (*Dombey and Son*) 111–12, 119, 120–4
Casby (the Patriarch) *see* Patriarch, the
characterization
  centrality of effigy and specters to 137
  Dickens as challenge to critical studies of 1
  French illustrators' influence on Dickens and Phiz 62–77
  limitations of critical thought and theorization 2
  representation and form 176–98
character(s) 11, 31–53
  "as if" applied to 203–4
  "flat" 22, 116, 205
  hauntology and 5–12
  spectral 54–79, 115–16
  structural concept of as pure representation 5
  as uncanny forms 11
  "unresolved" *vs.* "conscious" 4
  see also effigy-like characters; mimesis; spectral character(s); wooden characters

230

Index

Charley (*Bleak House*) 136–7, 154
Chesterton, G. K. 1, 12, 83, 113, 160, 222n1
  on caricature 31–3
  Dickens's "eerie realism" 97–8
  Dickens's style as "vital" and "animated" 177
  Dickens's "unbearable realism of a dream" 61, 119
  Little Dorrit as end in itself 204
  "MOOR EEFFOC" 113–16
  Old Curiosity Shop, The 103
Christopher Casby (the "Patriarch") *see* Patriarch, the
Clennam (*Little Dorrit*) 204–6, 208, 210, 219–20
clock(s)
  in *Dombey and Son* 104–6, 119
  in *Little Dorrit* 205, 208
  in *Pickwick Papers, The* 77
comedy, Dickens's use of 105
commodity fetish(ism) 110
  as central contradiction of capitalism 91–5
  Lukács, György 106
  play between entranced human subject under capital and 111–12
  see also Marx, Karl
consumption
  concepts of 66
  surplus jouissance of 101–3, 216
Court of Chancery 168–74
Crary, Jonathan, Dombey as effigy 116
crashes
  in *Little Dorrit* 219–20
criticism, Victorian 5
Cruikshank, George (illustrator) 3, 62
cut, in/of the Real 10–14, 19–21, 26, 54–79, 72
cut, the, as structuring principle 166–7

Daumier, Honoré 63, 132
  "Ah! His! ... Ah! His! Ah! His!" ("Heave-Ho! ... Heave-Ho! Heave-Ho!") (lithograph) 151
  caricature as radically new form of portraiture 92
  influence of on Phiz's illustrations 75
  "Masques de 1831" ("Masks of 1831") 91–2, 100–1
  "Poires, Les" ("The Pears") (lithograph) 36–8, 40, 62, 87–92
  "Sick Nurse" (lithograph) 62
  style as cutting through structural laws of mimetic portraiture 175
  "Ventre Législatif, Le" ("The Legislative Belly") 73–6
  see also expressive distortion(s); illustrated journals; Philipon, Charles
David Copperfield (character)
  blindness of 190–4
  doubling of 60–1
  as narrator 192–5
debt
  and alienation 98
  crippling power of 124–5
  Dickens's father as imprisoned for 181
  Micawber's 188
  Pickwick 217
  William Dorrit and 209
debtors' prison 76, 181, 209
Derrida, Jacques 10, 13–14, 18, 88, 154
  apparition of a specter 83
  hauntology 23
  "image script" 129
  Marx as associating image with specter 86
  see also jouissance; Lacan, Jacques; out-of-jointness
Descartes, René 48–9, 57

Index

desire 21, 51–3, 71, 86, 94, 122, 163–5, 183, 191, 210–18
  in *David Copperfield* 61, 192
  Esther's 137
  Kristeva, Julia 128
  object of 130, 136, 190
Dickens, Charles
  ability to take signifiers apart and play with them like material things 176
  breakthrough as new form 166
  as circumventing formal prose and clichés 67
  critique of British judicial system 72
  doubleness of voice 179
  dramatization of relation between word and image 63
  glissement 166–7
  interest in effigy/ies of 128
  materiality of words 173
  novels
    Bleak House 104, 111, 124–5, 128–56, 159, 166–7, 169, 172–3, 179
    David Copperfield 15, 58–62, 72, 181, 183, 190, 197, 198n4, 200, 202
    Dombey and Son 103–13, 116–27, 130, 141, 209, 213
    Hard Times 120, 202–3
    Little Dorrit 103–4, 199–222
    Martin Chuzzlewit 62
    Old Curiosity Shop, The 96–8, 102–4, 119, 130–1
    Oliver Twist, or the Parish Boy's Progress 178, 197
    Our Mutual Friend 104
    Pickwick Papers, The 63–79
  tapping into primary process of the unconscious 161–2, 221
  turning pictures into writing 65
  "unbearable realism of a dream" 61, 116, 119

  use of comedy and linguistic play to forge symbolic connections 105
  use of letters to circumvent formal prose and clichés 67
  working notes 61, 135
  see also "Allegory"; Dickens's style; *individual characters' names*; Phiz (Hablôt K. Browne)
Dickens's style 71–7, 177
  "as if" 203
  as dropping necessities of mimetic realism 175
  "energy of play" 178
  opening passages 167, 170–2, 175, 178–9
  of representing character 31
  radical change in representation 160
  as "vital" and "animated" 177
  see also Kucich, John; Marcus, Steven; Phiz (Hablôt K. Browne); Rosenberg, Brian
disparity 70
  as inscribed in signifier 72
  see also Žižek, Slavoj, disparity
distorting idea *see* Grandville, J. J.
distortion(s)
  of image 43
  as precondition for caricature 86–7
  role of in portrait, caricature, and modern art 92
  vs. likeness 32
  see also Grandville, J. J., distortion of perspective; expressive distortion(s)
Dolar, Mladen 1, 10, 12, 22, 26
doll/mask/key images of 143, 147
doll(s) 128–56, 130–1
  Caricature, La 89
  as effigy/ies 141
  hanging in effigy 153
  in illustrations 98, 104, 111, 141, 143–4, 146–7, 150–6
  Mrs. Skewton (Cleopatra) 120

Index

Dombey (character) 113, 116–19
Dora (*David Copperfield*) 190–1
doubling 17, 25, 54–6, 59, 101, 110, 128, 183, 209
  David and Rosa 15
  of mimesis 27
  Quilp and effigy 100
  see also splitting
dramatization
  of dream 164–5
  of relation between word and image 63
  of symbolic function of 161
  of symbolic function of effigy 138
Dürer, Albrecht, "window" 45

effigial
  gaze 141, 156
  substance 101–3
effigy/ies 56–7, 89, 91, 116, 124–5, 156
  Carker as 121–3
  figurehead as "substantial phantom" 99
  form of 86
  as form of likeness 130
  function of in *Bleak House* 141
  and the Gaze 155
  as nodal point connecting characters 103–4
  Old Curiosity Shop, The 98
  as Quilp's material double 100
  symbolic function of 138
  as on threshold between things and persons 130
  as ultimate "MOOR EEFFOC" 116–17
  unmasking 91
  of Uriah Heep's name 195
  violence of as directed at mimesis 86–7
  as visual signifier of subject 85
  as visual *vs.* linguistic image 128

  see also doll(s); imago(s); spectral character(s); Wooden Midshipman
effigy-like character(s) 104, 121–2
  Smallweed 111
  see also effigy/ies; spectral character(s)
"effigy of the absent", as crossing threshold of living and dead 139
ego-identification, as basis for all characterization 18
Eliot, George, on Dickens's failure to represent innerness 97, 116, 119
Eliot, T. S., Dickens's characters as belonging to poetry 32
Esther (*Bleak House*) 133–41, 143, 147, 151–5
  doll 15, 10–11, 130–1, 136–8, 140–1, 147, 174
ethics/hauntology, characterization grounded in 3
expressive distortion(s) 59, 63, 209
extimacy 49, 53, 61, 92, 116

Farina, Jonathan 202
  Everyday Words and the Character of Prose in Nineteenth-Century Britain 199
fetish(ism) 110–11
  Carker's teeth as 121
  in money form 212–13
  tribal 103
  unique relationship to signifier of 92
  see also commodity fetish(ism)
fictional agency *vs.* "real" 7
figurehead as effigy *see* Wooden Midshipman
fire 127n3
  image of 101–2
Flora (*Little Dorrit*) 206–7
Florence Dombey 120

Index

forms of representation
  and concept of subjectivity 6
  as "haunting and haunted by"
    one another 3
  linked to sociopolitical and
    ideological antagonisms 56
  visual 2, 3
Forster, John
  Life of Charles Dickens, The 113
  Micawber 181
French illustrators, influence of
  on Dickens's and Phiz's
    characterization 62–77
Freud, Sigmund 12–14, 16–17,
  19–22, 39, 51–4, 58, 72, 98,
  114–15, 125, 159, 161–6,
  168–9, 173, 190, 210,
  221–2
  dream representation 176
  essay on fetishism 183
  primacy of visual image 128–9
  primary processes 87–8
  uncanny 22, 26, 36
Frow, John 23
  Character and Person 6–9, 15–21
  mirror stage 16
  ontological aporia 7

Gaze, the 20, 44, 56, 60
  as contingent 53
  effigy and 141, 155–6
  in illustrations 77–9
  Lacan, Jacques 20, 48–53, 57
  of the Other 57–8, 76–7
  as spectral inscription 60, 62–79
Gérard, Jean Ignace Isidor *see*
  Grandville, J. J.
glissement 166
  and character 199
  internal splitting of sign allowing
    caricature to transform
    signifier 88
  narratives of 179

Gombrich, E. H. 33, 36
Gradgrind (*Hard Times*) 202–3
Grandville, J. J. 38, 56–7, 63, 75,
  83–4, 87–9, 100, 112, 123,
  132, 201
  anamorphosis in 43–4
  Baudelaire on 118
  "Duel Between a High and Low
    Soldier" (lithograph) 43,
    87–92
  expressive distortion 63
  "False Perspective" (lithograph)
    44
  Grandville as "tribal sorcerer" of
    commodity fetish 83–4
  "Il a beau faire, il n'aura pas la
    croix" ("No Matter How
    Hard He Tries, He Will
    Not Find the Cross")
    (lithograph) 54–6
  "Man and Animal Portraits
    Compared" (lithograph) 40,
    44–5, 46
  "Un peintre, à cheval sur son dada
    raphaélique" ("A Painter
    Astride His Raphael Hobby
    Horse") (lithograph) 46–7
  "Poachers of Small Stature"
    (lithograph) 44
  "Premier Rêve, Crime et expiation"
    ("First Dream: Crime
    and Atonement") (wood
    engraving) 203
  "A Quelle Sauce les Voulez-vous?"
    ("Which Sauce Do You
    Want?") (print) 89
  "Second Rêve, Une promenade
    dans le ciel" ("Second Dream:
    A Promenade Through
    the Sky") (engraving) 40,
    203
  Walter Benjamin on 83–4
  see also caricature(s)

Harvey, John, foundational study of Phiz's illustrations 62
hauntology 27
  and character 5–12
  of characterization 22
  Derrida and "out-of-jointness" 3
  short-circuit between representation and the real 166
Higbie, Robert 5
  Character and Structure in the English Novel 4
Hogarth, William 62
  "False Perspective" (lithograph) 44
  "Gin Lane" (etching and engraving) 151
Holbein, Hans 51–3
Hortense (*Bleak House*) 135–8

idealism 51–2
identification
  grounding in primary presence of an *I* 130
  as primary support of ego-formation 16
illustrated journals 36–8, 76
  Caricature, La 89, 151, 154
  Charivari 1, 75, 89
  illustrated novel(s) 2–3, 36–8
illustration(s)
  connections among in *Bleak House* 140–55
  as nontextual elements of Dickens' characterization 2
  relation to text 76
  see also Daumier, Honoré; Phiz (Hablôt K. Browne)
image
  interplay of with text 75
  primacy of 86
  self-reflexivity of in "The Valentine" 65

"image magic"
  Daumier, Honoré 10–11
  and desubjectifying the Real 36
  as origin of caricature 84–5
imago(s) 128–56
  Lacan and mirror stage 129–30
  as on threshold between things and persons 130
  Quilp as linked to 102
interiority
  as core characteristic of bourgeois art form 97

Jaffe, Audrey 11, 25–6, 140
  Esther's "reflexive" linguistic structure of 132–4
  Vanishing Points: Dickens, Narrative, and the Subject of Omniscience 5, 133, 155
  Victorian Novel Dreams of the Real: Conventions and Ideology, The 11, 25–6
Jarley's Waxworks (*The Old Curiosity Shop*) 98
Jarndyce (*Bleak House*) 134, 136–7
Jarndyce and Jarndyce (*Bleak House*) 126, 142, 170, 173–5, 205
Jenny (*Bleak House*) 138–9, 150, 152
Jo (*Bleak House* 135), 137–8, 148
Jordan, John O. 23, 143
Josh Bounderby (*Hard Times*) 120
jouissance 62, 70–1, 93–5, 115, 176, 179, 187–91, 194, 199
  of capital as spectral embodiment 122–3
  of language 196–7
  linguistic 191
  Real of 86
  surplus 92, 101–3, 122–3
Judy (*Bleak House*) 124, 126–7, 142

Kerr, David S. 91
  Philipon's pear effigy 154

Index

Kit Nubbles (*The Old Curiosity Shop*) 100
  effigy of 103–4
Kris, Ernst 33, 36
  and caricature 32–4, 221
    as play with magic power of visual image 85
  doodle 161
  effigy as short circuit between signifier and signified 86
  egocentric model 221
  "image magic" 84–8
  imago 129
  "Poires, Les" (lithograph) 36
  representational stages 100
  visual image as "more primitive" than linguistic 128–9
Kristeva, Julia
  interest of in visual language of cinema 128
  specular image and drive 86
Krook (*Bleak House*) 141, 146
  spontaneous combustion of 120–1
Kucich, John
  and character 160
  Dickens's style as "mechanical" 177–8
  Excess and Restraint in the Novels of Charles Dickens 177
  narratives of *glissement* 179
  Oliver Twist 177–8

Lacan, Jacques 14–22, 24, 26, 56–8, 61, 87, 222
  concept of the real 9–11
  dream representations 180
  Four Fundamental Concepts of Psychoanalysis, The 48–53
  Freud's dream of "Irma's injection" 162
  glissement 88, 199
  "the line and the light" 51–5
  and mapping oneself in the visual field 48
  mirror stage 129–30
  ontological status of the signifier 161
  primary processes as laws of the signifier 86–7
  psychosis 205, 208–9
  subject as split between imaginary and symbolic 213
  symbolic order 133
  see also Gaze, the; uncanny
Lady Dedlock (*Bleak House*) 135–40, 147, 154
language
  as constituting reality for subject 10
  intrinsic spectrality of 71–2
  materiality of in *David Copperfield* 198n4
  mechanical autonomy of 179
  as "Pickwickian" 161
  relation of to the Real 9
  as "writing itself" 160
Laplanche, Jacques 203
  "chains" of signification 129
  metonymy as bridge between signifiers 203
Leclaire, Serge 62, 203
  "chains" of signification 129
  metonymy as bridge between signifiers 203
letters, instability of 65–6
Lévi-Strauss, Claude
  mythological associations between "harelips," doubles, and twins 60–1
Little Dorrit (character)
  radical singularity of 215–18
Little Nell (*The Old Curiosity Shop*)
  see Nell

Liz (*Bleak House*) 138–40
logic
  of dreamlike quality of language 89
  as embodying gaze-beyond-death 140
  function of in *Bleak House* 140–1
  of Liz's baby for Jenny's 138–9
  use of to displace and channel retribution 154
logos, dramatizing 161
Louis-Philippe, King 54–6
  Roi Bourgeois 38, 56, 88–90
  see also Daumier, Honoré, "Poires, Les"; Philipon, Charles, "Poires, Les"
Lukács, György
  commodity fetish(ism) 103
  time 106

Maignan, Emmanuel 45
Major Bagstock (*Dombey and Son*) 103–4, 120
Marcus, Steven 1, 12, 66, 166, 176, 197, 198n1
  Dickens as turning pictures into writing 65–6
  Dickens's novels as using representational material as dreams do 161–2
  "Language into Structure: Pickwick Revisited" 155–62
  material aspect of Dicken's writing 71–2
  Pickwick Papers, The 74–5, 179
  style 221
Marx, Karl 86, 91–5, 106, 214
masked
  image 20
  Micawber 194
mask(s) 87, 100–1, 110, 122–4, 134–5
  "Lord Chancellor Copies from Memory, The" (etching) 141
  Nell sleeping among 98
  Uriah Heep's face as 189
  see also Daumier, Honoré, "Masques de 1831"; doll/mask/key images of
McGowan, Todd
  "Bankruptcy" 193
  text's ability to act as traumatic disruption 23
Merdle (*Little Dorrit*) 210–13, 219
Merleau-Ponty, Maurice
  "depth of field" 53
Michie, Helena, *Bleak House*'s reliance on unstable self 132
Miller, J. Hillis
  characterization *vs.* nontextual elements 2
  iconology as framing analysis of 3
mimesis 5–7, 15–16, 18, 31–53
  asymmetry of opposition to structure 5–6
  character as "autonomous" 2
  ideological force of linked with visual image 34
  as institutionalized form of representation 3
  mirror as metaphor for 16
  technologizing 45
  vanishing mediation of 94
  see also structuralism
mimetic characterization 5, 31
mimetic representation 33, 75
mirror, reflections as structuring image 104–5
money, as key to filling in gap of representation 95
"MOOR EEFFOC"
  Dickens's childhood encounter with 86, 113–14, 116
  and Dombey 116–18

Index

"MOOR EEFFOC" (*Cont.*)
  effigy as ultimate 115
  motto of all effective realism 83
Mr. Brogley (*Dombey and Son*) 104–3, 108–9, 118–19
Mr. Dick (*David Copperfield*) 182–4, 195–6
Mr. Dorrit
  crash of 219
  Father of the Marshalsea 210
  leaving debtors' prison in the realm of the "as if" 209
  see also Name-of-the-Father
Mr. Micawber (*David Copperfield*) 176–98, 190–202
  linguistic repetition and proliferation 193–4
  "Micawberisms" as darker aspect of his comic psyche 182–3
  see also Kucich, John
Mrs. Bardell (*The Pickwick Papers*) 68, 72, 76
Mrs. General (*Little Dorrit*) 215–17
Mrs. Skewton (Cleopatra) (*Dombey and Son*) 103–4, 120
Mr. Tangle (*Bleak House*) 74, 142, 175, 180–1

Nabokov, Vladimir 175
  on *Bleak House* 126
Name-of-the-Father
  Little Dorrit 215
  at stake in *Little Dorrit* 210–11
  see also paternal signifier(s)
naming/unnaming, and entrance into symbolism and symbolic castration 196
Nancy, Jean-Luc
  "effigy of the absent" 139
  Ground of the Image, The 155
Nathaniel Winkle (*The Pickwick Paper*) 68–70
Nell (*The Old Curiosity Shop*) 98–101

Newsome, Robert, *Bleak House* 167
Novak, Daniel 12, 24

ontological aporia 7–8
  see also Frow, John
ontological displacement 92, 114
ontological distortion, at heart of anamorphosis 48
ontological fiction, use-value and exchange-value 93
  spectrality 54, 135
  surplus 113
ontology 5
  "as if" 206
  of capitalism 220
  of characterization 3
  see also hauntology
order of representation, as haunting order of the real 9
order of the real, as haunted by order of representation 9
Other, gaze of 76–7
Otherness, as grounding characterization in ethics/hauntology 3
out-of-jointness 3, 10–11, 14, 21, 92, 116

paternal signifier(s) 210, 214
  see also Name-of-the-Father
Patriarch, the (*Little Dorrit*) 206, 210, 218–19
pear, image of as effigy competing with mimetic likeness of king 89
perspective 43–7
  devices in *Dombey and Son* 105
  geometral 49–52
  splitting of 72
Philipon, Charles 75

Index

Caricature, La (illustrated journal) 36, 75
Charivari (illustrated journal) 36, 75
  expressive distortion 63
  and "image magic" 36
  "Poires, Les" ("The Pears") (sketch) 34–6, 40, 54
  see also Daumier, Honoré
Phiz (Hablôt K. Browne) 2–3, 62, 65–7, 72–5, 127n4, 147–8, 151, 183
  as able to engage Dickens in creative interplay between text and image 75
  and English iconological tradition 62
  etchings as literal form of writing/scoring 67
  Grandville-type anamorphosis in "The Valentine" (etching) 63
  graphic parallel between Quilp and Wooden Midshipman 109
  influence of French illustrators on 75
  relationships among *Bleak House* illustrations 141
  style of 151
  as turning writing into pictures 65–7
  use of darkness in lithographs 151
Phiz (Hablôt K. Browne), illustrations
  "Appointed Time, The" (etching) 141, 146
  "Captain Cuttle Consoles His Friend" (etching) 106
  "Consecrated Ground" 150
  "Ghost's Walk, The" 148
  "Jo, the Crossing-Sweeper" 150
  "Lord Chancellor Copies from Memory, The" (etching) 141–3, 154
  "New Meaning in the Roman, A" (etching) 141–2
  "Pickwick Sits For His Portrait" (etching) 76–7
  "Tom-All-Alone's" (etching) 143, 148–51

"Trial, The" (etching) 68
"Valentine, The" (etching) 63–8
"Wooden Midshipman on the Lookout, The" (etching) 108, 110
pleasure principle, tension with reality principle 184
  see also Freud, Sigmund
"Poires, Les" ("The Pears") (lithograph) *see* Daumier, Honoré; Philipon, Charles
portraiture 31–53
  mock portrait gallery in *The Pickwick Papers* 75–7
  and position of self-identity before gaze of the Other 58
  and realist representation 31
  Rosa Dartle 58–9
Posthumous Papers of the Pickwick Club, The see Dickens, Charles, novels, *Pickwick Papers, The*
post-structuralism 2, 4
predatory capitalism *see* capitalism, predatory
presence 7
progress
  social fantasy of 101
prosopopoetic passages
  in *David Copperfield* 191–2

Quilp (*The Old Curiosity Shop*) 98–104

"reading" across text and illustration *see* Phiz (Hablôt K. Browne)
Real, the 9–11, 166
  cut in/of 10–14, 19–21, 54–79, 72
  emergence of subjectivity as cut in/of 11
  and "image magic" 36
  vs. representation 34
realism
  antagonism of 11
  bourgeois 95–6, 116

239

Index

realism (*Cont.*)
  as institutionalized form of representation 3
  as repressing ontological implications of anamorphosis 49
  Victorian 31
realist novel 96, 155
reality principle, struggle of with pleasure principle 184
reflections
  in *Dombey and Son* 118
  mirror 111–12, 119
  in *Old Curiosity Shop, The* 118–19
repetition compulsion, of Micawber and Mr. Dick 183
representation
  antagonism as inherent in 36
  as exclusively textual/linguistic 2
  prevalence of letters, writing, and documents always bound up with 154
  radical change in 155–62
  of subjectivity 120
  vs. the Real 34
  see also character; Dickens's style; spectral representation
Richard (*Bleak House*) 173–4
Roi Bourgeois see Louis-Philippe, King
Roman Allegory *see* "Allegory"
Rosa (*Bleak House*) 135–6
Rosa Dartle (*David Copperfield*) 58–61, 135–6
  see also scar(s)
Rosenberg, Brian
  David Copperfield 199–200
  Little Dorrit's Shadows: Character and Contradiction in Dickens. 177–8
Rubens, David 74

"Samive" *see* Sam Weller, as author's surrogate 70–1
Sampson Brass (*The Old Curiosity Shop*) 100
Samuel Pickwick (*The Pickwick Papers*) 66–7
Sam Weller (*The Pickwick Papers*) 63–8
  as author's surrogate 70–1
de Saussure, Ferdinand, signifier as arbitrary 176
scars
  Esther Summerson 132, 134
  Rosa Dartle 14–15, 21, 24, 58–62, 122
Schott, Gasper 45
  inverted perspective device as magical instrument 50
semiotics 2, 4
Serjeant Buzfuz (*The Pickwick Papers*) 68, 76
signifier(s)
  logic of 39
  remainder/materiality of 71–2
  verbal and visual 66
Smallweed (*Bleak House*) 126, 127, 170
  see also villains, and crippling power of debt
Smallweeds (family) (*Bleak House*) 22, 120
Snagsby (*Bleak House*) 147
space between representation and reality, the "as if" 199
spectral
  characterization 86
  embodiment, Carker as 122–3
  inscription, the gaze as 62–79
  materiality 115
  mimesis 40
  narrative 43
spectral character(s)
  Clennam as 205
  effigial 54–79
  vs. realist bourgeois subject 155
  vs. realist character(s) 115–16
spectral embodiment, Carker as 122–3
spectral form, caricature as 3
spectral representation 3, 97, 121
spectrality

as intrinsic to language 71–2
ontological 54
spectral materiality
  Dickens as positioning himself in language more radically 221
  property of signifier 161
  of signifier 196
  theorizing Dickens's breakthrough 165–6
spectral other, order of the real as 9
spectral representation 92
  "artistic truthfulness" 97
  as grounding subject in Disparity 92
  Carker's traits 121
  Dickens's form of *vs.* form of realist novel 155
  distortion as key technique of 63
speculative capitalism 106, 109, 210, 216
  see also Clennam
speculative entrepreneurism 123
speculative realism 10
splitting 66
  of perspective 72
  see also doubling
Steerforth (*David Copperfield*) 58–9
Steig, Michael 62, 130, 147, 150–1
  connections among plates in *Bleak House* 141
  Dickens's "new art form" 1–2
  foundational study of Phiz's illustrations 62
  "Tom-All-Alone's" (etching) 147
  "Valentine, The" and "The Trail" (etchings) 66–8
Stewart, Garrett
  Between Film and Screen 33
  Dickens and the Trials 192–3
  "montage thinking" 202
  syllepsis 201
structuralism
  and character 2
  language and semiotic theory 4
structure *vs.* mimesis, asymmetry of opposition 5–6

subject, the, as underlying concepts of character 3–4
subjectification, in mimetically informed criticism and theories of characterization 19
subjectivity
  bourgeois representation of 120
  conceptions of 5–6
  trauma of 86
  see also trauma, of subjectivity
symbolic exchange between word and image 65–6
symbolic order *see* Lacan, Jacques

text
  and illustration 68
  interplay of with image 75
  relation to illustration 76
Thackeray, William Makepeace
  advice to Phiz 62
  "the line," logic of 52
time, as linking clocks and debtors 106
Tom-All-Alone's (slum), *Bleak House* 137–45, 147–51, 153–6
Tony Weller (*The Pickwick Papers*) 63
transgression, and "image magic" 36
trauma
  Dickens's childhood 197
  Esther Summerson's 115–16, 135, 156
  Micawber's refuge from in words 184
  Mr. Dorrit's 218–19
  Rosa Dartle's 59
  social 156
  of subjectivity 86, 140, 156
  Žižek on 115–16
Trilling, Lionel
  biographical connection between Dickens and Clennam 204
  and question of ontology 160
Tulkinghorn (*Bleak House*) 15, 83, 135, 137–41, 146–8, 150, 172

Index

Twemlow (*Our Mutual Friend*) 119, 203–4

uncanny 1, 16
  Dolar, Mladen 22
  Lacan, Jacques 49
  ontology 12, 14, 15, 22, 27, 94, 129
  repetition compulsion of 36
unmasking 168
  Grandville's work 57
  of Micawber 196
  of mimesis 61
  of the Patriarch 219
  of Uriah Heep by Micawber 195
  see also mask(s)
Uriah Heep (*David Copperfield*) 186–9, 189, 190, 195, 197

Victorian novelists 31
Victorian novel(s) 1–2, 24, 200
  affect theory on 24
  as prehistory to cinema 39
  realism 31
  see also Jaffe, Audrey
villains, and crippling power of debt 124
Vincent, Howard P. 36–8, 75
  "Masques de 1831" ("Masks of 1831") 90
  "Poires, Les" as metamorphosis 40
  "Ventre Législatif, Le" ("The Legislative Belly") 73
visual images, as linked with ideological force of mimesis 34

Wain, John, *Little Dorrit* as Dickens's "most stationary novel" 204
Wellers (*The Pickwick Papers*), ekphrastic play 63–8
Welsh, Alexander, Uriah Heep as going "limp" 197

Woloch, Alex 8
  Bleak House 11
Woodcourt (*Bleak House*) 135, 147, 148, 150
wooden character(s)
  Brogley's metamorphosis into 112
  Dickens's use of as characters 116–18
  see also effigy/ies; Wooden Midshipman
Wooden Midshipman 100–1
  Cuttle's financial ruin as displaced onto 108–9
  Dombey and Son 103–4, 109–2, 121–2, 130, 213
  as effigy 103–4
writing
  on the body 61–2
  Phiz as turning into pictures 65

Žižek, Slavoj 14, 25–6, 86, 111–16, 202, 207, 214–15
  anamorphic stain 49–50
  anamorphosis 51–2
  "as if", function of in capitalism 213–14
  "call of the Other" 207
  critique of realist desire 139
  disparity 10–11, 34, 54
  gap between the Real and reality 202
  opening of signifier into the Real of jouissance 86
  out-of-jointness 10
  "primordial repression" and emergence of subjectivity 116
  Ticklish Subject, The 49, 187
  uncanny 31
  see also Real, the
Zupančič Alenka 26, 220
  Lacan's materialism 165–6
  out-of-jointness between symbolic and being 10–11

EU authorised representative for GPSR:
Easy Access System Europe, Mustamäe tee 50,
10621 Tallinn, Estonia
gpsr.requests@easproject.com

www.ingramcontent.com/pod-product-compliance
Lightning Source LLC
Chambersburg PA
CBHW051609230426
43668CB00013B/2046